A PANORAMA OF INDO-EUROPEAN LANGUAGES

Modern Languages

Editor

R. AUTY
M.A., DR. PHIL.
Professor of Comparative Slavonic Philology
in the University of Oxford

A PANORAMA OF
INDO-EUROPEAN
LANGUAGES

W. B. Lockwood
M.A., D.Litt.
Professor of Germanic and Indo-European Philology
in the University of Reading

HUTCHINSON UNIVERSITY LIBRARY
LONDON

HUTCHINSON & CO (*Publishers*) LTD
3 Fitzroy Square, London W1

London Melbourne Sydney Auckland
Wellington Johannesburg Cape Town
and agencies throughout the world

First published 1972

Printed in Great Britain by William Clowes & Sons Limited,
London, Colchester and Beccles, and bound by
Wm. Brendon, Tiptree, Essex

ISBN 0 09 111020 3 (cased)
0 09 111021 1 (paper)

For F.P.P.,
who read the first draft—
a generation ago.

CONTENTS

PREFACE

In compiling the present account of the Indo-European languages, I have in a literal sense been writing for myself. I have often wished for a volume which would both illustrate the salient features of the languages in question and at the same time provide summary information on their external history. In short, I missed what might be called an elementary background book. This I now attempt to supply, the aim being to include every known Indo-European language, past and present, and so to provide a volume which may have something of the character of a work of reference. Unless otherwise stated, population statistics refer to 1966. In assembling the material many hundreds of sources have been consulted over the years, but it seemed to offer no special advantage to reproduce this unwieldy bibliography here. The enquirer seeking further details will best turn to his library catalogue.

I am indebted to all those whose information has assisted me, directly or indirectly, in the composition of this work. In particular I am grateful to Mr J. Dingley, Dr D. N. MacKenzie, Mr C. Shackle, Dr R. Sternemann and Dr G. Uhlisch, who obligingly read sections of the draft typescript and gave me the benefit of their specialist knowledge. I also tender my thanks to those who kindly helped in procuring texts: Mr C. Alexiou, Professor Sir H. Bailey, Dr L. S. Baral, Mrs S. Bhattacharji, the late Professor T. W. Clark, Mr W. Crewe, Mr J. Dingley, Professor R. Djupedal, Drs A. Feitsma, Dr W. Fiedler, Dr R. Gutschmidt, Dr F. Hinze, Professor A. Isačenko, Professor E. D. Jones, Dr D. Kostov, Dr D. N. MacKenzie, Mr R. K. Mahanta, Mr J. Piette, Dr I. Raeside, Mr C. Reynolds, Professor E. Seidel, Mr C. Shackle, Mrs D. A. Sneddon, Dr E. Tumanian.

ABBREVIATIONS

Alban.	Albanian	Lat.	Latin
Armen.	Armenian	Latv.	Latvian
Eng.	English	Lith.	Lithuanian
Gaul.	Gaulish	OCS	Old Church Slavonic
Ger.	German	OEng.	Old English
Goth.	Gothic	OIr.	Old Irish
Gk.	Greek	OLith.	Old Lithuanian
Hitt.	Hittite	Russ.	Russian
Icel.	Icelandic	Skt.	Sanskrit
Ir.	Irish	Toch.	Tocharian

I

THE CONCEPT OF INDO-EUROPEAN

The Indo-European languages are so called since they have a common source in Primitive (or Proto-) Indo-European, an unwritten language conjectured to have existed as a continuum of closely connected dialects until the third millennium B.C. Chiefly because of the migrations of their speakers, these dialects became much differentiated and evolved into separate languages. Eventually the differences became so great that the original relationship of the languages in question was no longer spontaneously apparent. Not until 1786 was the existence of such a family of languages first mooted, and only in the next century was this surmise confirmed beyond doubt by the discoveries of the new science of comparative philology. The term Indo-European was then coined in reference to the geographical location of the languages in question, i.e., on territory from India to Europe. It was later realised, however, that Indo-European speech had been introduced into India from the west, so that Europe, particularly Central and Eastern Europe, now appears as the earliest known home of this family of languages.

The comparative study of the archaic Indo-European languages throws much light on the nature of Primitive Indo-European. It is seen to have developed the principle of grammatical gender, an earlier distinction between animate and inanimate being further divided as masculine, feminine and neuter. The distinction of two numbers, singular and plural, is very ancient, but later a dual developed to some extent. Nouns and adjectives were declined. On the evidence of Sanskrit, there were eight cases: nominative, vocative, accusative, genitive, dative, ablative, locative, instrumental. There is evidence of a pre-declensional stage, and it is likely that the very earliest case-endings formed a more or less uniform pattern, but later numerous classes arose to give a highly complex morphology. The Primitive Indo-European declension can often be theoretically postulated, e.g.

the evidence of Sanskrit, Latin and Greek indicates an Indo-European paradigm of the following order:

sg.nom. *ekwos* 'horse', voc. *ekwe*, acc. *ekwom*, gen. *ekwosyo*, dat. *ekwōy*, abl. *ekwōd*, loc. *ekwoy*, inst. *ekwō*, pl.nom.voc. *ekwōs*, acc. *ekwons*, gen. *ekwōm*, dat.abl. *ekwoybh(y)os*, loc. *ekwoysu* or *ekwoysi*, inst. *ekwōys*.

The declension of adjectives was in principle identical with that of nouns. Adjectives agreed with nouns in number and case. Most adjectives had three genders, but some distinguished only between animate and inanimate, and finally a few were, at least partly, indifferent to gender, these last reflecting the most archaic type. The three strata are indicated, for instance, in Latin, cf. *bonus* m. 'good', *bona* f., *bonum* n.; *facilis* m.f. 'easy', *facile* n.; *audāx* m.f.n. 'bold'.

Analysis of the verbal system has revealed that the many tenses of Indo-European developed from two basic forms, one denoting an action, the other a state. The tenses may express time, but also aspect and various sorts of modality. Very often etymologically unrelated roots were used to form the different tenses of the same verb, much as Eng. *go, went*; in fact the verbal morphology could be called typically irregular. It is to be noted, however, that some of the recorded languages continued to extend the inherited synthetic verbal system. There is, for example, no evidence that Primitive Indo-European developed a pluperfect, for though this tense occurs in Sanskrit, Greek and Latin, it will be of secondary origin, proper to the languages in question, since the manner of formation varies in each case. There were two voices: active and middle, the latter containing the notion that the subject was particularly involved in the action. The middle sometimes acquired a passive sense which in some languages became dominant. As with other parts of speech, reconstructions of the Indo-European verb are often possible, as pres.indic.act.sg.1 *bherō* '(I) bear', 2 *bheresi* or *bheris*, 3 *bhereti* or *bherei*, pl.1 *bheromes* or *-mos* or *-men*, 2 *bherete*, 3 *bheronti*—the alternatives most likely reflect dialect differences within Primitive Indo-European. Similarly the imperf.indic.act.sg.1 *bherom*, 2 *bheres*, 3 *bheret*, pl.1 *bherom..?*, 2 *bherete*, *bheront*; an augment could apparently be used with this tense as well, again a dialect feature no doubt, hence sg.1 *ebherom*, etc.

The reflexes of such theoretical Primitive Indo-European forms, together with illustrations of Common Indo-European vocabulary, are shown in the chapters which follow. Since no more than the briefest mention of these matters is feasible in the present publication, reference may be made for further details to the author's *Indo-European Philology, Historical and Comparative* (Hutchinson University Library) and the literature cited there.

The Branches of
the I-E Family

2

HELLENIC

This branch of the Indo-European family, philologically so important by reason of its great antiquity and rich documentation, is to all intents and purposes represented by a single language, Greek. Moreover, this language has remained essentially the language of one country, for its colonies, numerous and influential though they once were, have now vanished or are on the point of doing so.

Although the speech of Greece today is the direct descendant of the tongue used in antiquity, far-reaching evolutionary changes have taken place and Ancient Greek is no longer comprehensible to the speaker of Modern Greek. It is certain that if Plato were to walk the streets of Athens today, he would fail to recognise as Greek the language he heard spoken around him. On the other hand, he would often be able to make something of the printed word, since the script is the same and the spelling conservative in spite of root-and-branch changes in the pronunciation. Moreover, the literary language has always exerted a significant influence on the development of the spoken word and this has preserved a sense of continuity.

Ancient Greek

At what date the Greeks entered the country to which they gave their name is not known, but there is ample evidence that the new arrivals found a civilisation materially superior to their own, see 'Pelasgian' below. Epigraphical records, attested from the seventh century B.C. onwards, show that each city-state employed its own dialect officially. Above such local differences, four main dialect types may be distinguished: Arcadic, Aeolic, Doric and Ionic, distributed in a complex manner over the mainland of Greece, the islands and the coast of Asia Minor as the result of internal migrations. Attic, the speech of Attica and its capital Athens, forms part of Ionic. The classical works of Greek literature are written in one or other of these dialects, Attic taking the lead from the fifth century onwards. An exception, however, is the poetry ascribed to Homer. The Homeric or Epic dialect, as it is called, is not based on any one organic dialect, but is an artificial style evolved as the medium for the national epic. The chief constituents are, however, Ionic and Aeolic. The work stands at the beginning of Greek tradition and is dated to about 800 B.C.

With the rise of the Athenian Empire under Pericles at the middle of the fifth century, Attic spread rapidly as the state form of Greek, non-Attic Greek being reduced to the status of patois. Following the conquests of Alexander the Great (died 323), contemporary Attic, by then known as the koine (*koínē* 'common' dialect), became the official medium of a far-flung administration. It was something of an international medium, too, and not surprisingly the early Christians, though themselves mostly Aramaic speakers, compiled their New Testament in Hellenistic Greek, as the koine may also be termed. The Hellenistic period is regarded as coming to an end in A.D. 330, the date at which Constantinople became the capital of the Empire. During this period, the koine virtually obliterated the non-Attic dialects as spoken media also, so that Medieval and Modern Greek represent the further evolution of the koine. Only the Tsakonian dialect (below) contains a significant proportion of non-Attic forms.

Macedonian

Even in antiquity there appears to have been some doubt as to the antecedents of the Macedonians. Herodotus reports that Alexander I of Macedon was barred from taking part in the Olympic Games as he was a non-Hellene, but the same author describes the Macedonians as being akin to the Dorians. A number of Macedonian glosses and proper names have survived in ancient sources, but the material is too scanty to permit a positive identification of affinities. Some of the glosses have no correspondences in Greek, while others are close to it. It is generally held that the evidence suggests rather an aberrant form of Greek than an independent language. Since Macedonian was in contact with Illyrian and Thracian, borrowings from these languages could account for the exotic strain. Greek was being used at the Macedonian court by the fifth century and it is to be assumed that the Macedonian dialect (or language) succumbed to Attic Greek, like Ionic and the rest, during the Hellenistic Age.

Medieval and Modern Greek

Medieval or Byzantine Greek covers the period from the founding of Constantinople (until then Byzantium) as the capital of the Empire down to the sacking of the city by the Latins in 1204. The language since then is termed Modern Greek.

The sources for Medieval Greek are most meagre, since the written language of the age was essentially Attic, see 'Atticism' below. But the living, evolving language is attested in a few scraps of popular song and in some papyrus letters, the latter from Egypt. Documentation becomes fuller from the thirteenth century onwards, though continuing Atticistic tradition meant that texts in the current language are still in the great minority. Significant early prose texts are Jewish translations of Hebrew originals, see 'Yevanic' below. Modern Greek did not begin to come into its own as a written medium until towards the end of the last century. Creative writers led the movement for a national standard based on the usages of the living tongue; their goal seems now almost in sight.

Tsakonian

Tsakonian is the outlandish dialect of perhaps as many as 10,000 speakers in an area difficult of access along the forbidding coast of the Peloponnese between the Parnon Range and the Gulf of Argolis. It is generally agreed that this vernacular preserves a considerable number of features stemming directly from the local Laconian (Spartan) dialect of antiquity. Other modern dialects are derived essentially from the koine (p. 6).

Yevanic

The Jews have a place of note in the history of Modern Greek. They were unaffected by Atticism (see below) and employed the current colloquial which they transcribed in Hebrew letters. There is a small literature in this Jewish-tinged Greek, which may be termed Yevanic (Hebrew *Yevanim* 'Greeks', lit. 'Ionians'); it dates from the early part of the modern period, the most extensive document being a translation of the Pentateuch. In its context, this exceptional cultivation of the vernacular has its analogue in the choice of Hellenistic Greek by the translators of the Septuagint—and in the New Testament.

Atticism

In the second century B.C. certain writers began to imitate the Attic of the Classical Period, despising the then living koine as too debased for literary composition. This development is called Atticism; it became usual and has continued in principle ever since. Attic Greek has played a role in Eastern Europe comparable to that of Latin in the West. But whereas Latin was largely replaced by the vernaculars about the beginning of modern times, Atticising Greek persisted down to the early years of the last century as the habitual literary form. Liberation in 1829 brought no decisive break with the past, though by now a certain amount of Modern Greek was being regularly written. The official medium of the new Greek state was the *kathareúousa*, the 'purist' style based on ancient models. True, this style, even at its most austere, now made concessions to the living language, especially in idiom and syntax. Nevertheless, from about 1880 more and more writers took to *dēmotiké*, the 'popular' language in its contemporary form. Greece had thus two literary languages. Each had its own protagonists who struggled acrimoniously, even violently, as in the Gospel riots of 1901 when demonstrating students demolished the printing works where a translation of the New Testament into Demotic Greek had just come off the press. Animosities in this, the language question, are less extreme nowadays, for meanwhile the two styles have drawn closer together. The Demotic has taken the lead and will, most likely in the not too distant future, become the sole national standard. But it has absorbed a number of purist elements, especially from the lexicon of its rival.

The Greek-speaking area, past and present

As we have said (p. 5) the beginnings of the hellenisation of Greece cannot be dated, though one may confidently assume that Greek had become dominant throughout the area by 1000 B.C. The process was not confined to the mainland and adjacent islands. By 800 B.C., at the latest, Greek-speaking urban centres were flourishing along the Aegean littoral of Asia Minor. By way of Rhodes, colonists reached Cyprus. The area of Greek speech in antiquity was thus bounded to the north by Illyrian, Macedonian (see above) and Thracian, across the Hellespont again by Thracian, and various local tongues, such as Lydian, Carian, Lycian. Within the central area, enclaves of Pelasgian still existed.

About the middle of the eighth century, Greek was carried by colonists to southern Italy and Sicily. In 623 B.C. a colony was established at Cyrene—here Greek was presumably in contact with Berber—and about 600 B.C. the city of Massalia, the modern Marseilles, was founded in Liguria. From the seventh century onwards, important colonies came into being along the Illyrian coast and about the same time other settlements were arising at points on the shores of the Euxine (Black Sea).

In the Hellenistic Age, expansion was chiefly confined to the East where, in Asia Minor especially, Greek extended its range at the expense of Thracian and Anatolian languages. A notable event was the founding of Alexandria as a Greek-speaking centre in 331 B.C. We have already spoken of the role of the koine as an international medium. With the rise of Rome, however, the Greek colonies in the

West lay open to romanisation. Marseilles and Naples (Gk. *Néa Pólis* 'New Town') appear to have remained predominantly Greek until the third and fourth centuries A.D. respectively. In the extreme south the language survived even better. In Sicily, Greek appears to have still been spoken along the east coast in later medieval times, while in Calabria and Apulia pockets of Greek speech are found to this day, see 'Italiot Greek' below.

In the post-Hellenistic period, Greek continued to extend its range in the East, a development encouraged when Byzantium (renamed Constantinople) became the capital of the Empire in A.D. 330, even though Latin remained in official use for another two hundred years. Thracian was eliminated and Greek made great headway in Asia Minor, obliterating many local languages and only coming to a halt in face of Armenian and Iranian. Greek continued to be used in Alexandria and other Egyptian centres of Hellenism, though Coptic remained the tongue of the mass of the population of the country as a whole. Then, in 639, the Arab invasion dramatically reversed all previous linguistic trends: Greek, and eventually Coptic, too, had to give way to the speech of the conqueror. The Greek colony of Cyrene was likewise overrun by the Arabs two years later with analogous consequences.

A little later, Greek suffered another set-back, this time in its very heartland. Slavonic tribes broke into Mainland Greece in the eighth century and established themselves in strength in many parts of the country, not least in the Peloponnese. For a time, it may have looked as though the newcomers were to become the dominant linguistic force, but as it turned out, the Greeks in due course assimilated the Slavs.

But while Greek was thus reasserting itself in Greece proper, it was suddenly overwhelmed in Asia Minor. Following military victory north-west of Lake Van in 1071, Turks began to flood in from the East, and by the thirteenth century had crossed the Bosphorus so that Turkish now began to replace Greek in Eastern Thrace, too. Constantinople itself fell in 1453. All the same, some enclaves of Greek speech remained in the now predominantly Turkish territory. Greek continued in use in Cappadocia and on the Pontus down to the present century. It similarly survived in areas along the Aegean coast. But the explusion of a million and a quarter Greeks in 1922 and 1923 left only a mere 100,000 survivors, by now largely assimilated.

In the eighteenth century and later, the Greeks on the Pontus were strong enough to send colonists across the Black Sea to Russia, and in the 1930s about 100,000 villagers in the Rostov district were using Pontic Greek. Not far away another, slightly smaller colony, of uncertain origin, existed in the Mariupol (now Zhdanov) region. At the time referred to, a fair amount of publishing in Greek, including school books, was taking place, some of it in these two local forms of the language, both very different from the language of Greece itself, in this respect comparable to Italiot (below).

During the period of Ottoman rule from 1461 to 1829, many Turkish settlements were made in Greece, and an even greater number of Albanians were brought in. Most of the Turks were transferred to Turkey in 1922 and 1923, while the Albanians have by now generally been assimilated. The Arumanians in Greece, too, are a declining entity, so that Greece is today much more homogeneous linguistically than before.

Greek is the native language of well over nine millions: upwards of eight and a half in the Kingdom of Greece, including a few thousands in the frontier areas of Albania and other neighbouring countries, with a further 450,000 in the Republic of Cyprus.

Cyprus

Writing in Cyprus is attested as far back as the middle of the second millennium B.C. When the first Greek colonists arrived is not known, but they were evidently ignorant of the alphabet, since the earlier Cypriot Greek inscriptions, from the seventh to the third centuries B.C., employ a cumbersome syllabary taken over from the auto-chthonous inhabitants. This syllabary is most unsuitable for the writing of Greek and was apparently constructed for a non-Indo-European language. The pre-Greek inhabitants, whatever their affinities, preserved their identity for some centuries, as inscriptions in their language continue until the fourth century B.C. These cannot as yet be interpreted; the language is provisionally known as Eteo-cypriot. With the extinction of this language and of Phoenician, which gained a foothold in the island in antiquity, Cyprus remained to all intents and purposes purely Greek-speaking until the establishment of Turkish rule in 1571. Turkish hegemony lasted until 1878, when Cyprus passed under British control. During this time, Turkish peasants and artisans settled widely throughout the island. Their descendants have generally retained their native language and today number 120,000 or one-fifth of the population. Owing to the troubles of the last two decades, the Turkish minority has tended to congregate so forming predominantly Turkish neighbourhoods. British rule ceased in 1960 when the present republic was proclaimed with Greek and Turkish as its official languages.

Italiot Greek

The Greeks in southern Italy were still significant enough to be known to Roger Bacon in the thirteenth century, who recommended that

Greek books be acquired there. But the Greek-speaking area has greatly diminished since then and the language is today heard only in two small enclaves in Calabria and Apulia, in the 'toe' and 'heel' of Italy respectively. The former comprises Bova and four neighbouring hamlets. Here the language is disintegrating as it rapidly yields to Italian, being now used by hardly more than a thousand persons. But Greek is much stronger in the other enclave, where quite 20,000 persons living in Calimera and eight surrounding villages retain it as their patois. Italiot Greek is not officially recognised today and plays no part in church or school, where proceedings are conducted in Italian. Nevertheless, occasional publications in the Apulian dialect appear; they employ the Latin character.

Since Italiot Greek has for so long evolved independently of other Greek and has been much influenced by Italian, it occupies a special position among Greek dialects. It is scarcely comprehensible to a speaker of Balkan Greek. We would characterise Italiot Greek as a separate language, falling into two quite considerably differentiated dialects, Calabrian and Apulian.

Greek alphabet

The Greek alphabet was borrowed from a North Semitic type used by the Phoenicians. The earliest Greek inscriptions are assigned to the seventh century B.C. with the exception of a graffito incised on a wine jug (the Dipylon oinochoe) regarded as belonging to the late eighth century. The shape of the letters, however, is considerably different from the Phoenician prototype, indicating a period of independent evolution. Just how the vowelless Semitic script was transmitted and adapted is not known but borrowing appears to have taken place early in the first millennium.

Two main types of alphabet developed in Greece: Ionic, from which the standard Greek alphabet is derived, and Chalkidic. The latter died out in its homeland, but survived in the colonial West, where it was eventually employed to write local Italian languages (p. 25).

Texts in linear script

Excavations in Crete, especially at Knossos (1900–1904) and on the Greek mainland at Pylos (since 1939) and Mycenae (since 1952) have brought to light over 3,000 clay tablets, and a still greater number of fragments, inscribed with both ideograms and linear writing. As the texts are accompanied by numerical signs, they appear to be accounts or inventories. They have been dated archaeologically to the period from the fifteenth to the twelfth centuries B.C. and are thus witnesses to Minoan–Mycenaean culture. Two forms of linear writing occur, an older one, called Linear A and a development of this, Linear B.

Most of the tablets are inscribed in the latter. It consists of 89 different signs, too high a number for an alphabet, but about right for a syllabary. The texts also contain some 130 ideograms.

In 1953, M. Ventris and J. Chadwick surprised the learned world with a publication which offered, at one stroke, a virtually complete decipherment of Linear B. The language was declared to be an early form of Greek and named Mycenaean. Most scholars accept these findings, but there are some dissenters. The minority holds that the syllabary, as deciphered, presents an intolerable number of homograms; for instance, *pa-te* can stand for (later Gk.) *pa-tér* 'father' or *pán-tes* m.pl. 'all'. Ideograms may have a peculiar function. Thus a drawing like a pot on three legs is stated to be preceded by syllables spelling out 'tripod', a redundancy unparalleled in other scripts of this age. It may be emphasised that only a fraction of the material—of the order of, say, one-tenth—has been interpreted more or less. Not one of these brief documents could as yet be explained in its entirety and new finds of tablets have not led to any general improvement in the understanding of the materials. In view of such difficulties, it would be important to learn exactly by what steps Ventris, the prime mover, achieved his decipherment in the first place. This information, however, has never been fully presented. Most unfortunately, Ventris lost his life just after he had sprung into fame and before he could answer his critics. Chadwick, his collaborator in the later stages, has been content to argue 'It is no longer of any consequence to know how the values were obtained; the words they yield constitute their own proof' (*Decipherment of Linear B*, 1958 and various issues since, p. 92).

In this predicament, the outsider may prefer to regard the Ventris decipherment as conjectural and reckon with the possibility that the language behind the mysterious script could in fact be pre-Greek, as is usually thought to be the case with texts in Linear A, and also in various other pre-alphabetic inscriptions found here and there by archaeologists both in Mainland Greece and on the islands.

Pelasgian

There is abundant evidence for a pre-Greek population both in the toponomy of the country and in the ordinary vocabulary of Greek. The Greeks themselves called these people Pelasgians, and Herodotus specifically states that the original inhabitants of Attica were Pelasgians who had adopted the Greek language. Pelasgian was apparently a living language locally in the Aegean until the fifth century B.C.

Modern investigators, however, are inclined to posit the existence of several ethnic groups in pre-Hellenic Greece. It is seen that many place names contain elements not known in Indo-European, as

-ēnai in *Mukēnai* 'Mycenae' and *Athēnai* 'Athens' or *-issós* in the Attica river names *Ilissós, Kephissós*. Similar things apply to those parts of the Greek vocabulary which provide evidence of an advanced culture, e.g. *plínthos* 'brick', *asáminthos* 'bath tub', showing the ending seen again in the place name *Kórinthos* 'Corinth', or the exotic *basileús* 'king' with its unique feminine *basílissa* 'queen'. These are loan words from a substratum to all appearances non-Indo-European. It is likely that pre-Greek languages are attested in pictographic and linear scripts of great antiquity unearthed by archaeologists, cf. 'Texts in linear script' above. A few non-Greek alphabetic inscriptions, hitherto unread, have also been found in Greece.

There are a number of items in the Greek lexicon which, while being apparently non-Greek in origin, nevertheless make an Indo-European impression. Thus *púrgos* 'castle, stronghold' seems to be cognate with synonymous OEng., Old German *burg*, but the form of the Greek word is unexpected. It is therefore sometimes assumed that Gk. *púrgos* is a borrowing from a lost Indo-European language submerged by Greek. Such a language would naturally develop sound laws of its own, of which *púrgos* would be an illustration. This putative Indo-European language is generally identified with Pelasgian.

THE STRUCTURE OF HELLENIC

ANCIENT GREEK

We quote below Classical Attic forms. The Homeric poems in particular contain a considerable number of archaic elements, but these do not significantly affect the overall picture and are accordingly omitted here.

Phonetics

There are five vowels: *a, e, i, o, u*, each long or short, and numerous diphthongs: *ai, au*, etc. Differences in length are indicated in the native script by special letters in the case of *e* and *o*; we transliterate *ē, ō*. The consonants transcribed *ph, th, kh*, were pronounced *p + h*, etc. The diacritics denote types of pitch accent.

Accidence

There are three genders, three numbers and five cases, and the Indo-European declensional classes are easily recognisable. IE **ekwos* 'horse' appears as *íkkos* or, much more commonly, as *híppos*. Paradigm:

Sg.nom.	*híppos*	Pl.	*híppoi*	Du.	*híppō*
voc.	*híppe*		*híppoi*		*híppō*
acc.	*híppon*		*híppous*		*híppō*
gen.	*híppou*		*híppōn*		*híppoin*
dat.	*híppōi*		*híppois*		*híppoin*

The adjectives have comparable declensional schemes.

The verb is highly synthetic and rich in tenses and moods, being in this respect second only to Sanskrit. It has six basic tenses in the indicative (pres., fut., imperf., aor., perf., pluperf.), three in the imperative (pres., aor., perf.) and the same in the subjunctive, four in the optative (pres., fut., aor., pluperf.). There are five infinitives and five participles (pres., fut., aor., perf., pluperf.). There are two voices: active and middle, the latter increasingly with passive meaning. Sample paradigm:

ACTIVE
Present

Infin. *phérein* 'to bear'

		Indicative	Subjunctive	Optative	Imperative
Sg.1		*phérō*	*phérō*	*phéroimi*	
	2	*phéreis*	*phérēis*	*phérois*	*phére*
	3	*phérei*	*phérēi*	*phéroi*	*pherétō*
Pl.1		*phéromen*	*phérōmen*	*phéroimen*	
	2	*phérete*	*phérēte*	*phéroite*	*phérete*
	3	*phérousi*	*phérōsi*	*phéroien*	*pheróntōn*
Du.2		*phéreton*	*phérēton*	*phéroiton*	*phéreton*
	3	*phéreton*	*phérēton*	*pheroítēn*	*pherétōn*

Participle sg.nom. *phérōn* m., *phérousa* f., *phéron* n.

Imperfect (indic. only) sg.1 *épheron*, 2 *épheres*, 3 *éphere*, pl.1 *ephéromen*, 2 *ephérete*, 3 *épheron*, du.2 *ephéreton*, 3 *epherétēn*

MIDDLE/PASSIVE
Present

Infin. *phéresthai* 'to bear (in one's own interest)' or 'to be borne'

		Indicative	Subjunctive	Optative	Imperative
Sg.1		*phéromai*	*phérōmai*	*pheroímēn*	
	2	*phérei*	*phérēi*	*phéroio*	*phérou*
	3	*phéretai*	*phérētai*	*phéroito*	*pherésthō*
Pl.1		*pherómetha*	*pherṓmetha*	*pheroímetha*	
	2	*phéresthe*	*phérēsthe*	*phéroisthe*	*phéresthe*
	3	*phérontai*	*phérōntai*	*phérointo*	*pherésthōn*

Du.2   *phéresthon*   *phérēsthon*   *phéroisthon*   *phéresthon*
   3   *phéresthon*   *phérēsthon*   *pheroísthēn*   *pherésthōn*

Participle sg.nom. *pherómenos* m., *pheroménē* f., *pherómenon* n.
Imperfect (indic. only) sg.1 *epherómēn*, 2 *ephérou*, 3 *ephéreto*, pl.1
epherómetha, 2 *ephéresthe*, 3 *ephéronto*, du.2 *ephéresthon*, 3 *epherésthēn*

The future is formed from another root, hence *oísō* '(I) shall bear',
etc., the remaining tenses from a third, e.g. perf. *enénokha* '(I) have
borne', aor. *énenka* '(I) bore', etc.

Numbers: 1 *heîs*, 2 *dúo*, 3 *treîs*, 4 *téssares*, 5 *pénte*, 6 *héx*, 7 *heptá*,
8 *oktṓ*, 9 *ennéa*,10 *déka*, 100 *hekatón*

Vocabulary

The Indo-European character of Greek shows unmistakeably in
the major part of the word stock, as

taûros 'bull': Lat. *taurus*, Ir. *tarbh*, Welsh *tarw*, Icel. *þjór*, also Lith.
taûras, Russ. *tur* with the specialised meaning 'aurochs'
agrós 'field': Skt. *ájras*, Lat. *ager*, Eng. *acre* (original sense in
green acres)
zugón 'yoke': Skt. *yugám*, Lat. *jugum*, Hittite *yugan*, Russ. *ígo*,
Welsh *iau*, Eng. *yoke*
thugátēr 'daughter': Skt. *duhitár-*, Lith. *duktě̃*, gen. *duktêrs*, Russ.
doč', gen. *dóčeri*, Armen. *dustr*, Toch.A *ckācar*, B *tkācer*
ophrûs 'brow': Skt. *bhrûs*, Eng. *brow*, Russ. *brov*', Lith. *bruvìs*
polús 'much': Skt. *purús*, Goth. *filu*, Ir. *il-*
hérpei 'creeps': Skt. *sárpati*, Lat. *serpit*

Texts

From Xenophon, *Anábasis* 'Expedition', *c.* 400 B.C.

Kaì euthùs anagóntes   toùs   anthrṓpous élenkhon
and at-once bringing-up the (two) men   (they) interrogated

dialabóntes   eí tina eideîen   állēn hodòn ḕ   tḕn
taken-separately if any (they) knew other way   than the

phanerán.   Ho mèn oûn héteros ouk
visible (one) the however one   not

éphē   mála pollõn phóbōn
said ('said he didn't') (in spite of) very many threats

prosagoménōn. Epeì dè   oudèn   ōphélimon élegen,
made   since however nothing useful   (he) was saying

horõntos toũ hetérou   katesphágē.
seeing   the other ('in sight of the other') (he) was-slaughtered

Ho dè   loipòs   élexen hóti hoũtos
the however remaining (one) said   that this (one) ('the first man')

mèn   ou phaíē dià taũta
indeed not said for these

eidénai,   hóti autõi
to-know ('said he didn't know for the reason') that to-him

etúnkhane   thugátēr ekeĩ par'   andrì
was-happening daughter there beside husband

ekdedoménē.   Autòs
given-out ('he happened to have a daughter married there') he

d'   éphē hēgésesthai   dunatèn
however said to-lead ('that-he-would-lead') (them along an) able

kaì hupozugíois   poreúesthai   hodón.
also by-baggage-animals to-be-traversed way

Matthew vi.9–13

Páter hēmõn, ho en toĩs ouranoĩs: hagiasthétō tò ónomá sou.
father of-us the in the heavens be-hallowed the name of-thee

Elthátō hē basileía sou.   Genēthétō tò thélēmá sou,   hōs en
come the kingdom of-thee be-done the will   of-thee as in

ouranõi kaì epì gẽs.   Tòn árton hēmõn tòn epioúsion dòs hēmĩn
heaven and on earth the bread of-us the daily   give to-us

sémeron. Kaì áphes hēmĩn tà opheilémata hēmõn, hōs kaì hēmeĩs
today   and forgive to-us the debts   of-us   as also we

aphíemen toĩs opheilétais hēmõn. Kaì mè eisenénkēis hēmãs eis
forgive the debtors   of-us   and not into-lead us   into

peirasmón, allà rhũsai hēmas apò toũ ponēroũ. Hóti soũ   estin
temptation but deliver us   from the evil   for of-thee is

hē basileía kaì hē dúnamis kaì hē dóxa eis toùs aiõnas.
the kingdom and the power   and the glory into the ages

MODERN GREEK

Phonetics

The spelling of Modern Greek is the traditional one, giving the language a superficially archaic appearance. The ancient vowel system has been drastically simplified. The phonemic distinction between short and long has vanished, differences today being purely phonetic in that any vowel is lengthened somewhat in stressed position. Moreover, *ē, i, u* and various diphthongs, notably *ei* and *oi*, have fallen together as [i], old *e* and *ai* are now both [ɛ], *au* and *eu* are [av,ɛv], *ou* is [u]. The consonants transliterated *ph, th, kh* have become voiceless spirants, while *b, d, g* have become the corresponding voiced spirants, *kh* and *g* having a palatal pronunciation before front vowels. Voiced occlusives are now less common and are written *mp, nt, gk*, i.e. [b,d,g]. The aspirate *h* is lost. The modern accent is predominantly one of stress.

Accidence

The language preserves the three genders, but has lost the dual number and the dative case. It continues the ancient word for 'horse', though only as a literary form. We therefore substitute *aderphós* 'brother'. Paradigm:

Sg.nom.	*aderphós*	Pl.	*aderphoí*
voc.	*aderphé*		*aderphoí*
acc.	*aderphó*		*aderphoús*
gen.	*aderphoũ*		*aderphõn*

The adjective has retained a comparable inflectional system.

The morphology of the verb has been simplified. The infinitive system and the optative conjugation have gone. The subjunctive is formally reduced to the present and aorist, indeed in the former only orthographic differences distinguish it from the indicative. New analytic forms have developed for the future and perfect. Middle voice as such has given way to passive use. Ancient *phérō* survives in the modern language as *phérnō* and has been generalised throughout the conjugation. Sample paradigm:

ACTIVE

	Present		Aorist	
	Indicative	Subjunctive	Indicative	Subjunctive
Sg.1	*phérnō*	*phérnō*	*éphera*	*phérō*
2	*phérneis*	*phérnēs*	*épheres*	*phérēs*
3	*phérnei*	*phérnē*	*éphere*	*phérē*

Pl.1	*phérnome*	*phérnōme*	*phérame*	*phéroume*
2	*phérnete*	*phérnete*	*phérate*	*phérete*
3	*phérnoun*	*phérnoun*	*épheran*	*phéroun*

Imperf.pres.sg. *phérne*, pl. *phérnete*, aor.sg. *phére*, pl. *phérete*
Participle pres. *phérontas*
Imperf. (indic. only) sg.1 *épherna*, etc. (as for aorist)
Future (continuous) sg.1 *thà phérnō*, etc., (momentary) *thà phérō*, etc.
Conditional: sg.1 *thà épherna*, etc., *thà éphera*, etc.
Perf. *ékhō phérei* '(I) have borne', etc.

PASSIVE

	Present		Aorist	
	Indicative	Subjunctive	Indicative	Subjunctive
Sg.1	*phérnomai*	*phérnōmai*	*phértheka*	*phérthō̃*
2	*phérnesai*	*phérnesai*	*phérthēkes*	*pherthē̃s*
3	*phérnetai*	*phérnetai*	*phérthēke*	*pherthē̃*
Pl.1	*phernómaste*	*phernómaste*	*pherthékame*	*pherthoũme*
2	*phérneste*	*phérneste*	*pherthékate*	*pherthē̃te*
3	*phérnontai*	*phérnōntai*	*phérthēkan*	*pherthoũn*

Imperf.pres.sg. *phérnou*, pl. *phérneste*, aor.sg. *phérou*, pl. *pherthē̃te*
Participle pres. *phernoúmenos*, perf. *pherménos*
Imperf. (indic. only) sg.1 *phernómoun*, 2 *phernósoun*, 3 *phernótan*, pl.1 *phernómaste*, 2 *phernósaste*, 3 *phernóntan*
Future (continuous) sg.1 *thà phérnomai*, etc., (momentary) *thà pherthō̃*, etc.
Conditional *thà phernómoun*, etc., *thà phérthēka*, etc.
Perf. *ékhō pherthe*̃ '(I) have been borne', etc.

Numbers: 1 *hénas*, 2 *dúo*, 3 *treîs*, 4 *téssereis*, 5 *pénte*, 6 *héxi*, 7 *hephtá*, 8 *okhtṓ*, 9 *enniá*, 10 *déka*, 100 *hekató*

A note on vocabulary

Demotic Greek employs many foreign words, among which a Turkish element is noticeable, e.g. *manávēs* 'greengrocer', *ntoulápi* 'cupboard', *touphéki* 'rifle' (T. *manav, dolap, tüfek*). As a result of the two styles current in Greek today, a large number of doublets occur, e.g. essentially literary *híppos* 'horse', *ártos* 'bread', *lakhanopṓlēs* 'greengrocer' beside demotic *álogo, psōmí, manávēs*. Often the difference is one of morphology, e.g. literary *géphura* f. 'bridge', *glukús* 'sweet', *patḗr* 'father', *Athē̃nai* pl. 'Athens', demotic *gephúri* n., *glukós, patéras, Athḗna* sg.

Texts

From G. Oikonomídēs, *Homérou Odusseía* 'Homer's
Odyssey', Athens, pp. 181–2

Hē Pēnelópē mpḗke stèn   aíthousa kaì eîpe stoùs mnēstḗres:
the Penelope came into-the room   and said to-the suitors

'*Akoûste me,   mnēstḗres, aphoû epiménete kápoion nà*
listen   to-me suitors   since you-insist someone in-order-that

pantreutõ apò sãs   érkhomai
I-marry from you ('you insist that I marry one of you') I-come

loipòn nà   sãs   proteínō héna agṓnisma. Edõ eînai tò
then in-order-that to-you I-propose a   contest   here is   the

megálo tóxo toũ   Odusséa. Hópoios mporései ákopa nà tanúsē mè
great bow of-the Odysseus whoever is-able   easily to draw with

tà khéria tou   tè khordè kaì nà perásē tò
the hands of-him ('with his hands') the string and to shoot the

bélos mésa ki' ap' tà dṓdeka pelékia, autòs thà gínē   ántras
arrow right-through the twelve axes   he   shall become husband

mou, autòn th' akolouthḗsō, tò spíti tò suzugikó mou
of-me him shall I-follow   the house the conjugal of-me

aphénontas, poù oúte stòn húpno mou, tharrõ, dè thà tò
leaving   which even in-the sleep of-me I-think not shall it

lēsmonḗsō.
I-forget

Matthew vi.9–13

Patéra mas, poù eîsai stoùs ouranoús: às hagiastẽ t' ónomá
father our who art in-the heavens   be-hallowed the name

sou.   Às érthē hē basileía sou.   Às gínē tò thélēmá sou,
of-thee come the kingdom of-thee be-done the will   of-thee

hópōs stòn ouranò étsi kaì stè   gẽ. Tò psōmí mas tò
as   in-the heaven so   also on-the earth the bread of-us the

kathēmerinò dõse mas sémera. Kaì sukhóresé mas tà khréē mas,
daily   give us today   and forgive   us   the debts of-us

hópōs ki' emeîs sukhōroûme toùs khreōpheilétes mas. Kaì mè mâs
as   also we   forgive   the debtors   of-us and not us

phérēs sè peirasmó allà leutérōsé mas apò tòn ponēró. Giatì
lead   into temptation but deliver   us   from the evil-one for

dikế sou eînai hē basileía kaì hē dúnamē kaì hē dóxa stoùs
thine   is   the kingdom and the power   and the glory into-the

aiõnes.
ages

3

ITALIC

The linguistic configuration of Ancient Italy was highly complex. Venetic was spoken in the north-east, and Celtic in the Po Valley. Between the Celts and the Tyrrhenian Sea lay the Ligurians, of unknown affinities. To the south were the non-Indo-European Etruscans, whose territory stretched from the sea to the Apennines as far south as the Tiber. East of them lived the Umbrians and related peoples; south of the Tiber, the Latins inhabited Latium. The Samnites, whose language was Oscan, disputed the southern half of the peninsula with Messapians and Greeks. A people known as Siculi, of uncertain connections, lived in Sicily side by side with influential colonies of Greeks. Sardinia and Corsica seem to have held autochthonous populations of unknown stock.

Latin is seen to have originally been a member of a group of closely related dialects, usually termed Latin-Faliscan after the better known ones. Faliscan was the speech of the town and environs of Falerii. But none of the Latin-like dialects is attested in more than a few words in archaic inscriptions. With the rise of Rome they were early replaced by Latin, say before the end of the second century B.C. The Latin-Faliscan dialects occupied a very restricted area. They had, however, much in common with a larger group known as Osco-Umbrian, and the two groups have been traditionally linked together as the Italic branch of the Indo-European family. But it is now argued that whereas the two groups do share many features, there are also a number of differences which seem to be more fundamental than the similarities. It is therefore likely that the latter are relatively recent and due to the subsequent co-existence in Italy of two originally distinct branches of Indo-European. But though distinct, the two branches all the same stood in close genetic relationship to each other, and to Celtic.

It was the speech of the minor district of Latium, in particular that variety current in the city of Rome, which was destined to supersede all the multifarious languages of Ancient Italy and many more beside. The success of Latin was the linguistic consequence of the Roman Empire.

The expansion of Latin

From the fifth century B.C., Rome was an aggressive force. Before the middle of the following century, she had come to dominate Latium. As a result of final victory in the Samnite Wars in 290 B.C., Roman armies advanced to the far south and overcame the Greek cities there by 275. Meanwhile Etruria had been subdued, resistance ceasing in 265. During the next few decades, first Sicily and then Sardinia and Corsica became Roman provinces. By 192, the Gauls of the Po Valley had laid down their arms, whereupon the Veneti voluntarily became subjects of Rome, so that all Italy was then effectively controlled by a single government.

At the end of the Second Punic War in 201, Rome received the whole of the Iberian Peninsula, though many decades were to pass before the centre, west and north were subjugated. Part of Illyria had fallen to Rome as early as 229, the rest was subdued by 168. The kings of Thrace became Roman vassals. Macedonia was turned into a Roman province in 146, the rest of Greece forgoing its independence a few years later. Asia Minor, Syria, Palestine, and eventually Egypt likewise passed into Roman hands. On the destruction of Carthage in 146, the whole of its territory was reconstituted as the Roman province of Africa. About the same time, Rome was very active in southern Gaul, which in 121 also became a Roman province—the modern Provence. The remainder of Gaul was conquered by Julius Caesar between 58 and 51. In 15 B.C., Rhaetia was occupied and the way to southern Germany lay open. In A.D. 43 began the Roman occupation of Britain.

The dates of linguistic conquests are naturally not so precise as those marking military or political victories. But the general line of development is not in doubt. Latin automatically carried official status and enjoyed immense prestige throughout the Empire, so that very soon the language of the conqueror began to replace the multifarious languages of the conquered. In Italy itself the non-Latin languages had generally succumbed by the beginning of the Christian era, though Oscan seems to have survived into the second century A.D. Only the immigrant Greek of the far south resisted with some success and even today is not quite extinct. The pattern of linguistic

assimilation was repeated in Western and Central Europe, in the
Balkans and in Africa. With the exception of Basque in the Western
Pyrenees, the indigenous languages of the Iberian Peninsula probably
disappeared as quickly as the non-Latin languages of Italy. In Gaul,
both the non-Indo-European Aquitanian and the Celtic Gaulish had
in the main yielded to Latin by the end of the fourth century. It is likely
that Latin was naturalised in Britain, too, at least in the more accessible
south-east. Latin certainly made great headway in the Balkans,
dominating the western half, then penetrating further east. The sphere
of Latin also extended into the Central European Plain. It embraced
the Alpine area, where it replaced Rhaetian, a language of unknown
affinities attested in a handful of inscriptions, and spread to the *limes*
on the Upper Danube. After the fall of Carthage, Latin established
itself in the new province of Africa. Malta, oddly enough, does not
appear to have become Latin-speaking. So much at least has been
deduced from the absence of Latin loanwords in Maltese (a form of
Arabic introduced in the ninth century). It is generally thought that
Malta was previously Punic (i.e., Phoenician) in speech, like Carthage.
It is less surprising that Latin did not supersede the languages of the
highly cultured eastern part of the Empire, among which Greek was
pre-eminent. As the medium of a civilisation greatly admired by the
Romans, Greek remained the chief literary language of the Near East
throughout the period of Roman domination, though Latin came into
official use there and remained so until the sixth century.

Not all the linguistic gains made by Latin, as catalogued above,
proved permanent. The language disappeared from Africa following
the Arabic conquest of 675. Latin in Britain will have been threatened
by resurgent British in the sub-Roman period and finally obliterated
by the invading Anglo-Saxons. Across the Channel, British formed an
overseas colony in Armorica. Latin further lost ground to German
advancing across the Rhine and Danube. Details of the position in
the Balkans are obscure, but though Latin survived vigorously in
some areas, it also yielded much territory to languages introduced
from the north and east, especially to Slavonic. The indigenous
Albanian also drove Latin from some of its strongholds. But in Gaul,
in the Iberian Peninsula and in Italy itself, Latin remained unquestionably master, though often suffering foreign inroads and the establishment of enclaves of alien speech. The area over which Latin became
the popular language is technically called Romania.

Periodisation

The documented history of Latin begins with an inscription of the
sixth century B.C. By the middle of the third century, a written literature on the Greek model was coming into being. These beginnings were

followed by the Classical Period, conventionally divided into the Golden Age, from 80 B.C. to the death of Augustus in A.D. 14, and the Silver Age from then until 120. During the latter part of the Classical Period, spoken Latin is seen to have been changing rapidly. The spoken style of the first to the fifth centuries, often attested in non-literary inscriptions, is termed Vulgar Latin. This oral medium was, of course, anything but uniform over the wide area of Romania, but rather a continuum of closely related dialects, of which defined types are recognisable: Italian, Iberian, Gallic, Rhaetian, Balkan. Out of these arose the medieval and modern Romance or Neo-Latin languages. The influence of Latin spread far beyond the boundaries of Romania. Neighbouring languages absorbed a large quantity of Latin loanwords and structural features of Latin were often imitated, too.

Latin as a dead language

Although it was not long before Classical Latin became virtually a foreign tongue to speakers of Vulgar Latin, it alone was regarded as the proper literary medium. As a dead language in the sense that it was no longer anybody's mother tongue, literary Latin remained in use throughout the Middle Ages, even though classical correctness was by no means always achieved. The Catholic Church adopted literary Latin as its official medium, in this as in other respects continuing Imperial tradition. By the same token, Latin remained the language of law, administration and scholarship. Not only in Romania was Latin thus employed, but also to a considerable extent in Celtic, Germanic and in some Slavonic countries. It was in the Romance-speaking area, however, that Latin was most influential and its employment undoubtedly delayed the literary development of the nascent Romance languages.

From the thirteenth century Latin faced serious competition from the vernaculars, before which it gradually retreated. By the beginning of modern times, Latin was chiefly used as the language of international diplomacy, of learning and the Church. John Milton is often re-membered as Cromwell's Latin Secretary. Shortly afterwards, thanks to the prestige of France under Louis XIV, French replaced Latin as the recognised medium of international negotiations. In the world of learning, Latin held its own until about the end of the seventeenth century, when its place was taken by the main vernaculars. The Catholic Church has been the most conservative. Though by recent enactment largely banished from the Mass, Latin remains the official language of the Church.

It should not be forgotten that Latin was commonly used as an oral medium throughout the Middle Ages and even later. This tradition is not entirely defunct. For example, at the Catholic seminary *Collegium Urbani* in Rome intending missionaries from forty countries hear their lectures and formally discuss their subjects in Latin. But outside the classroom, the common language of these students is—Italian.

The Latin alphabet

The Romans were not only indebted to Greece for literary models, they were ultimately indebted to her for the very alphabet they wrote with. The Greek alphabet developed two main types, Ionic and Chalkidic. The latter was used by those Greeks who about the middle of the eighth century B.C. began to set up colonies in Italy. This alphabet was at once taken over by the Etruscans, then the most advanced of the Italian races. Subsequently this alphabet, in variant forms, was transmitted by the Etruscans to the other peoples of Ancient Italy, among them the Romans.

ROMANCE LANGUAGES

French

On the territory of modern France one recognises two divergent types of Romance. They are the descendants of the languages known in medieval times as Langue d'Oïl and Langue d'Oc, spoken in the northern and southern halves of the country respectively, the terms *oïl* and *oc* being the contemporary forms of the word for 'yes'. The linguistic boundary runs along the Gironde and Dordogne to Lussac, then north through Angoulême, sweeping in an arc through Montluçon and St Etienne to reach the Italian frontier opposite Grenoble. Modern Standard French derives from the northern language; on the southern language, see Provençal.

French is the earliest and best-attested Neo-Latin language, first in a few lines in the Strasbourg Oaths of 842, literature proper starting with a poem in praise of St Eulalia from the end of the same century. French is richly documented in various medieval dialects, the language up to 1350 being termed Old French. In the middle period from 1350 to 1550, the dialect of the Ile de France with Paris at its centre emerges as the dominant literary form, continuing since then as Modern French. The fame of France's culture and the power of her kings led to the general acceptance of French instead of Latin as the language of international affairs (p. 24) and French was avidly studied in educated circles throughout Europe. French hegemony in this respect remained until the beginning of the present century, by which time English had clearly established itself as the chief world language.

But French retains a few relics of its erstwhile standing, for example as the official medium of the World Postal Union.

Northern French early gained access to the south following the destruction of the independents courts there in the early thirteenth century. Standard French has meanwhile replaced many of the spoken dialects both in the north and south, and at the present time all the remaining dialect speakers, even in the south, can also speak the standard language with ease. Standard French is also gaining at the expense of various non-French languages spoken on the territory of Metropolitan France: Basque in the Basses Pyrénées, Catalan in Roussillon, Breton in Brittany, Flemish in French Flanders and German in Alsace-Lorraine.

The French-speaking area extends into Belgium, where the dialect is called Walloon. Here French has been in sharp conflict with Flemish, both languages now having official status (p. 104). Though only spoken in one frontier village in Luxembourg, French is by reason of a long tradition the usual official language of the Grand Duchy (p. 100). French is the language of the western parts of Switzerland and one of the four official languages of the Confederacy. French is further the native language of the great majority of the inhabitants of the Aosta Region in N.W. Italy. French has official status in Andorra, beside Catalan, which is the language of the native inhabitants.

French was the traditional language of the Channel Islanders in spite of the long association with England which goes back to the Norman Conquest. When Philip II of France annexed Normandy in 1204, the Channel Islands remained in English (properly Anglo-Norman) hands, but only at the commencement of the nineteenth century did French start to give way to English. French remains an official language in Jersey and was so in Guernsey until 1946. The language is still found in these two larger islands, spoken by a dwindling minority. The dialect is Norman, used as a patois by perhaps 30,000 in Jersey and a smaller number in Guernsey. According to the 1961 census, nearly 2,000 persons counted in Jersey had no English, but whether these were native Jerriais or simply French visitors was not stated.

While French was thus yielding ground in its outposts in the Channel, it was compensating for these losses in a new island possession in the Mediterranean. France acquired Corsica in 1758. The island-born population speaks an Italian dialect (p. 42), but the only official language is French, and in the towns at least the native dialect is much gallicised.

French in Europe is spoken as the first language by 52 millions in France (47 m.), Belgium (3,800,000), Switzerland (1,100,000), Italy

(100,000). French is further spoken by upwards of 7 millions overseas, chiefly in Canada (see below).

Anglo-Norman

French became domiciled in England at the time of the Norman Conquest as the native language of the new ruling class and was to remain so for a century and a half at least. Beside Latin, French now appeared as a language of administration, justice and business, while the vogue of French literature is well evidenced by the large number of surviving manuscripts. During this time English was, relatively speaking, much neglected as a literary idiom. But with the loss of Normandy in 1204, life in England became more insular. Those barons who preferred their English to their French estates naturally grew more English in outlook. If they had not already done so, they now began to acquire the English language. A sign of the changing linguistic situation, albeit still an isolated one of its kind, was a royal proclamation of 1258 drawn up not only in Latin and French, but also in English. Though more and more an acquired language, French in England continued as a usual written medium until the end of the fourteenth century. In pure literature its last notable representative was Gower, who also wrote in Latin and English; he died in 1401. Official French survived longest in the courts. Parliament was first opened in English in 1368. At the same time was enacted the Statute of Pleading whereby English was to replace French as the language of court proceedings. But this dispensation could only tardily be obeyed, since the law was still scarcely expressible in English. Law French, as it came to be called, though progressively corrupted by anglicisation, seems to have been common in 'pleadings' until Henry VIII's day. It was not finally abolished until 1731. It remains to add that the royal court itself was the most persistent centre of French culture and language. The first king after the Conquest to speak English as his mother tongue was Bolingbroke, born 1367, who ascended the throne as Henry IV in 1399.

The French employed in England is technically known as Anglo-Norman. It was essentially Norman, though it admitted forms from other dialects and in due course evolved a number of insular peculiarities. After 1204, it became more and more a book language. It will be remembered that the native French speakers never formed more than a tiny fraction of the total population. But thanks to their special status in the society of their time, they exercised an influence out of all proportion to their relative numerical strength. The position of French in England was peculiar in that it was a class language; it had no dialects.

French overseas

Colonisation carried the French language to the New World, to
Africa, to the East and the South Seas.

New World. French in the New World has best survived in Canada,
where today 6½ millions, close on one-third of the dominion total,
use French as their mother tongue. French, beside English, is an
official language in Canada, though at state level it is admittedly very
much the junior partner. However, the number of French speakers is
increasing, not only absolutely, but also relatively, and there is a
noticeable element of rivalry between the two languages. There are
two distinct areas of French settlement, each going back to the
beginning of the colonial period: the 'Canadian' of Quebec and the
'Acadian' of the Maritime Provinces.

Canadian is now by far the more influential and its speakers constitute well over 80 per cent of the inhabitants of Quebec Province.
Quebec itself is to all intents and purposes a French-speaking city,
while in Montreal two-thirds of the population are *francophone*. For
these, education is through the medium of the native tongue and they
may pass all their lives in an entirely French milieu. But urban
dwellers, at any rate, usually know English well, so that some 2½
millions are reckoned bilingual.

In the Maritime Provinces, French is very much less significant and
the number of speakers does not exceed 200,000, two-thirds of whom
live in New Brunswick where they form 40 per cent of the population.
The remainder are scattered over purely rural parts of Nova Scotia
and Prince Edward Island, accounting for 10 and 15 per cent of the
inhabitants respectively. The Acadians are bilingual, their French
having the inferior status of a patois; for official purposes their
medium is, in practice, English. Nevertheless, in spite of some
anglicisation, the number of Acadians continues to grow. Finally, in
this area, we notice the 5,000 French-speaking inhabitants of St
Pierre and Miquelon, off the south coast of Newfoundland; these two
small islands belong politically to France.

The Maritime Provinces would likely have remained as thoroughly
French as Quebec had not large numbers of the French inhabitants
been expelled by the British government as a consequence of the
decree of 1753. By the 1760s Acadian refugees—their situation im-
mortalised in Longfellow's *Evangeline*—were arriving in Louisiana
where French colonists were already established. The Acadians
occupied the empty coastal belt from the Mississippi to the Texas
border where their descendants retain their dialect, locally known as
Cajun 'Acadian'. The French of the older colonists who came and
named the territory in the seventeenth century also survives to some
extent; its speakers are found in New Orleans and environs. Louisiana

French has no official status and is essentially a patois. It is used by about 200,000, now all bilingual, and its continued existence is naturally imperilled by English. In addition, Creole French is spoken in Louisiana, see pp. 30f. where the French of the Antilles and South America is also referred to.

Africa. The French got off to a good start in the scramble for Africa. They initiated a successful war against Algeria in 1830 which ended with the annexation of that country. From this base, French power expanded eastwards and westwards. In 1881, Tunisia became a French protectorate, and by this time French influence was dominant in Morocco also. By 1954 there were 850,000 French settlers in Algeria, 300,000 in Morocco, 250,000 in Tunisia. French enjoyed official and high social status, it appeared to have gained a permanent hold on North Africa. But political changes dramatically reversed the situation. Morocco and Tunisia declared their independence in 1956, followed after a fierce struggle by Algeria in 1962. In all these countries, Arabic was made the sole official language. Moreover, since independence, the French population has been leaving. By 1964 it was down to half in Morocco and Tunisia, while in Algeria the exodus was cataclysmic, with less than 100,000 remaining. Today the French element is merely nominal and quite extraneous. But the French language is widely known in North Africa and will continue as the first European tongue, but otherwise the future belongs to Arabic as the chief indigenous medium.

French influence spread south of the Sahara, increasing rapidly from about 1890 and leading to the formation of French West Africa and French Equatorial Africa. The French language was introduced into the Congo by the Belgians. These territories, however, never attracted European settlers in any numbers. Meanwhile they have become independent (mostly in 1960), but the succession states, without exception, have retained French as their official medium. Indeed, this was inevitable in view of the multiplicity of indigenous languages, several hundred in all, most of which are used by relatively small groups and none of which have been adapted to cope adequately with modern administrative requirements. The Republic of the Cameroons unites former British as well as French territory; here English shares official status with French. French remains the official medium of the French Somali Coast, but one-time French Somaliland is now part of the Republic of Somalia where Arabic is official. Madagascar was a French colony from 1895 to 1960, when the island became independent with the native Malagasy as well as French official for all purposes. French is the primary medium chiefly of settlers from France, not above 20,000 in number. The mainly Swahili-speaking Comoro Islands were declared a French Overseas

Territory in 1958, retaining the official use of French. On the position in Reunion and Mauritius, see p. 32.

The East and South Seas. French has played a notable part in the Near East. Syria and the Lebanon became French mandates in 1920 and 1922 respectively, but French influence in that area dated from the previous century. These two countries became independent in 1944 with Arabic as the sole official language. French may, however, be expected to remain the European language best known in these countries.

The French were thwarted in their main designs on India in the eighteenth century, but retained Pondicherry and four smaller ports until 1956. The primary use of French, however, was essentially confined to persons of European descent.

The occupation of what was to be known as French Indo-China began in 1863, and with it the introduction of French as an official medium. It became widely known as a second language among the educated classes. But the emergence of the republics of Vietnam, Laos and Cambodia in 1946 prepared the way for the demise of French and the establishment of Vietnamese, Laotian and Cambodian as sole official languages. But, as elsewhere in the circumstances, French remains the best known European language.

French has become a significant language in the South Seas. It is the sole official medium of New Caledonia, French since 1853. In Tahiti, it shares official status with the native Tahitian. Of some 180,000 under the French flag in Polynesia, about 50,000 have French as their first language.

Creole French

The genesis of all forms of Creole French is traced to the Pidgin, the so-called Petit Nègre, developing on the west coast of Africa, especially in Senegal, as the result of French slave-trading activities in the early seventeenth century. It doubtless owed something to the Creole Portuguese already present in the same area. The Pidgin was transplanted with the slaves to the various colonies where it formed the nucleus of the emergent Creole which quickly replaced the autochthonous languages of the Africans. Five types of Creole French have evolved; they were developing in their main areas by the middle of the seventeenth century, and are as follows.

Louisiana Creole, the patois of perhaps 80,000 descendants of plantation slaves living in the southern part of the state of Louisiana, is now speedily giving way to English.

Closely related to the foregoing is Haiti Creole or Haitian, the mother tongue of the entire population of the Republic of Haiti. But the official language is Standard French. Even after independence in

1804, the ruling circles continued to look down upon Creole. But a change of heart has recently been taking place, and since 1961 Creole has played some part in elementary state education. Haiti is an impoverished and backward country with 89 per cent illiteracy. This accounts in large measure for the universal presence of Creole as well as for the fact that a language spoken by over $4\frac{1}{2}$ millions has only just received a modest measure of recognition in its own territory. How the Haitians will solve their language problem remains to be seen. Only since the 1940s has any mentionable amount of publishing been done in Creole, but the rate of production is on the increase and this will strengthen the position of Creole *vis-à-vis* Standard French. The issue will become more and more: Is Creole in education to be merely a bridge to the acquisition of French, or is Creole a language in its own right and one to be cultivated for its own sake? If the latter opinion prevails, Haitian will be seen as the national language, which could one day lead to its supplanting French as the official language of the country. It may be emphasised that French is a foreign language to the Haitians, the great majority of whom understand only Creole. French lexical elements predominate in the Creole, but are often drastically reshaped. The inflexional system of French, on the other hand, has been virtually discarded and new grammatical devices introduced, some of them reflecting African syntax. Several thousands of African words have also been found, though most survive only locally in rural districts. Haitian retains a few traces of the Carib Indian language of the original inhabitants of Hispaniola.

Antilles Creole is spoken in Guadeloupe, Dominica, Martinique, St Lucia, Grenada, and Trinidad and Tobago. Of these, only Guadeloupe (pop. 310,000) and Martinique (pop. 330,000) are now French—technically Overseas Departments—and here Creole is fairly strong though subject more and more to the influence of the official language, Standard French. The other islands passed into British hands and the resultant introduction of English adversely affected the French-based Creole. It is now on the verge of extinction in Grenada and almost so in Trinidad and Tobago. In St Lucia, however, it has maintained itself fairly well, especially in rural districts, though its speakers have usually acquired English as well. Altogether something like 700,000 persons use forms of Antillan Creole as their mother tongue. The Carib and Arawak dialects spoken in the islands at the time of European settlement died out long ago, except in Dominica where about a hundred Caribs have not yet entirely abandoned their ancestral tongue.

French Guiana Creole is spoken by some 30,000 living in Cayenne and the coastal region of this backward overseas department of France.

Indian Ocean Creole is the colloquial in Reunion (a French overseas department), in the Republic of Mauritius, and in the Seychelles.
The French colonisation of Reunion began in 1650 and Creole developed here as in the New World as the common language of the introduced slave population. Creole is still generally spoken throughout
the island by its 400,000 inhabitants, but Standard French is said to be
so well known that the Creole is presumably being modified by the
official language much as it is in Guadeloupe and Martinique. The
French took possession of Mauritius in 1712. This involved some
movement of population from Reunion, but Mauritian Creole is
nevertheless considerably different from that of the older colony, so
that the speech of other immigrants has had an important affect on
its development. Mauritius became British in 1814, and English
became the main official language; French has remained official,
though is much less used. But both English and French are native
languages only to the few thousand European residents. After the
abolition of slavery in 1835, a large influx of Indian coolies introduced a new ethnic element, and Indian languages, chiefly Hindu
stani, are still widely used in country districts. However, Creole is the
lingua franca of Mauritius' fast increasing population, now exceeding
800,000. Creole has hitherto played no part in education, where the
medium is usually English or French, but it seems certain that Creole
will one day become the ubiquitous oral medium. It is already the
cultural hallmark of Mauritian nationality and the use of the national
vernacular as a literary medium can hardly be long delayed. The French
occupied the Seychelles in 1768, the labour force coming mainly from
Mauritius and with it the Creole. The Seychelles (pop. 50,000) became
British in 1814 and today only English is official. A degree of anglicisation has been inevitable, but Creole continues to be the patois of the
native population, though a knowledge of English is widespread and
increasing. All these Indian Ocean islands were uninhabited at the
time of settlement.

Provençal

Provençal is properly the language of Provence with its capital
Marseilles, but the term is also used more widely to designate all the
dialects of the Langue d'Oc. These cover the whole of southern
France—excepting the small areas of Basque and Catalan (pp. 37f.)—
bounded on the east by Italian and on the north by the dialects of the
Langue d'Oïl (p. 25). Having first appeared in legal texts from the
end of the eleventh century, Provençal burst onto the European
literary scene in the twelfth century as the medium of the courtly lyric
of the troubadours. The language, Old Provençal, is remarkably
uniform, testifying it would seem to the existence of standardised

poetic diction comparable to that of their German imitators (p. 99). Yet this early glory was short-lived. The princely courts of the south were allegedly implicated in the Albigensian heresy and their political power destroyed by the armed forces of the north. After the battle of Muret in 1213, little is heard of the independence of the south in politics or thought. The Provençal language, however, lived on, though never again cultivated extensively as a written language. For such purposes, French was now usual. In the second half of the nineteenth century, however, a literary movement flickered into life around the work of the poet Mistral, who employed the dialect of Provence proper. But the language was already doomed, even before its last champion appeared. Already by the time of the Revolution and the Empire the towns were going over to French, and Provençal had acquired the stigma of a socially inferior rustic patois. Then compulsory French-medium education from 1870–80 spread an active knowledge of the state language throughout the countryside and hastened the break-up of the native tongue. Provençal survives today in certain rural localities, dialectally much diversified, and in spite of the efforts of some of its adepts, continues to retreat before French, the language of prestige, which by now all can handle with ease. It will be seen that, in this respect, Provençal occupies a position in France quite analogous to that of Plattdeutsch in Germany. Provençal is sometimes termed Occitan.

Spanish

It is not surprising that the Neo-Latin dialects of a well-defined geographical area such as the Iberian Peninsula should develop many features in common. Had historical processes led to the emergence of a single Iberian state, then surely there would have arisen out of the continuum of spoken dialects a single Iberian language. But here, as elsewhere, standard languages owe their existence to political configurations. Thus events in the eleventh and twelfth centuries laid a firm basis for the rise of Portugal as an independent political unit which would one day evolve its own national language. Similarly the political unity of Medieval Catalonia led to the creation of a Catalan literary language. But at the beginning of modern times, Catalonia unlike Portugal, was absorbed into the Kingdom of Spain and accepted Castilian, the dominant language of that kingdom, as its official medium also.

All three Iberian languages originated in the north. In 711, the Moors invaded the Iberian Peninsula and quickly made themselves masters of all but the most northerly districts. The Arabic of the conquerors did not replace the native Romance dialects, though those in the Moorish-ruled part, the Mozarabic dialects as they are called, took over numerous loan-words from Arabic. The position of the Moors in Spain was somewhat comparable to that of the Normans in England. Over the centuries, the unsubdued north regained more and more territory until the Moors were finally expelled in 1492. This gradual Reconquest was accompanied by a corresponding southward movement of the northern dialects, notably of Galician, Castilian and Catalan. Galician in the north-west provided the basis of Portuguese, Catalan spread down the east coast as far as the outskirts of Murcia, while Castilian, centrally situated between the two, became the official language of Spain. In this capacity it eventually displaced or overlaid the various other dialects, Galician and even Catalan not excepted. Only Portugal was protected by its political frontier. From the start, Castilian was the most significant literary dialect; it is the language of the mid-twelfth century epic *Poem of the Cid*. The most archaic Spanish, however, belongs to the eleventh century. The texts are a few stanzas of Mozarabic popular poetry, written in Arabic script, only recently recovered from unedited Arabic manuscripts discovered in North Africa.

Spanish is the native medium of some 26½ millions in Peninsular Spain and of an estimated 135 millions overseas.

Spanish overseas

Spanish has established itself in Africa, America and the Far East.

Africa. Spanish is the official language of Spain's overseas provinces: the Canary Islands, Spanish West Africa (Ifni and Spanish Sahara), and Spanish Guinea (Rio Muni with the islands Fernando Po and Annobón). Further, Spain has certain rights in Céuta and Melilla, where Spanish is also in use. The colonisation of the Canaries (pop. one million) began as early as 1402. They have been entirely Spanish-speaking since the extinction, in the seventeenth century at the latest, of the indigenous Guanche, a language of the Berber family. Fernando Po, with 70,000 inhabitants, is also Spanish-speaking, apart from a small residue of Bubi, a Bantu language. The island was ceded by Portugal in 1777. Elsewhere the native populations speak local languages as their primary medium; in Annobón the vernacular is Creole Portuguese.

America. Spain's overseas possessions were formerly, of course, far more extensive. Spanish was introduced into the Caribbean before the end of the fifteenth century, and the sixteenth saw its expansion in both North and (especially) Central and South America. But this immense colonial realm was lost to the mother country. The northern part fell to the United States, the rest declared itself independent. On US territory, Spanish has in general yielded to English, but immigration from Mexico has meant that there is never a shortage of native Spanish-speakers in the southern states. At present one can think in terms of a million such persons.

South of the Rio Grande, however, all the emergent states have continued the official use of Spanish. The states in question, with their populations, are: (Central America) Mexico 42.2 m., Guatemala 4.6 m., Republic of Honduras 2.4 m. (and about 25,000 in British Honduras), El Salvador 3.0 m., Nicaragua 1.7 m., Costa Rica 1.5 m., Panama 1.3 m., (Antilles) Cuba 7.8 m., Puerto Rico 2.7 m., Dominican Republic 3.8 m., (South America) Colombia 18.1 m., Venezuela 9.0 m., Ecuador 5.3 m., Peru 12.0 m., Bolivia 3.8 m., Paraguay 2.1 m., Uruguay 2.7 m., Chile 8.8 m., Argentina 22.7 m. The Spanish-speaking states in America have thus a total population of 155,500,000.

As in the case of North America (p. 110), the above population figures include an unknown, but certainly considerable proportion of immigrants whose mother tongue is not Spanish and who indeed may not even have acquired it. More significantly, the figures include about 18 million speakers (perhaps half of them monoglots) of autochthonous Indian languages, for these have survived much better than in North America. True, in the majority of Latin American countries today the proportion of those speaking Indian languages is small—from nil in the Antilles to, say, four per cent on the mainland—but in the so-called Indian countries the picture is rather different. In Mexico, especially in the southern part, something like four millions still have as their mother tongue an American Indian language, of whom perhaps a million understand no Spanish. The main languages concerned are, firstly, Nahuatl, the speech of the Aztecs and the most numerous constituent of the Uto-Aztecan family (p. 117), known to three-quarters of a million, and secondly Maya, spoken by over 300,000. In Guatemala, about one and a half million speak indigenous languages, the most prominent being Quiché and the very similar Cakchiquel (300,000 each) and Quekchi (200,000), all members of the Mayan family. But the greatest concentration is in Ecuador, Peru, Bolivia, and Paraguay where, perhaps propitiously, the number of speakers of the three main Amerindian languages is growing. Guaraní (1,800,000) is the language predominantly spoken throughout Paraguay and is regularly used in journalism, though Spanish is the medium of state education; both have official status. Dialects of the Guaraní type formerly dominated over the territory of present-day Brazil as far north as the Amazon Basin. Aymará is the native language of a million Indians in Bolivia and of half that number in Peru. In this latter country, some five and a half millions use Quechua, which claims another million and a half in Bolivia and well over a million in Ecuador. Both these languages appear to be genetically isolated. A large majority of Aymarans and Quechuans are monoglots. They inhabit the Andean highlands and play only a minor role in state politics. It is possible that acculturation and economic progress may lead to the hispanisation of these peoples, as has happened elsewhere. On the other hand, given present-day conditions, modernisation of life may lend prestige to these important autochthonous tongues, especially Quechua. This language had already spread widely as the official medium of the Inca Empire, and its influence was further extended by the Spanish Catholic mission, which adopted Quechua for its propaganda among the Indians. This expansion has taken place at the expense of lesser native languages, of which a number have become extinct. Aymará, too, has in many places yielded to Quechua. With its estimated eight million adherents, Quechua could become a powerful claimant for official recognition, at least in those parts where it is predominantly spoken.

Far East. Spanish was also carried to the Far East, firstly to the Philippines, later to Guam. Spanish colonists had settled in the former by the end of the sixteenth century. Spanish became the official language of the colony and was learnt as a second language by the native intelligentsia, but did not supplant any of the multifarious local languages in the archipelago, except in a creolised form and only to a limited extent (see below). When the United States took over in 1898, Spanish was retained as an official language, but had to take second place to English. Its influence rapidly declined, but it remains one of the three official languages of the present Republic of the Philippines (p. 115). According to the 1960 census, some 9,600 returned Spanish as their mother tongue. Spain occupied Guam and the rest of the Marianas in the seventeenth century and ruled there until 1898 (p. 115). Spanish did not replace the native Polynesian language Chamorro, but affected it to the extent that borrowings from Spanish account for something like nine-tenths of the vocabulary now in use.

Judeo-Spanish

In 1492, the year in which Columbus was preparing the way for Spanish in America, refugee Jews, expelled from Spain, were carrying the language to North Africa and Italy. Here they founded new communities which preserved the Spanish language. Many of these Sephardic ('Spanish') Jews later moved to the Balkans and the Levant which, together with North Africa, remained their chief strongholds down to recent times. Latterly, however, the greatest number of Sephardim are to be found in the United States or in Israel. Judeo-Spanish has remained fairly close to Iberian Spanish, but has evolved features of its own and regional differences are also present. Judeo-Spanish is often called Ladino; it may also be termed

Judezmo 'Jewish'. Its speakers are bilingual. The exclusive communal life of former times enabled the language to survive so well, but given modern conditions, rapid assimilation is the rule, so that this variety of Spanish can now hardly be expected to last for more than a couple of generations or so. We guess that about a quarter of a million know the language, which is still employed in journalism. In general, Hebrew characters are used, preferably in Rabbinical form, but there is some publishing in Latin letters.

Creole Spanish

Papiamento 'Speech' (*papia* 'speak'), the vernacular of Curaçao and the adjacent islands of Aruba and Bonaire, is considered to be a Spanish-based creole with an old Portuguese component. Its provenance and early history are obscure. The Spaniards are known to have made a settlement on Curaçao in 1527. The Dutch took over in 1634 and the present population does not appear to be older than this. Since Dutch has been the official language, Papiamento has absorbed many words from this source. It is the ubiquitous spoken language of the native-born population numbering about 175,000. It has some status in journalism, but Dutch is the medium of education.

Spanish contact vernaculars are in use in the Philippines. They are stated to be hispanised varieties of the Creole Portuguese brought to Manila in 1658 by a couple of hundred families evacuated from Ternate in the Moluccas. Two such dialects in Bataan are Caviteño and Ermitaño, said to have been spoken in 1942 by 18,000 and 12,000 bilinguals respectively, the speakers also knowing Tagalog (p. 115). A much more influential dialect is Zamboangueño, the colloquial of Zamboanga and district, also called Chabacano 'Vulgar', spoken according to the census of 1960 by over 125,000 persons. A study of this speech describes the census figure as too low and states that Chabacano is increasing its geographic range. An offshoot of Chabacano is Davaueño, spoken by an unknown number in Davao.

A note on Basque

The provinces at the angle of the Bay of Biscay, protected by the ranges of the Pyrenees, preserve an isolated pre-Indo-European language—Basque. There is no standard form of this language, only a cluster of numerous, often highly divergent dialects. The Basque-speaking country is bounded by a line running in an arc from Bilbao through to Navarre a few miles south of Pamplona, then north-east to the Pic d'Anie, whence westwards through the northern foothills to the sea. In former times the area was much larger. Place names show that an earlier linguistic frontier ran through Tafalla to Huesca, whence north-east to take in the whole of the Central Pyrenees, then

north-west to the Garonne, following it to the sea. On the Spanish
side this territory was still Basque in the Middle Ages, but the language
disappeared earlier from the plain on the French side. It is thought to
have been the non-Celtic language of Aquitaine referred to by Julius
Caesar in *De Bello Gallico*. Today about half-a-million villagers,
four out of five of them on the Spanish side, speak Basque. The towns
in the area have abandoned the language and all speakers of Basque
are now bilingual. In general the language is declining in much the
same way as minority languages elsewhere in Europe.

Basque appears to have been close to its neighbour Cantabrian,
once spoken along the north coast of Spain, but further affinities are
problematic.

Catalan

Catalan, a transitional form between the Iberian type of Romance and
Provençal, is proper to Catalonia and Roussillon. In the first half of
the thirteenth century, the language was introduced by conquest into
Valencia and the Balearic Islands, submerging the earlier dialects.
It was carried to Sardinia in 1326, where it remains to this day in the
patois of Alghero and environs (p. 43).

An important medieval literature was produced in Catalan, the
first texts dating from the late twelfth century. A high degree of
standardisation was reached and the language enjoyed full official
recognition. But when the Kingdom of Aragon, of which the Catalan-
speaking districts formed part, joined with Castille in 1479, the
official use of Catalan was discontinued in favour of Castilian.
Catalan now became a chiefly oral medium. However, regional feeling
remained strong and when, in recent times, Catalonia came to the
fore as the main industrial region of Spain, separatists worked for the
restoration of Catalan as an official language, an aim briefly achieved
during the Republican period 1936–9. The Falangist government
immediately outlawed the language, but attitudes have meanwhile
grown more tolerant and there is now a considerable amount of
publishing in Catalan. Together with French, Catalan is an official
language in Andorra; it is also the vernacular of the 12,000 inhabitants of that diminutive republic. On the whole, Catalan has maintained itself well in spite of disabilities, though it has lost ground to
Castilian especially in Valencia, and also to French in Roussillon. It
seems that the language is used by some seven millions. They are,
however, essentially bilingual, employing their respective state
language as the usual literary medium.

It goes without saying that Spanish and Catalan on the one hand,
and Catalan and Provençal on the other, are linguistically so close
that mutual comprehension in essentials is not difficult. Their mutual

relationship is of about the same degree as obtains between the Continental Scandinavian languages.

Portuguese

The old province of Lusitania, substantially the territory of the modern Portugal, was overrun by the Moors in 711. The Reconquest began in the eleventh century from Galicia, the province immediately to the north. Lisbon was reached in 1147, the present political boundaries being fixed by 1267. During this period the Galician dialect imposed itself on the emerging state language to provide the essential basis for Standard Portuguese. The earliest texts from the late twelfth century begin an unbroken tradition in the writing of Portuguese. Galicia itself, however, was not united to Portugal but was annexed by Spain and, with the extension of Castilian, the native dialect here sank to the level of a patois. Portuguese is rather like Spanish, so that speakers of these languages soon learn to understand each other for practical purposes.

Portuguese is spoken by some $8\frac{1}{2}$ millions in Portugal itself. It is also the language of Madeira, the Azores and elsewhere overseas, especially Brazil. Altogether about 90 million people have Portuguese as their mother tongue.

Portuguese overseas

Portuguese was the first European language to be carried overseas, thanks to the enterprise of Portugal's master mariners. Madeira and the Azores, both uninhabited, were discovered in 1430 and 1439 respectively. In 1415, the first African settlement was effected at Céuta and voyages of exploration down the west coast of Africa continued throughout the century, culminating in Vasco da Gama's rounding of the Cape in 1497. At last the sea road to India had been found and in the next century the Portuguese went on to reach the Far East. All along the trade routes leading via Africa and India to the Moluccas or Macao or Nagasaki the newcomers established their outposts of Portuguese commerce and language alike.

Nor was the New World neglected, where Brazil was claimed for Portugal in 1500. Settlement began in 1532 and here sprang up the giant colony which assumed independent statehood in 1822. Portuguese first displaced the native Indian languages along the seaboard and then advanced inland. Today Portuguese is the language of 85 million Brazilians. The Indian population numbers about one million; perhaps half of these speak no Portuguese. But elsewhere the spread of Portuguese has not been so dramatic. Portuguese is, of course, the language of Madeira (pop. 300,000) and the Azores (pop. 350,000). It is also the official language of Portugal's overseas provinces: Cape Verde Islands, Portuguese Guinea, St Thomas and Príncipe, Angola, Mozambique, Timor, Macao. But in all these places, except Príncipe, the vernaculars of the native populations are as a rule either Creole Portuguese as in the Cape Verde Islands and St Thomas, or exotic languages as in Angola, Mozambique, Timor, Macao. The inhabitants of Príncipe, population now 8,000, formerly spoke Creole, but in this century have gone over to Standard Portuguese. Otherwise Standard Portuguese is the mother tongue mainly of European settlers. These are found chiefly in Angola (about 200,000) and Mozambique (about 50,000). Until 1961, Portugal held Goa and two smaller enclaves on the west coast of India. The census of 1961 reported over 12,000 persons in that country speaking Portuguese as their first language, but as Portuguese has now no official status, it cannot be expected to survive there for long.

Creole Portuguese

Pidgin came into being wherever the Portuguese had contact with non-Europeans. It received a great impetus from the slave trade, since Pidgin became the common medium of slaves taken from different territories and speaking different languages. For their children, Pidgin would be the most familiar form of speech which they would adopt as their primary medium thus turning it into a fully-fledged Creole. Several Portuguese-based creole languages survive to this day.

Cape Verde Islands Creole is the spoken medium of the 150,000 coloured inhabitants of these islands. The language goes back to the slave population introduced in the sixteenth century, the islands being uninhabited when first sighted about 1456. Latterly, lusitanisation has increasingly modified this speech. Closely related to the foregoing is Guinean Creole, the native medium of some 50,000 inhabitants of Portuguese Guinea. The remainder almost universally retain their multifarious tribal languages, but Creole is the lingua franca of the country, known in varying degrees to perhaps one half of the colony's 525,000 inhabitants. Creole extends into Senegal, where its centre is Ziguinchor, chief town of Casamance, the province immediately to the north-west of Guinea. Technically known as Casamançais, it is the native medium of over 40,000 persons and an acquired language of 15,000 more. Unlike the form in Guinea, it is unaffected by Standard Portuguese. Judging by loanwords in African languages further north, this Creole was once more widely disseminated in Senegal than it is today. The origins of Guinean Creole will certainly go back to the sixteenth century. St Thomas Creole is the spoken medium of 70,000 coloured inhabitants of that island, first settled in 1485. A related dialect was formerly the vernacular of Príncipe, settled about the same time. It is still remembered by a few old people, but has generally given way to Standard Portuguese. A third dialect is used by the 2,000 inhabitants of Annobón, ceded to Spain in 1777. The three islands were uninhabited at the time of their discovery by the Portuguese. All the above-mentioned Creoles are related, having developed from West African Pidgin. They are entirely non-literary.

Malayo-Portuguese, a creole language which arose in the East, was at one time very important, but is now extinct. However, the Creole of the island of Ternate in the Moluccas was transported to the Philippines where it has spread to some extent, though being thoroughly overlaid with Spanish in the process (p. 37). Macanese, the Creole of Macao, has been largely decreolised in its native territory, but immigrants to Hong Kong after the British occupation in 1841 escaped the levelling influence of Standard Portuguese, and here the Creole has been preserved as a communal patois by perhaps as many as 4,000 speakers.

Creole was without a doubt once extensively used in Brazil, but has generally succumbed to lusitanisation. On the other hand, semi-Creole forms of Portuguese may still be heard in the interior. Creole Portuguese was once present in Surinam, where it forms a component in Sranan and Saramaccan (p. 118). The Papiamento of Curaçao also contains a Portuguese element (p. 37).

In conclusion we mention that some investigators find a Portuguese substratum in other creoles spoken by Africans, whether Dutch, English, French or Spanish. If this is true, then these languages are ultimately the outcome of graftings onto the Pidgin Portuguese of the fifteenth and sixteenth centuries.

Italian

The first purely Italian text, a short deposition in connection with a lawsuit, is dated 960. According to Dante, Italian was being used for literary purposes by the end of the twelfth century, but the oldest surviving specimens—poetry—belong to the thirteenth. Dante himself (1265–1321) was the creator of Standard Italian. He employed the Tuscan dialect with many specifically Florentine forms, as did also Petrarch and Boccaccio in the fourteenth century, from which time the supremacy of Tuscan was unquestionably established. But even today spoken Italian is still to a considerable extent broadly dialectal, and not only in the countryside, some cities have a local dialect, too, e.g., Napolitan, Venetian. But all know the standard language which, under modern conditions, is replacing the motley throng of spoken dialects.

Standard Italian is also replacing the Sardinian and Rhaetian dialects, the latter once stretching in a band across the northern periphery of Italy from the Swiss Grisons to the Yugoslav frontier. In the north-east, Italian has struggled against Croat and Slovene and lost ground here after 1945 when the frontier was redrawn; the same applies to the Adriatic Islands and Zara/Zadar transferred to Yugoslavia at the same time. Since the end of World War I, Italian has been gaining in South Tyrol at the expense of German. The inhabitants of the Region of Aosta, traditionally French-speaking, use Italian for official purposes, and Italian is making some headway as a spoken language also. The small enclaves of Greek and Albanian speech which still survive in the southern part of Italy are everywhere threatened by the encroachment of the major language. The Arabic of Pantellaria was completely replaced by Italian in the eighteenth century.

Italian is mainly confined to the territory of the Italian State. It extends, however, into Switzerland where 600,000 speakers live, chiefly in Tessin and the south-east tip of the Grisons; it is one of the official languages of that country. Italian is further the native idiom of Corsica (250,000 speakers), but here French has been the official language since 1758, the indigenous Corsican being purely a patois. There are about 75,000 Italian-speakers, mostly bilingual, living in areas ceded to Yugoslavia in 1945. All in all, Italian is the first language of some 53 millions, speakers of Sardinian and Rhaetian included (see below).

Italian overseas

Italian colonisation developed too late for success on the scale of the great colonial powers. Eritrea was an Italian possession from 1890 to 1945. It is now part of Ethiopia, whose official language is Amharic. The former Italian Somaliland is incorporated in the present Republic of Somalia (pp. 29, 112). Italy occupied Libya in 1912 and the number of Italian settlers grew year by year. But these were evacuated in 1943 and after the war Libya became an independent state with Arabic as its official language. Italian government of the Greek-speaking Dodecanese from 1923 to 1945 had no affect on the basic linguistic situation there. Italian was formerly an official language in Malta (p. 114).

Although Italian never became the source of any creole, it has the distinction of being associated with Lingua Franca, the first known pidgin. This was one of the languages which Gulliver tried out on the Liliputians. It arose in the Middle Ages in the ports on the Riviera from Marseilles to Genoa and was widely used in the Levant from the time of the Crusaders down to the eighteenth century. It latterly became known as Sabir.

Sardinian

The dialects of Sardinia are often considered as forming a separate language. Those of the south (Campidanian) and centre (Logudorian) are among the most conservative of Neo-Latin speeches. Those of the north, however, form a transition to the Central Italian dialects of Corsica. The Spanish occupation from 1326 to 1714 resulted in many borrowings, first from Catalan, later from Castilian, and an enclave of the former language remains in and around Alghero (p. 38). Sardinian is not normally written, though a few old texts have come down to us, the earliest from the eleventh century. Attempts to develop a literary language for the impoverished and largely illiterate population have always failed. Sardinian is used by about one million persons. To all intents and purposes a purely oral medium, it plays no part in education which is conducted through Italian. Sardinians are generally bilingual, but many have gone over to Italian entirely, and this tendency is gaining momentum.

Rhaetian

The dialects once spoken in a continuous band from the Carnic Alps to the Swiss Grisons are generally classified as a separate Romance entity. They are known as Rhaetian or Rhaeto-Romance and are admittedly close to Italian. They early yielded to German on what is now the Austrian side of the state frontier with Italy, while on the Italian side they have been extensively replaced by Italian. The remaining Rhaetian strongholds on Italian soil are the Tagliamento area (Carnic Alps and the northern part of the Friulan Plain) with maybe half a million speakers; here the dialect is termed Friulan. Rhaetian also survives in a few valleys in South Tyrol, this time under the name of Ladin; the total number of those using the dialect will not exceed 15,000. Even these surviving Rhaetian outposts have been considerably influenced by Italian, which is of course the language of education and literacy. All the same, a small literature exists in Friulan, which can boast of a text as early as the thirteenth century.

In the west, Rhaetian has likewise yielded to German and Italian. Since the tenth century it has retreated from the shores of Lake Constance and today is confined to certain parts of the Grisons. But Rhaetian here is no mere patois; it is a recognised literary medium. Apart from an isolated twelfth-century text, a considerable literature has developed since the Reformation (beginning in 1552) and in 1938 Romaunsch, as it may be called, acquired official status for local purposes. Yet the Romaunsch speakers do not total much more than 40,000. Moreover their speech falls into five rather considerably differentiated dialects, namely Sursilvan/Obwaldisch (Hither Rhine Valley), Sutsilvan/Nidwaldisch (Tungleasta, Mantogna, Schona),

Surmiran/Oberhalbsteinisch (Sursés and Val d'Alvra), Ladin/
Oberengadinisch (Upper Engadine), Ladin/Unterengadinisch (Lower
Engadine and Munster Valley). Printing is done in all five forms,
though principally in Sursilvan and (the two forms of) Ladin.
Romaunsch speakers use German as their second language. In spite
of provincial patronage, a certain amount of publishing and elementary education in Rhaetian, not to mention the patriotic efforts of
the Romaunsch League, the position of the language is dangerously
threatened by the advance of German. It goes without saying that the
practical impossibility of creating a single literary form suitable for
all the members of this small minority is a most serious handicap in its
struggle for survival in the modern world.

The term Rhaetian derives from Rhaetia, the Alpine province
occupied by the Romans in 15 B.C. and eventually latinised. The
earlier language of the inhabitants is recorded in a number of inscriptions, but the material is too exiguous to permit conclusions about its
affinities. The language of these monuments is also named Rhaetian.

Dalmatian

In addition to Sardinian and Rhaetian, it is usual to posit a further
separate branch of Romance close to Italian, namely Dalmatian. The
Dalmatian dialects formerly ranged down the east coast of the Adriatic, perhaps reaching as far as the northern limit of the compact
Greek-speaking area in what is now South Albania. Dalmatian is
believed to have survived best in urban districts, but by the end of the
Middle Ages it appears to have succumbed to Croat and Albanian
advancing from the surrounding countryside, possibly also to
Italian colonies planted on the islands by the Venetians. There are no
documents for this branch of Romance except for a few texts taken
down from oral tradition at the end of the last century in Veglia/Krk
just before the language became extinct. Vegliot is seen to be particularly close to Italian, due maybe to its geographical position on the
very edge of the old Dalmatian region. It was of course also much
influenced by Croat, the language of the island today.

Rumanian

Rumanian is the most easterly of the Romance languages. There are
really four Rumanian languages, although only one of them—
latterly in two varieties—has attained full literary and official status.
The four Rumanian languages are these:

1. Daco-Rumanian, i.e., Rumanian in the most usual sense of the
word, the native language of over $16\frac{1}{4}$ millions or 85 per cent of the
population of Rumania and close on two millions or 65 per cent of the
population of Soviet Moldavia, to which must be added small groups

living at various points on or near the Rumanian frontier in Bulgaria, Yugoslavia and Hungary, perhaps a quarter of a million in all.

Dialect differences in Daco-Rumanian are not great. The literary language is based, in essentials, on the dialect of Walachia centred on Bucharest. The emergence of written Rumanian was retarded by the official use of Church Slavonic which, until the middle of the seventeenth century, was the language of church and chancery among the Rumanians, with the result that their own idiom is only known from the modern period. The earliest texts date from the sixteenth century, the first being a letter dated 1521, and until after the middle of the last century, Rumanian was written in Cyrillic characters. Rumanian has been vastly influenced by Slavonic, some three-fifths of its basic lexicon being borrowed from this source. We may say that Church Slavonic has been to Rumanian what Latin has been to the languages of the west. But for over a century now, Rumanian has consciously turned away from Slavonic and instead draws freely on French for its neologisms. The change from Cyrillic to Roman letters was likewise a reflection of westernising tendencies.

Rumanian extends across the present frontier on the Pruth into the Moldavian SSR. Some little distance to the east, however, the compact Rumanian-speaking area gives way to a mixed zone of Rumanian and Ukrainian. The Rumanian on Soviet territory is officially called Moldavian. Here Ukrainian influence has been strong, especially in matters of modern vocabulary, but otherwise Moldavian can hardly be called anything else but a separatist form of Rumanian. It is written in Cyrillic.

The other three Rumanian languages are sometimes loosely referred to as Vlachic, but philologically speaking, they are to be distinguished as follows.

2. Macedo-Rumanian or Aromunian (sometimes Arumanian) is the language of the Aromuni, the Rumanians of the south, often known also as Vlachi. Originally shepherds practising transhumance, they ranged over Macedonia and down through the Pindus Mountains. From here they spread east and west, especially into southern Albania, Epirus and Thessaly. Where they later became sedentary, living as scattered minorities among Albanians, Macedonians, Bulgarians or Greeks, they tended to lose their native language in a process of denationalisation which conditions in this century have accelerated. In the absence of reliable statistics, it is not possible to say how many know or use the Aromunian language today. At the beginning of the present century one could think in terms of 300,000 or more; today the number is—perhaps—half as many and certainly rapidly shrinking. There are two main dialect groups, a northern (Macedonia) and a southern (Pindus), each of which falls into a number

of somewhat divergent sub-dialects as is understandable in a language so widely dispersed, normally unwritten and without official standing. Aromunian speakers are bilingual.

3. Megleno-Rumanian or Meglenitic is still used by a few hundred bilinguals in some parishes in the Plain of (Vlacho-) Meglen on the west bank of the Vardar, north-west of Salonika, and by a similarly small number in the village of Cerna in the (Rumanian) Dobrudja. At the turn of the century probably as many as 10,000 persons knew the language, but about a third left for Rumania after World War I. Grammatically it is close to Daco-Rumanian, but has many lexical elements in common with Macedo-Rumanian.

4. Istro-Rumanian is now in use only in one locality in the Učka Gora (Monte Maggiore) region in Istria. At the beginning of the present century some 3,000 spoke this form of Rumanian; the official census of 1921 gave 1,644. The Istro-Rumanians, who call themselves Vlash (singular Vlach), are the remnants of the Western Rumanians, formerly widespread throughout present-day Yugo-slavia; they retreated with their flocks to this infertile, depopulated corner of Istria to escape from the Turkish administration. It goes without saying that their now moribund language, which has the closest affinities with Daco-Rumanian, is permeated with elements from Croatian, the second language of the Vlach.

Origin of Rumanian

The main area in which Rumanian is spoken, i.e., within the borders of the modern state of Rumania, corresponds roughly to the Roman province of Dacia, created in A.D. 107 following Trajan's defeat of the native chieftains. Settlers *ex toto orbe*, as Eutropius reports, streamed into the new province in such numbers that the area must soon have been very largely romanised in speech as well as in custom. It was natural to assume that the present-day Rumanians are the descendants of these Roman colonists. Throughout the centuries, apparently, they had weathered the heavy storms that came their way, especially in the shape of Germanic (third cent.), Slavonic (sixth cent.) and Magyar (ninth cent.) invasions, and though their speech was considerably influenced by the last two, they had nevertheless re-mained true to their national identity as erstwhile Romans—as their name would indicate—and had preserved the Latin speech of their forbears in Dacia. All this seems obvious enough, yet in reality it is largely unproven supposition, for historical records give hardly any information on the crucial questions of Rumanian ethnogenesis.

Philologists were the first to voice doubts about the 'self-evident' origin of the Rumanian people. Nor is this surprising, since a scholarly investigation is almost entirely dependent on linguistic criteria. The discussion which followed was, however, not always objective. Many Rumanians seemed to feel that their national honour was being impugned if they were not allowed to be directly descended from Trajan's stalwart settlers. Let us consider the facts observed.

From the middle of the third century, pressure from East Germanic tribesmen constituted a most serious threat to the Roman position in Dacia and in 270 Aurelian decided on the evacuation of this frontier province; the evacuation was completed by 275. The garrisons and civilian authorities were withdrawn to the south across the Danube which became the new frontier. It is reasonable to suppose that great numbers of refugees accompanied this withdrawal. The Germanic tribesmen, mainly Goths and Gepids, now took possession of the abandoned province and remained there undisturbed for a century. It is a remarkable fact that the Rumanian language contains no certain traces of ancient Germanic influence.

Rumanian also has a number of features in common with Albanian, notably elements of pre-Latin vocabulary found nowhere else in the Balkans. These similarities are held to indicate more than a common substratum, so that one envisages a period of contact between the two languages at an early date. The most likely place for such contact is the triangle between Nish, Sofia and Skopje, i.e., the ancient Dardania, the district which received the evacuees from Dacia. Subsequently, so it is argued, the Albanians moved westward, while part of the Rumanians re-immigrated to Dacia. Other Rumanians, of whom a tiny band remains in Istria, wandered to the west and north, the rest went south; their descendants are the Aromunians and the Meglenites. The beginnings of these movements are considered to go back to the end of the first millennium.

It has recently been claimed that especially the eastern dialects of Rumanian contain a considerable number of appellatives of pre-Latin origin, not found in Albanian, and identifiable as Dacian. This fact, if such it is, speaks for some continuity of linguistic tradition in Dacia.

In general it may be said that the known facts often permit various explanations. What makes research into these matters so difficult and hazardous is the complete absence of early records in Rumanian. A 'compromise' theory of the origins of the Rumanian language would be as follows. The romanised peasantry of Dacia remained in the less fertile parts of the country after the collapse of the Roman administration. Their variety of Vulgar Latin contained a fair number of Dacian elements. The influence of Germanic on their language was not great, as the Germanic tribes took the best land, and subsequently disappeared when this autochthonous peasantry fused with the re-immigrants from south of the Danube and possibly with other romanised peoples still surviving west of the Danube. For a long time they shared their land with Slavonic invaders—the evidence of place names makes it clear that the Rumanian and Slav lived side by side—but finally assimilated them, by which time they were powerful enough to survive pressure from the Magyars.

THE STRUCTURE OF ITALIC

LATIN

The records of Old Latin understandably preserve many archaisms, but the essential character of Italic, as we know it, is adequately exemplified by the classical language, which we quote here.

Phonetics

There are five vowels, *a, e, i, o, u*, and a small number of diphthongs, chiefly *ae, au, oe*. Vowel length, though normally unmarked in writing, is phonemic, e.g. *sagitta* 'arrow', *sagittā* 'by an arrow'. The consonants *c, g* are always [k, g], *v* is [w]. Double consonants are long.

Accidence

There are three genders, two numbers and six cases. IE declensional classes are easily recognisable. IE **ekwos* appears as follows:

sg.nom. *equus* 'horse', voc. *eque*, acc. *equum*, gen. *equī*, dat.abl. *equō*, pl.nom.voc. *equī*, acc. *equōs*, gen. *equōrum*, dat.abl. *equīs*

Adjectives follow comparable declensional schemes.

The morphology of the verb is complex, though less so than that of Greek. It is, however, more regular. There are six tenses of the indicative (pres., fut., imperf., perf., fut.perf., pluperf.) and four of the subjunctive (pres., imperf., perf., pluperf.), present imperative, further sundry infinitives, participles and verbal nouns. There are two voices, active and passive, the latter (with the deponent class) continuing the IE middle. Sample paradigm:

ACTIVE

Infin. *ferre* 'to bear'

	Present		Imperfect	
	Indicative	Subjunctive	Indicative	Subjunctive
Sg.1	*ferō*	*feram*	*ferēbam*	*ferrem*
2	*fers*	*ferās*	*ferēbās*	*ferrēs*
3	*fert*	*ferat*	*ferēbat*	*ferret*

Pl.1	*ferimus*	*ferāmus*	*ferēbāmus*	*ferrēmus*
2	*fertis*	*ferātis*	*ferēbātis*	*ferrētis*
3	*ferunt*	*ferant*	*ferēbant*	*ferrent*

Imperf.sg.2 *fer*, 3 *fertō*, pl.2 *ferte*, 3 *feruntō*
Pres.part.sg.nom. *ferēns* m.f.n.
Future sg.1 *feram*, 2 *ferēs*, 3 *feret*, pl.1 *ferēmus*, 2 *ferētis*, 3 *ferent*

PASSIVE

Infin. *ferrī*

	Present		Imperfect	
	Indicative	Subjunctive	Indicative	Subjunctive
Sg.1	*feror*	*ferar*	*ferēbar*	*ferrer*
2	*ferris*	*ferāris*	*ferēbāris*	*ferrēris*
3	*fertur*	*ferātur*	*ferēbātur*	*ferrētur*
Pl.1	*ferimur*	*ferāmur*	*ferēbāmur*	*ferrēmur*
2	*feriminī*	*ferāminī*	*ferēbāminī*	*ferrēminī*
3	*feruntur*	*ferantur*	*ferēbantur*	*ferrentur*

Imperf.sg.2 *ferre*, 3 *fertor*, pl.2 *feriminī*, 3 *feruntur*
(No pres.part.)
Future sg.1 *ferar*, 2 *ferēris*, 3 *ferētur*, pl.1 *ferēmur*, 2 *ferēminī*, 3 *ferentur*
Other tenses are formed from a different stem, hence *tulī* '(I) have borne', *lātus* (< **tlātus*) *sum* '(I) have been borne', etc.
Numbers: 1 *ūnus*, 2 *duo*, 3 *trēs*, 4 *quattuor*, 5 *quīnque*, 6 *sex*, 7 *septem*, 8 *octō*, 9 *novem*, 10 *decem*, 100 *centum*

Vocabulary
Latin preserves an abundance of traditional IE words, e.g.,

nōmen 'name': Skt. *nā́man-*, Gk. *ónoma*, Eng. *name*, Ir. *ainm*, Welsh *enw* Russ. *ímya*, Toch. A *ñom*, B *ñem*, Hitt. *laman*
dēns, gen. *dentis* 'tooth': Skt. *dánta-*, Gk. *odṓn*, gen. *odóntos*, Lith. *dantìs*, Ir. *déad* ('set of teeth'), Welsh *dant*, Goth. *tunþus*, Eng. *tooth*
rex 'king': Skt. *rā́jā*, Ir. *rí*, Welsh *rhi*
deus 'god': Skt. *devás*, Lith. *diẽvas*, Ir. *dia*, Icel. (pl.) *tívar*
dexter 'right' (as opposed to 'left'): Gk. *dexiterós, dexiós*, Ir. *deas*, Skt. *dákṣinas*, Lith. *dẽšinas*, Goth. *taíhswa*
juvenis 'young': Skt. *yúvān-*, Lith. *jáunas*, OCS *junŭ*, Eng. *young*, Ir. *óg*, Welsh *ieuanc*
edō '(I) eat': Skt. *ádmi*, Gk. *édō*, Armen. *utem*, Eng. *eat*, Lith. *ĕmi*, Russ. *yem*

Texts

From Julius Caesar, *De Bello Gallico* 'Concerning the
Gallic War'. (First landing in Britain, 55 B.C.)

Exigua parte aestatis   reliqua   Caesar, etsi   in his
small   part   of-summer remaining C.   although in these

locis,   quod omnis Gallia ad septentriones vergit, maturae sunt
places since all   Gaul to north   turns early   are

hiemes, tamen   in   Britanniam proficisci contendit. . .
winters all-the-same into Britain   to-set-out decided

His   constitutis rebus
these arranged   things ('these arrangements made')

nactus   idoneam   ad navigandum tempestatem tertia
having-obtained favourable to sailing   weather   at-third

fere   vigilia solvit   equitesque in   ulteriorem
about watch (he) weighed anchor cavalry-and into further

portum progredi   et naves conscendere et se   sequi
port   to-proceed and ships to-go-aboard and him to-follow

iussit. . .   Ipse   hora   circiter diei
(he) commanded himself at-hour around of-day

quarta   cum primis navibus
fourth ('about the fourth hour of day') with first   ships

Britanniam attigit atque ibi   in omnibus collibus expositas
Britain   reached and there on all   hills   displayed

hostium   copias armatas conspexit.   Cuius   loci haec erat
of-enemies forces armed   (he) perceived of-which place this was

natura, atque ita montibus   angustis mare continebatur, ubi
nature and   so with-heights steep   sea   was-contained where

ex   locis superioribus in   litus telum adigi   posset.
from places higher   onto shore javelin be-thrown could

Matthew vi.9–13

Pater noster qui es in caelis: sanctificetur nomen tuum. Adveniat
father our   who art in heavens be-hallowed name thy   come

regnum   tuum. Fiat   voluntas tua, sicut in caelo   et   in terra.
kingdom thy   be-done will   thy as   in heaven and on earth

Panem nostrum quotidianum da   nobis hodie. Et   dimitte nobis
bread our   daily   give us   today and forgive us

debita nostra, sicut et   nos dimittimus debitoribus nostris. Et   ne
debts our   as   and we forgive   debtors   our   and not

nos inducas in   temptationem, sed libera nos a   malo. Quoniam
us lead   into temptation   but free   us from evil for

tibi   est regnum   et   potestas et   gloria in   saecula.
to-thee is kingdom and power   and glory into ages

ITALIAN

Phonetics

The phonemic distinction between long and short vowels, character-istic of Classical Latin, was lost in later spoken Latin. In Italian, stressed vowels are longer than unstressed. The consonants *c, g* before front vowels are pronounced [ʧ], [ʤ], *gl, gn* are palatalised *l, n,* respectively, *ch* is [k], *z* variously [ts] or [dz]. Double consonants are long.

Accidence

A feature of later spoken Latin was the reduction of the case system to two terms, nominative and accusative. In the daughter languages even this difference was eventually given up, so that today only the distinction between singular and plural can be expressed by the end-ing—we disregard here Balkan-type innovations in Rumanian—hence Ital. *cavallo* m. 'horse', pl. *cavalli.* A further development was the loss of the neuter gender; old neuters are commonly masculines today, e.g., Ital. *foglio* m. 'leaf' from Lat. *folium* n.

The conjugation of the verb, on the other hand, has been much better preserved. True, a large number of ancient formations have been replaced by analytic forms, as in the case of the passive, but certain new synthetic forms have arisen, too, notably the future, e.g., Ital. *amerò* '(I) shall love' from Late Lat. *amare habeo* lit. '(I) have to love', a periphrasis which replaced Cl. Lat. *amabo,* and similarly the con-ditional *amerei* '(I) should love' from *amare habui* originally '(I) had to love'. Sample paradigms:

Infin. *amare* 'to love' (Lat. *ferre* 'to bear' has not survived in Romance)

	Present		Imperfect	
	Indicative	Subjunctive	Indicative	Subjunctive
Sg.1	amo	ami	amavo	amassi
2	ami	ami	amavi	amassi
3	ama	ami	amava	amasse
Pl.1	amiamo	amiamo	amavamo	amassimo
2	amate	amiate	amavate	amaste
3	amano	amino	amavano	amassero

(Historically, the imperf. subj. continues the Latin pluperf. subj.: sg.1 *amavissem*, etc.)

	Remote Past	Conditional
Sg.1	amai	amerei
2	amasti	ameresti
3	amò	amerebbe
Pl.1	amammo	ameremmo
2	amaste	amereste
3	amarono	amerebbero

(These tenses correspond to the Latin perfect and a spoken *amare habui*, etc.—see above)

Imperf.sg.2 *ama*, pl.2 *amate*

The perfect system is formed periphrastically, e.g., *ho amato* '(I) have loved', similarly the passive, e.g., *sono amato* '(I) am loved'.

Numbers: 1 *uno*, 2 *due*, 3 *tre*, 4 *quattro*, 5 *cinque*, 6 *sei*, 7 *sette*, 8 *otto*, 9 *nove*, 10 *dieci*, 100 *cento*

Texts

From the novel *Cuore* ('Heart', i.e., 'Goodness of Heart')
by E. de Amicis

Allora il   maestro disse alla   classe: '*Oggi entra nella   scuola*
then   the master said to-the class   today enters into-the school

un piccolo italiano nato a   Reggio di   Calabria, a più   di
a little   Italian born at R.   of ('in') C.   at more than

cinquecento   miglia di   qua. Egli è nato in una terra gloriosa,
five-hundred miles from here he   is born in a   land glorious

che   diede all'Italia   degli uomini illustri,   e   le   da
which gave to-the Italy of-the men   illustrious and to-it gives

dei   forti   lavoratori e   dei   bravi soldati; in una delle
of-the strong workers   and of-the brave soldiers in one of-the

più   belle   terre   della   nostra patria,
more ('most') beautiful lands ('districts') of-the our   native country

abitata   da un popolo pieno d'ingegno e   di coraggio. Vogliategli
inhabited by a people full   of spirit and of courage wish-him

bene,   in maniera che   non s'accorga
well ('be friends with him') in manner that not (he) notices-himself

di esser lontano dalla   città dove   è nato;
to be   far   from-the town where (he) is born

fategli   vedere che un ragazzo italiano, in qualunque
make-him ('let-him') see   that a boy   Italian in whatever

scuola   italiano metta il   piede, ci   trova dei   fratelli.'
school (he) Italian puts   the foot   there finds of-the brothers.

Matthew vi.9–13

Padre nostro, che sei nei   cieli: sia santificato il   tuo nome.
father our   who art in-the heavens be hallowed   the thy name

Il   tuo regno   venga. La tua volontà sia fatta in terra come in
the thy kingdom come the thy will   be done in earth as   in

cielo. Dacci oggi il   nostro pane cotidiano. E   rimettici i
heaven give-us today the our   bread daily   and forgive-us the

nostri debiti, come noi ancora li   rimettiamo ai   nostri debitori.
our debts as   we still   them forgive   to-the our   debtors

E   non indurci in   tentazione, ma liberaci dal   maligno.
and not lead-us into temptation but deliver-us from-the evil

Perciocchè tuo è il   regno   e   la potenza e   la gloria
for   thine is the kingdom and the power   and the glory

in sempiterno.
in eternal

    3

OTHER MODERN ROMANCE LANGUAGES

(The Paternoster)

Sardinian (Logudorian dialect)

9   *Babbu nostru, qui stas in sos chelos: sanctificadu siat su nomen tou.*
10   *Benzat a nois su regnu tou. Fiacta siat sa voluntade tua, comente in su chelu asi in sa terra.*
11   *Su pane nostru de ogni die donanostu haë.*
12   *Et perdònanus sos peccados nostros, comente nos ateros perdonamus sos inimigos nostros.*
13   *Et ne nos lasses ruere in sa tentatione, sinò liberanos de male.*

Vegliot

9   *Tuota nuester, che te sante intel sil: sait santificuot el naun to.*
10   *Vigna el raigno to. Sait fuot la voluntuot toa, coisa in sil, coisa in tiara.*
11   *Duote costa dai el pun nuester cotidiun.*
12   *E remetiaj le nuestre debete, coisa nojiltri remetiaime a i nuestri debetuar.*
13   *E naun ne menur in tentatiaun, mui deliberiajne dal mal.*

Rumanian

9   *Tatăl nostru carele eşti în ceruri: sfinţească-se numele taŭ.*
10   *Vie împărăţia ta. Facă-se voia ta, precum în cer aşa şi pe pămînt.*
11   *Pâinea noastră cea spre fiinţa dă-ne-o nouă astăzi.*
12   *Şi ne iartă nouă greşalele noastre, precum şi noi iertăm greşiţilor noştri.*
13   *Şi nu ne duce pe noi în ispită, ci ne izbăveşte de cel rău. Că a ta este împărăţia şi puterea şi mărirea în veci.*

Rhaetian (Sursilvan dialect)

9   *Bab nos, ti che eis en tschiel: sogns vegni fatgs tiu num.*
10   *Tiu reginavel vegni neutier. Tia veglia daventi sin tiara sco en tschiel.*
11   *Nies paun de mintga gi dai a nus oz.*
12   *E perduna a nus nos puccaus, sco era nus perdunein a nos culponts.*
13   *E meina nus buc en empruament, mo spendra nus dal mal. Pertgei tes ein il reginavel e la pussonza e la gliergia a semper.*

French

9   *Notre père, qui es aux cieux: que ton nom soit sanctifié.*
10 *Que ton règne vienne. Que ta volonté soit faite sur la terre comme
    au ciel.*
11 *Donne-nous aujourd'hui notre pain quotidien.*
12 *Et pardonne-nous nos offenses, comme nous pardonnons à ceux qui
    nous ont offensés.*
13 *Et ne nous induis point en tentation, mais délivre-nous du mal. Car
    c'est à toi qu'appartiennent le règne et la puissance et la gloire aux
    siècles des siècles.*

Catalan

9   *Pare nostre que estau en lo cel: sia santificat lo vostre nom.*
10 *Vinga lo vostre regne. Fassas la vostra voluntat, axí en la terra com
    en lo cel.*
11 *Lo nostre pá de cada dia, donáunoslo avuy.*
12 *Y perdonau nostres deutes, axí com nosaltres perdonam á nostres
    deutors.*
13 *Y no permetáu que nosaltres caigam en la tentació, ans deslliur-
    aunos de mal.*

Spanish

9   *Padre nuestro, que estás en los cielos: santificado sea tu nombre.*
10 *Venga tu reyno. Hágase tu voluntad, así en la tierra como en el
    cielo.*
11 *Danos hoy nuestro pan cotidiano.*
12 *Y perdónanos nuestras deudas, así como nosotros perdonamos á
    nuestros deudores.*
13 *Y no nos metas en tentación, mas líbranos de mal. Porque tuyo es
    el reyno y la potencia y la gloria por los siglos.*

Portuguese

9   *Pai nosso, que estás nos céus: santificado seja o teu nome.*
10 *Venha o teu reino. Seja feita a tua vontade, assim na terra, como
    no céu.*
11 *O pão nosso de cada dia nos dá hoje.*
12 *E perdoa-nos as nossas dívidas, assim como nós perdoamos aos
    nossos devedores.*
13 *E não nos induzas à tentação, mas livra-nos do mal. Porque teu é o
    reino e o poder e a glória para sempre.*

Papiamento

9 *Nos tata, cu ta na cielo: cu bo nomber ta santificado.*
10 *Cu bo reina bini. Cu bo voluntad ta cumpli, ariba tera, asina cu na cielo.*
11 *Duna nos ave nos pam di cada dia.*
12 *Pordona nos nos debe, asina cu nos ta pordona nan debe na nos debedor nan.*
13 *I no pone nos den tentacion, ma libra nos di malo. Posoba di bo ta reina i poder i gloria pa siemper.*

Haitian

9 *Papa nou, ki nan sièl: ké non ou jouinn tout réspè.*
10 *Ké règn ou vini. Ké volonté ou akonpli sou tè a tankou nan sièl.*
11 *Ban nou, jodi a, pin chak jou nou.*
12 *Padonnin nou péché nou, tankou nou padonnin moun ki ofansé nou.*
13 *Pa minnin nou nan tantasion, min délivré nou an-ba malin an. Paské règn, puisans, avèk la gloua sé pou ou nan tout létènité.*

In conclusion, an Anglo-Norman version of the early thirteenth century:

9 *Li nostre pere, qui ies es ciels: saintefiez seit li tuens nums.*
10 *Avienget li tuns regnes. Seit faite la tue voluntet, sicum en ciel e en la terre.*
11 *Nostre pain cotidian dun a nus oi.*
12 *E pardune a nus les noz detes, eissi cume nus pardunums a noz deturs.*
13 *E ne nus mener en temtatiun, mais delivre nus de mal (. . .)*

4

OSCO-UMBRIAN

The exact position within the Indo-European family of the languages collectively known as Osco-Umbrian or, more precisely, the degree of their genetic relationship to Italic has not yet been definitively established, as explained on p. 21.

Oscan

Oscan was the language of the Samnites who occupied the major part of Ancient Italy south of Latium. The use of the term Oscan to denote the language follows classical precedent, the Oscans of Campania being the first of the Samnite tribes with whom the Romans came into intimate contact. Though the Samnites acknowledged the supremacy of Rome in 290, the official use of Oscan continued until the Social War of 90–89 B.C. which removed the last elements of independence. The majority of the surviving Samnites eventually adopted Latin as their spoken language, too, but some were hellenised. Oscan probably survived into the second century A.D.

Apart from personal and place names quoted in Latin or Greek texts and a few glosses, Oscan is known from about two hundred inscriptions, the longest with some 300 words, but the rest chiefly very brief, half of them containing only proper names. These records cover a period of five centuries, from coin legends going back to the end of the fifth century to graffiti found at Pompei after A.D. 63. About three-quarters of the inscriptions come from Campania. A native alphabet derived from Greek via Etruscan was in use, though inscriptions are also found both in Latin and Greek characters. The generally uniform nature of the language, especially of the monuments from Campania, suggests that Oscan possessed a developed literary style.

A few early inscriptions characterised as Sabellian show that this dialect was closely akin to Oscan.

Umbrian

Apart from a handful of short inscriptions, the chief evidence for Umbrian comes from the ritual texts inscribed on seven (originally nine) bronze tablets—the Iguvine Tables—discovered in the ruins of the temple of Jupiter at Gubbio, the ancient Iguvium, in 1444. Amounting to some 4,000 words, it is by far the longest record of any ancient Italian language other than Latin. The major part is written in a native script derived from Etruscan and may be as old as 200 B.C., the remainder in Latin characters seems to be about a century later. The orthography is erratic.

A few early inscriptions in the dialect of the Volscans, a people of Latium subdued by Rome in 338 B.C., show that their native idiom was close to Umbrian. Volscan early succumbed to Latin.

THE STRUCTURE OF OSCO-UMBRIAN

The translation of the Oscan and Umbrian texts has been largely successful thanks in the main to the fairly close relationship of these languages to Latin. Scanty though the material is, there is nevertheless sufficient to prove that in essentials the grammar followed the Latin pattern. Similar declensional and conjugational types are recognised and the syntax is directly comparable. However, Oscan in particular preserves a number of archaic features, the vowel system being most conservative. Umbrian, on the other hand, is remarkable for phonetic innovation.

It goes without saying that the vocabulary of Osco-Umbrian has most in common with Latin, including terms not found outside Italy, as O *vio*, U *via* 'way': Lat. *via*. Lexical correspondences of Indo-European range include: U *fer-* 'bear', cf. Lat. *ferre*, etc. Further examples:

O *deicum* (infin.), U *deitu* (imper.) 'say': Lat. *dīcere*, Goth. *ga-teihan* ('announce'), Gk. *deiknúnai* ('show')

O *aragetud* (abl.) 'silver': Lat. *argentum*, Ir. *airgead*, Welsh *arian* older *ariant*, also Armen. *arcat'*, Toch. A *ārkyant*, also Skt. *rajatám*, further Gk. *árguros*

U *kaprum* (acc.sg.) 'goat, buck': Lat. *caper*, Icel. *hafur*, Gk. *kápros* ('boar'), Ir. *caora* ('sheep'), Welsh *caer-iwrch* ('roe-buck')

A few numerals are known, e.g. 1 U *un-*, 2 U *du-*, 3 O *tris*, U *trif*, 4 O *petor-*, 5 OU **pempe* deduced from derived forms.

Texts

Oscan

From the Bantine Bye-Laws, last quarter of second century
B.C. (C. D. Buck, *A Grammar of Oscan and Umbrian*, 1928,
p. 233)

Pon   censtur Bansae   toutam censazet, pis   ceus   Bantins
when censors at-Bantia people shall-tax whoever citizen Bantine

fust,   censamur   esuf   in. (= *inim*) *eituam   poizad   ligud*
shall-be let-be-taxed himself and   property by-which law

iusc   censtur censaum angetuzet.   Aut suaepis (= *suae pis*)
these censors to-tax   shall-have-proposed but if anyone

censtomen (= *censtom-en*) *nei cebnust   dolud   mallud*
census-into   not shall-have-come with-deceit wicked

in. eizeic uincter,   esuf   comenei   lamatir
and for-it is-convicted himself in-assembly (?)let-be-scourged

pr. (= **praetoreis*) *meddixud   toutad*
of-praetor   under-magistracy (the) people (being)

praesentid perum   dolum mallom, in.   amiricatud   allo
present   without deceit wicked and without-compensation other

famelo   in. ei. (= **eituo*) *siuom   paei   eizeis   fust,*
household and property   entirely which of-him shall-be

pae   ancesto fust,   toutico
which untaxed shall-be public

estud.
let-be ('the rest of his household and all his untaxed property shall
without compensation become public property)

Umbrian

From the Iguvine Tables, *c.* 200 B.C. (C. D. Buck, op. cit.,
p. 297)

(řř believed to have been a sibilant *r*)

Inuk uhturu urtes   puntis   frater
then augur having-risen pentads ('groups of five') brothers

ustentuta   puře fratru   mersus
let-them-show as   of-brothers by-customs

fust
let-it-be ('let the Brothers, rising in pentads, elect the augur according
to the customs of their Fraternity')

kumnakle. Inuk uhtur vapeře   kumnakle   sistu.
in-assembly then augur on-stone-(seat) in-assembly let-him-sit

Sakre uvem   *uhtur*
victim sheep ('a victim and a sheep'; 'victim' perhaps 'pig') augur

teitu.   Puntes terkantur.   Inumek sakre uvem
let-him-designate pentads ?shall-inspect then   victim sheep

urtas   puntes fratrum   upetuta.   Inumek via
having-risen pentads of-brothers ?let-them-choose then   by-way

mersuva   arvamen (= arvam-en) etuta.   Erak pir
?accustomed field-into   let-them-go ?then fire

persklu   *uřetu. Sakre uvem kletra*
with-prayer ('a prayer being said') let-it-burn victim sheep in-litter

fertuta   aituta.
let-them-bear let-them-drive (?'let them lift and carry')

Arven (= arv-en) kletram amparitu.   Eruk esunu
field-in   litter   ?let-him-set-down ?then sacrifice

futu.
let-it-be

5

VENETIC

In antiquity, the area which became the Roman province of Venetia, i.e., the Venetian Plain and Istria together with the Alpine foothills to the north, held a population whose language, judging by its scanty remains, may have constituted a distinct branch of the Indo-European family. This, the Venetic language, is attested in some two hundred short inscriptions dating from the sixth to the first centuries B.C., most of them from Este (the ancient Adeste). The monuments are written in an alphabet of the so-called North Etruscan type.

Venetic had features in common with Italic, e.g., *vhraterei* 'brother' (dat.) where *vh = f*, cf. Lat. *frātrī*. The form *leuzorophos* 'children' (dat.) is referred to IE **leudhero-* seen in Gk. *eleútheros* 'free' akin to Lat. *līberī* '(free-born) children'; the Venetic ending *-ophos* is reminiscent of Lat. *-ibus*, Skt. *-ibhyas*, Ir. *-ibh*. The Venetic treatment of IE **dh > z* is seen again in *zonasto* '(he) gave', where *zon-* may be compared with Lat. *dōn-* in *dōnāre* 'to give', further Lat. *dōnum*, Skt. *dánam* 'gift'.

The language eventually succumbed to Latin introduced into the area about 183 B.C., when the Romans founded a colony at Aquileia. Presumably the hilly districts were the last refuge of the language which perhaps ceased to be spoken in the second or third centuries A.D.

CELTIC

We have, in a previous chapter, witnessed the remarkable career of the dialect of the minor province of Latium which, through the pre-eminence of its chief town Rome, became the language of more than half of Europe and exerted a memorable influence on the rest. In the present chapter we shall consider a group of languages whose fortune has been entirely the opposite. These are the Celtic languages. At a time when Latin was still no more than a local dialect, Celtic languages were in use over a vast area from Britain to Spain and from Spain to the Danubian Plain and beyond. But theirs was an unlucky star. And it was Latin which was destined to strike the most telling blows against Celtic, to storm its main strongholds on the continent and finally to isolate it in the less accessible parts of the British Isles.

The first notices of the Celts in history are from the fifth century B.C. Combining the casual remarks of Hekataios and Herodotus, we find Keltoi ranging from the upper reaches of the Danube to Pyrene, beyond the Pillars of Hercules, and in evidence in the hinterland of the Greek colony of Marseilles. In the next century another Greek, Epiphoros by name, enumerates the Keltoi among the four great barbarian peoples, and well he might, since in this century Celtic prestige reached its culminating point.

CONTINENTAL CELTIC

Galatian

Judging by references in Greek writings and by archaeological evidence, Celtic tribesmen began to move into the Balkan area and settle among Illyrians and Thracians during the course of the fourth century B.C. They burst into Greece, but were repulsed. The Greeks often refer to these Celts as Galatai, i.e., Galatians. In 277 or 278 B.C., two such Galatian tribes, involving themselves in local politics, were

invited into Asia Minor, where they were shortly afterwards joined
by a third Galatian tribe. These confederates roved through the
countryside pillaging and exacting tribute until restrained by Attalus
of Pergamon about 230, who settled them among the Phrygians in
the region of the modern Ankara. They had their cult centre called
Drunemeton, a term containing the well-known Celtic word *nemēton*
'sanctuary'. Though cut off entirely from other Celts, the Galatians
preserved their national identity for many centuries and were certainly still using the Galatian language at the turn of the fifth century
A.D. This we are told by Jerome, the celebrated translator of the Vul-
gate, who noted that the Galatians, in addition to speaking Greek,
also spoke a language of their own which was akin to that of the
Treveri, a tribe of Celtic Gaul (see 'Gaulish'). How long the Galatians
survived as such in the Balkans is not known. From the silence of
contemporary authors, we are led to assume that they were assimilated by the beginning of the Christian era.

Gaulish

Celtic appears to have been established in Italy by the end of the fifth
century B.C. Taking advantage of the decline of Etruscan power, Celts
crossed the Alps to establish themselves first in the upper valley of the
Po and later in parts of Emilia and Umbria. Known to the Romans
as Galli, i.e., Gauls, they were soon raiding far to the south and Rome
itself, except for the Capitol, was destroyed about 387. The Roman
victory over the Gauls at Telamon in 225 marked a turning point and,
after a final victory near Bologna in 192, the Celts south of the Alps
submitted to Roman rule. Their main territory became the Roman
province of *Gallia Cisalpina* 'Gaul this side of the Alps', *Gallia
Transalpina* being the still largely unknown Gaulish-speaking territory beyond the Alps. Romanisation of Cisalpine Gaul proceeded
apace and was most likely completed by the beginning of the Christian period, except for the remoter Alpine foothills where Celtic may
have maintained itself for—at a guess—three or four centuries longer.
It is perhaps present in inscriptions from the second century B.C.
onwards found in Tessin (Switzerland); the language of these inscriptions is often referred to as Lepontic.

The Romans came into close contact with the other Gauls when
they created their province of *Gallia Narbonensis*, the modern
Provence, between 125 and 120 B.C., but it was not until Julius
Caesar's famous campaigns from 58 to 51 B.C. that the rest of Gaul
was subjugated. Then, for the first time, the Celts appear in the full
light of history. Caesar opens his account of the war by stating that
independent Gaul was divided into three parts, inhabited by peoples
calling themselves respectively Aquitani, Belgae and Celtae, the last

being the native name for Galli; each part, according to Caesar, had
its own language. This last assertion, however, needs qualification.
Classical authors are notoriously uncritical where barbarian languages
are concerned. Certainly the Aquitani in the south-west (Aquitaine)
were not Celts. They are believed to have used a non-IE language
perhaps akin to Basque which is found to this day in the mountainous
country at the angle of the Bay of Biscay both on the French and
(especially) on the Spanish side of the frontier. But there is no other
evidence that the speech of the Belgae differed very appreciably from
that of the Celtae. A number of Belgic personal names are known and
these are not unlike types current elsewhere in Celtic-speaking Gaul.
The Belgae lived in the north-east—in modern times the newly formed
state of Belgium was called after them—and they are said by Caesar
to have recently crossed into Gaul from beyond the Rhine. This
statement accords with the findings of archaeology. At the time of
their greatest expansion, Celts lived in Central and Southern Germany.
They ranged eastwards into Bohemia, which takes its name from the
Celtic Boii, and southwards into Austria; Vienna derives its name
from the Celtic settlement Vindobona. But Germanic pressure from
the north subsequently ousted them from these parts. Many Celts
crossed the Rhine into Gaul and about the time of Caesar's campaigns,
the Middle Rhine was rapidly becoming the linguistic frontier between
Germanic and Celtic. What Celtic remained to the east was doomed
to extinction within the next two or three centuries.

Nor was the fate of Celtic in Gaul to be very different. Under the
Roman administration, Latin made such rapid progress that the
native language was soon moribund. At the turn of the fifth century
we hear of the still Gaulish-speaking Treveri, a powerful tribe inhabiting the then somewhat inaccessible country around Trier, shortly to
be overwhelmed and assimilated by Germanic invaders. At the other
end of the country, among the Alps of present-day Switzerland, Celtic
seems to have lingered on here and there for a century or two longer.
It is sometimes suggested that Gaulish may have lived on in Armorica
(see 'Breton' below). But apart from such peripheral survivals it is
certain that, by A.D. 400, Gaulish was effectively banished from what
had been the most thoroughly Celtic country on the continent of
Europe.

The Gaulish language is known mainly through the many native
names transmitted by classical authors or found in the half a hundred
or so inscriptions discovered in Gaul and Northern Italy. A few
Gaulish words are quoted by various ancient authorities and others
have been detected as loan words in Latin, especially as written in
Gaul, and in French. Lastly, thousands of geographical names survive, many still in use. But no literary texts have come down to us.

Indeed, it is doubtful if such ever existed. The druids, at any rate, are said to have prohibited the writing down of their traditional lore. For inscriptional and business purposes the independent Gauls used a variety of the Greek alphabet—a sign of the influence of Greek-speaking Marseilles.

Celtiberian

We now refer briefly to the most westerly of the continental Celts. Herodotus knew of Keltoi living beyond the Pillars of Hercules. This seems reasonable testimony that Celts were established in the Iberian Peninsula by the mid-fifth century B.C. Onomastic evidence, e.g., the occurrence of the names *briga* and *dūnum*, meaning something like 'hill settlement' and 'enclosed settlement' respectively, helps to delimit the areas where Celts once lived. They presumably mingled with the earlier, so-called Iberian population of unknown provenance. At any rate, Celtiberi are mentioned in Greek and Roman sources from the end of the third century B.C. At this time the territory of this people seems to have been the mountainous area of central Spain. The Celtiberi were the most warlike of the Hispanic peoples, often in active revolt against the Romans and not entirely subdued until 49 B.C. Their language is believed to be recorded in a considerable number of inscriptions, some in Latin characters, but many in a peculiarly Iberian script not yet adequately deciphered. Speculation unbounded is characteristic of many of the studies of the admittedly difficult problems connected with the Celtic element in the Iberian Peninsula. But one general conclusion may be mentioned here. The distribution of the place names containing *briga* and *dūnum* strongly suggests that the Iberian Celts arrived in two waves. The earlier immigrants are responsible for the *briga*-names, common in the centre and south. A later immigration is reflected in the *dūnum*-names which are confined to Catalonia just south of the Pyrenees. Since this word is common in Gaul (where *briga* is rare), the second immigration would be merely an overspill from Celtic Gaul.

The Roman occupation, dating from 218 to 219 B.C., led to the romanisation of the peninsula within a relatively short time, so that Celtiberian along with other languages in the area, except Basque, must have finally died out some time about the beginning of the Christian era or a little later.

INSULAR CELTIC

BRITTONIC

As a result of his military successes in Gaul, Caesar found himself in a position to invade the legendary island of Britannia. He marched through the south-east of the country in the summers of 55 and 54 B.C., encountering a Belgic population who, so he learnt, had not been in the country more than a generation or two. When, in A.D. 43, the Roman occupation became permanent, we infer that Celts inhabited the whole of the island up to a line running from the Forth to the Clyde. Beyond them were the unsubduable, sandy-haired Caledonians. But though these Caledonians constituted the backbone of the resistance to Roman penetration in the north, they were not the sole inhabitants of that part of the country. It seems, from archaeological finds, that a northward movement of Celts, beginning in the first century B.C., had lead to settlements along the east coast. For this we have also the evidence of place names; we may compare *Aberdeen* which means 'Estuary of the Dee' with *Aberystwyth* 'Estuary of the Ystwyth'.

When did the Celts reach Britain? Except for Caesar's note on the immigrant Belgae, historical sources are silent. But archaeology provides a general answer. In the first half of the fifth century B.C., the parts of Britain nearest the Continent were overrun by invaders coming from the north of France and the Low Countries. This seems to have been an invasion on an unprecedented scale, comparable to the coming of the Anglo-Saxons a thousand years later. The new arrivals, known as the bearers of the British Iron Age A Culture, quickly spread over the whole country as far as the Cheviots. Penetration into Scotland seems to have taken place much later, at the beginning of the historical period, perhaps as a reflex of Belgic activity in the first century B.C. Another significant, but smaller invasion from the same direction occurred about the middle of the third century B.C. These invaders established themselves at various places throughout the country; they were the bearers of the British Iron Age B Culture who introduced La Tène art into these islands. The general linguistic configuration both in Britain and on the Continent leaves no doubt that these two groups of pre-historic invaders were indeed Celts. One is tempted to connect the earlier invasion with the great build-up of Celtic power north of the Alps about the middle of the first millennium, which was, as we have seen, soon to intrude into the Mediterranean world.

Connections between Britain and Gaul at this period are not only demonstrable archaeologically, they are also implicit in the onomastic evidence. The modern city of Paris takes its name from the Gaulish Parisii who held tribal lands there; Parisii were settled in Yorkshire as well. Contemporary sources for our knowledge of Celtic in Britain are of the same character as those available for the study of Celtic in Gaul, though more exiguous. But it is plain that the Celtic spoken in Britain was a language of the same general type as Gaulish; the two were closely related languages just as Tacitus (*Agricola* XI) states *sermo haud multum diversus* 'the tongue (of the Britons) is not very different (from that of the Gauls)'. We may call it British. Another term is Brythonic, an anglicisation of Welsh *Brythonig* from *Brython* 'Briton'. Perhaps the best term is Brittonic from the ancient British form *Brittones* 'Britons'. It is often useful to be able to refer to Gaulish and British together; we may then speak of Gallo-Brittonic.

Brittonic in Ireland

When we considered the position of Brittonic at the beginning of the historical period, we saw that it was expansive in a northerly direction. It had just reached the Scottish Lowlands and was making its way up the east coast beyond the Firth of Forth. There is good reason for believing that Brittonic was expansive in another direction as well. There is archaeological evidence for a considerable La Tène immigration into Northern Ireland from the north of England in the second century B.C. Irish records down to the eighth century A.D. speak of *Cruithni* as a foreign race inhabiting various parts of Ireland, notably the north-east. It is philologically quite possible to interpret *Cruithni* as 'Britons', from which one could conclude that Brittonic was in use in Ireland until the eighth century. Other factors lend some support to this view. Firstly, the Irish language contains a fair proportion of loan words from Brittonic. These are not only words of culture acquired from the more civilised Britons, but many quite ordinary words as well, a fact which implies a period of coexistence. Secondly, it is remarkable that the epithet 'Irish' was not traditionally applied to the language of the country. In native idiom, the Irish language is always called Gaelic. This could mean that Irish was, at one time, not the only language spoken in Ireland.

THE ROMAN PERIOD AND AFTER

There is no direct information on the development of the linguistic situation in Roman Britain. From what is known of developments elsewhere in the Empire, it is pretty clear that the urban centres would be Latin-speaking and most likely that the accessible parts of the lowland areas of the south and east were also romanised. But in the remote and upland areas of the west and north, where the mode of life was but little altered, Celtic speech persisted, though undoubtedly a knowledge of Latin was widespread among the educated. Even in purely Celtic areas, Latin was the written language as is proved by funerary inscriptions far to the west.

It is to be supposed that the Roman withdrawal gave a new lease of life to British. But whatever the trends may have been in this historically obscure period, they were rudely interrupted by the arrival of Germanic invaders—Angles, Saxons, Jutes—who began to settle in the country in A.D. 449. By the early seventh century, the newcomers were in possession of all the land south of the Firth of Forth with the exception of the mountainous area of the North-West, Wales and the Dumnonian Peninsula (Devon and Cornwall). Here, reinforced by refugees, the Celtic populations managed to maintain themselves. In the North-West, British survived until the ninth and tenth centuries, when it was displaced by Norse introduced by Viking settlers from the Gaelic area (p. 122). Nevertheless, part of the region retained the tell-tale name of *Cumberland*, where *Cumber-* is from Brittonic **Combrogo-* 'compatriot', evidently a term by which the native Celts distinguished themselves from foreign immigrants and which had superseded the older tribal names. At any rate the appellation was widespread. It is not recorded in the South-West, perhaps fortuitously, but it is common enough in Wales: *Cymro* means 'Welshman', *Cymru* 'Wales, Cambria', *Cymreig* 'Welsh'.

Such British north of the Cheviots as did not yield to Anglo-Saxon succumbed to Gaelic introduced from Ireland, though not immediately. Organised in the kingdom of Strathclyde, the Britons between the Clyde and the Solway maintained their identity until the eleventh century. Their language, distinctly traceable in three words preserved as technical terms in a twelfth-century legal document, may be called Cumbric. How long the large British-speaking population north-east of the Antonine Wall resisted gaelicisation is uncertain; we hazard a guess that it became extinct by the end of the tenth century.

Welsh

Four periods may be distinguished. Early Welsh is preliterary, and attested only in names, e.g., in Bede. Old Welsh, from 800 to 1100, consists of glosses and a few short passages. The language appears in its full stature in Middle Welsh, 1100–1400, as the vehicle of an extensive literature in prose and verse. The basis of the modern literary language is Morgan's bible of 1588, the archaic diction of which goes back to the previous century. There has been a standard literary language since the Middle Welsh period, but this development has not been matched in the spoken language, due to the official neglect of Welsh. Most spoken Welsh is dialect Welsh, but many are able to speak the standard language as well. The main dialects are those of Gwynedd (N.W.), Powys (N.E. and Mid-Wales), Dyfed (S.W.), and

Gwent (S.E.). Pure dialect speakers from the north and south do not understand each other easily. Furthermore, all dialects vary considerably from the written language.

Until the Act of Union, which came into force in 1536, Wales was to all intents and purposes a monoglot country where the native language flourished as the ordinarily spoken and most usually written medium. The Goidelic-speaking enclaves (see below) had long been eliminated. Only in South Pembrokeshire—'Little England beyond Wales'—was there a really substantial English-speaking population. Here the native Welsh had been driven from their lands in the twelfth century to make room for Flemish colonists who were subsequently anglicised, p. 104. But the Act of Union contained a provision that English alone should be employed in the law courts and that no one could hold an official position in Wales who was not able to use the English tongue. Even if, for practical reasons, the whole of this provision could not be implemented immediately, it nevertheless opened the door to anglicisation. Now that the national language was deprived of its official status, its prestige inevitably waned. The upper classes were the first to abandon their native language, but the bulk of the peasantry and the artisan class remained Welsh monoglots down to the beginning of the nineteenth century. From then on a knowledge of English began to spread, slowly at first, but rapidly after about 1850. The industrialisation of the south attracted so many workers from outside Wales that Welsh began to yield to English, particularly in the main centres. The towns on the north coast, too, became largely anglicised during the second half of the last century, by which time most of those who continued to use Welsh were becoming bilingual. Not unnaturally, great store was set on a knowledge of English and here the schools, where English was the sole official medium of instruction, played a decisive part.

The mentality of the Welsh speakers in this situation is certainly worthy of remark. Many saw in English a means to better things for themselves and their families. Having become conscious of the big world outside Wales, they developed an inferiority complex in the language question. Some of those who had acquired English, especially if they lived in an area of mixed speech, either abandoned their native tongue entirely or at least made a point of never using it with their children: they, at any rate, should go forth into the world with a clean start. Not a few Welsh speakers were reluctant to admit that they knew Welsh, especially if only monoglot English speakers were present. Even the Welshman who had no English was affected by this spirit of abasement. George Borrow's *Wild Wales* is an unsurpassed source of information on these matters. Borrow walked through

Wales in 1854 and tells how he identified a labourer as a Welsh monoglot merely by the way the Welshman turned his head away as Borrow was about to pass him on the road. The poor man without English was afraid the gentlemanly stranger might address him in the Saxon!

In all fairness to the Welsh, we must state that they have not been alone in this. Indeed, wherever analogous conditions obtain, identical attitudes can be observed. It is the same with the Bretons, or the Frisians, or the Rhaetians. Some will even deny their nationality altogether. The Aromunian shepherd may well declare himself a Greek or a Macedonian according to where one finds him, and many a Lusatian, in spite of the recent official recognition and encourage-ment of his minority language, will announce himself as a German. To come nearer home, the Welsh story can be equally well documented from Ireland, from the Isle of Man, from the Highlands and Islands of Scotland, and even from Cornwall where the language died out long ago. Nicholas Boson of Newlyn, born in 1624, tells how his mother tried to prevent him learning Cornish by forbidding the servants and neighbours to speak to him in that language. But he learnt it all the same, came to respect it and regretted that such a fine medium should be in danger of being lost. It is to Boson that we owe the only surviving folktale in Cornish.

But, as Boson's story illustrates, reactions are not all negative and defeatist; far from it. Pride in one's heritage is often a factor deter-mining conduct. So it was in Wales, too. Many Welshmen deplored the neglect of the native tongue. After a hard struggle with officialdom, Welsh was finally introduced into the schools as a grant-earning subject in 1890. Official hostility to Welsh has grown milder of late, so that Welsh is now taught in many schools and has become the ordinary medium in some. But the main crippling disability remains: Welsh has not obtained proper and full official status. No language can maintain itself in the modern world without such recognition. Small wonder then that the language continues to lose ground. The number of those able to speak Welsh is shrinking rather rapidly. According to the census of 1931, there were 909,000 Welsh speakers, but in 1951 these had become 714,000, of whom a large proportion belonged to the higher age-groups. In spite of the decline, however, Welsh still predominates in most of rural Wales.

We may conclude with a note on Welsh overseas. During the last century occasional attempts were made to establish Welsh-speaking settlements abroad, but only one such attempt met with any measure of success. In 1865, about 150 Welsh settled in the lower Chibut valley in Patagonia with the help of the Argentine government. They eventually prospered and were joined by new arrivals from Wales, the population growing to 2,500 in 1891. Welsh is still used, mainly by members of the older generation; the young people now prefer Spanish.

Cornish

Celtic survived in Devon until the tenth century when the Tamar became the boundary between Saxon and Celt. Cornwall ceased to be an independent kingdom about 900, but the Celtic population was not dispersed. Theirs was a small country, however, and no natural obstacles offered protection against outside influences. Throughout the Middle Ages the linguistic frontier moved slowly but surely westward. By 1600 it was approaching Truro, so that Cornish was then confined to an area too small for survival. The remaining Cornish speakers now became bilingual and rapidly went over to English; after 1700 the language was nowhere being passed on to children. We hear that in 1776 four or five old people in Mousehole (near Penzance) could still use Cornish. Before the end of the century the language must have become extinct.

Cornish was never used as an official written language. In the Middle Ages, Latin or French were the languages of the courts; they were superseded by English in 1392. Nevertheless, the literary remains of Cornish are not inconsiderable. Like Early Welsh, Early Cornish is attested in a few names from the preliterary period. Old Cornish is the language of glosses written from 900 to 1100. A number of passion plays of the fourteenth and fifteenth centuries are written in Middle Cornish. Another play, dated 1611, prose passages amounting to, say, 150 pages, various antiquarian jottings made when the language was in its final stage, together with Celtic words still surviving in the dialect English of Cornwall, constitute our records of Modern Cornish.

Cornish is closely related to Welsh, but a number of differences of long standing show that, at the end of Brittonic times, the languages of the South-West and of Wales were well on the way to becoming separate entities.

We should not conclude this brief account of Cornish without mentioning that small band of enthusiasts in Cornwall who, in this century, have taught themselves the extinct speech of their forbears and even produced original compositions in it. Their revived Cornish is, however, based on Middle Cornish, i.e., on the language of the best-preserved period. We do not know if in any other place the patriotic feelings and intellectual aspirations of a group of people have found such an outlet, unless it be the Isle of Man, but here native speakers of Manx were to be found until recently.

Breton

According to venerable tradition, the irruptions of the Saxons into Southern Britain caused many of the Celts to cross over into the Gallo-Roman province of Armorica, later to be known as Brittany. It is not clear how the arrival of invaders in S.E. Britain could have triggered off a mass emigration from the extreme South-West, for such it appears to have been, and it has recently been suggested that not Saxon, but Irish pressure was most likely the essential factor. However that may be, British Celts carried their language across the Channel, where it came to be called Breton. It is not known if a Gaulish-speaking population still survived in Armorica which might conceivably have attracted British-speaking refugees. At all events the language which imposed itself on Armorica bears the closest affinities with Cornish, so that one may speak of Corno-Breton as contrasting with Welsh. The settlement is regarded as having begun in the fifth and lasted until the early seventh century.

Breton is today spoken in rural areas of Basse-Bretagne west of a line from Saint-Brieuc to Vannes. At the time of its maximum extent, it occupied almost the whole of Brittany, though never reaching Rennes or Nantes. Subsequently, the Bretons came under the rule of feudal houses of French origin, and since the eleventh century, Latin and French have been the only languages used officially in Brittany. The influential circles knew the native tongue, but neglected it in favour of French, so that Breton never became the medium of a rich, national literature as Welsh did, nor could it under such circumstances achieve any degree of standardisation.

Periodisation in Breton is as follows: Early Breton (names only) before 800, Old Breton (chiefly glosses) 800–1100, Middle Breton 1100–1650, afterwards Modern Breton. Middle Breton is not represented by continuous texts until the fifteenth century; these are nearly all religious plays (as in Middle Cornish) and poems of considerable linguistic, but little literary interest. During the last hundred years or so, Breton has been cultivated in writing by a nationalistic-minded élite and an approximate literary norm has emerged, though a standard orthography has still not been agreed upon. But most Breton speakers are illiterate in their mother tongue. For long, Breton was officially barred from the schools, though it had to be used unofficially at least in the infants' department as so many children began school with no French. Since 1951, however, Breton has been recognised by the ministry as a school subject (only). As is to be expected, dialect speaking is the rule in Brittany. There are four main dialects, those of Cornouailles, Léon (which has contributed most to the literary norm), Tréguier and Vannes, the last being very appreciably different from the others.

During the latter half of the nineteenth century, the Breton peasantry became bilingual, French being acquired through the schools. At the same time, the urban populations, now growing rapidly, tended to become monoglot French. These trends run parallel to contemporary developments in Wales. How many speak Breton? French census returns are not concerned with linguistic matters, so one must turn to unofficial estimates. In 1945 perhaps as many as a million persons knew Breton, though a large percentage of speakers was in the higher age-groups. In the last two decades the number of persons speaking Breton has certainly dropped very considerably, if not catastrophically.

We saw that Breton is, in origin, much closer to Cornish than Welsh. Writing at the turn of the twelfth century, Giraldus Cambrensis observed that the languages of Brittany and Cornwall were almost identical and, to a considerable extent, comprehensible to a Welshman. Later, however, Breton and Cornish came more and more under the influence of their powerful neighbours. Breton was profoundly modified by French, while Cornish (like Welsh) was wide open to English influence. Today Breton is, apart from various words spoken in isolation, quite incomprehensible to a Welshman and vice versa, so that the often-related stories of Breton onion-men understanding Welsh conversation must be dismissed as pure romance. Differences today are so great that a Welshman can make no sense of a Breton magazine, no more than a Breton can read a Welsh newspaper. Of course, the underlying genius of the languages is the same and much of the vocabulary is common to both, though as often as not obscured by secondary sound changes. With a bit of perseverance, however, these fellow Celts can fairly soon learn to read each other's language.

GOIDELIC

Had the Romans established their power in Ireland as they did over the greater part of Britain, they would perhaps have left some testimony of the linguistic situation in that country. As it is, we are entirely dependent on the later native sources and on inferences drawn from internal linguistic evidence. These indicate that the language known as Irish was the dominant tongue, but that British had from, say, the second century B.C. established bridgeheads in Ireland and may have survived there until the eighth century.

The Irish language is first mentioned in the late seventh century; it is called Goidelic (Goedelic), from which is descended the modern term Gaelic. As already mentioned, native tradition refers to the language only as Gaelic, never as Irish. When the language was carried abroad (to Scotland and the Isle of Man), it continued to be known as Gaelic to native speakers everywhere, but one may, of course, also use the distinguishing terms Irish Gaelic, Scottish Gaelic and Manx Gaelic.

Goidelic is a Celtic language, related to, but quite distinct from Brittonic. At what prehistoric period the Goidelic-speaking Celts arrived in Ireland is quite undetermined, nor can it be said whence or by what route they came. Many theories have been propounded; none of them are warranted by the known facts, or rather by the absence of known facts.

The term Goidelic is chiefly used to denote Irish as distinct from British or, more technically speaking, to denote Q-Celtic as opposed to P-Celtic. It may be used, however, in reference to the earliest phase of the Irish language which is attested in just over 300 funerary inscriptions dating from the fourth to the eighth centuries A.D. They consist almost exclusively of personal names. A few are written in the Latin alphabet, but the great majority are engraved in a sort of linear cypher, known as the Ogam script, considered to be an invention of the fourth century.

Goidelic outside Ireland

At the end of the third century, the Irish became expansive and Goidelic was carried overseas. Irish colonies were established in North and South Wales, where they doubtless survived into the Dark Ages. For example, an Irish dynasty ruled in Dyfed (S.W. Wales) until the eighth century. Ogam inscriptions imply that the language was in use there until the seventh century at least. By the same means it may be postulated that Irish was still in use in North Wales in the sixth century. Devon and Cornwall also received influential settlers about the same time. As in Wales, the Irish here, too, were eventually assimilated.

Further north, however, Goidelic was to make more lasting conquests. The Isle of Man was overrun and at length completely gaelicised. The forms of a name in a fourth century Ogam inscription suggest that in that century Irish and British were in use side by side.

Irish activity in the north is first noted in fourth-century references to the Scots, so often mentioned together with the Picts, as raiders harassing the Roman province from the north. Scotti appears to have originally been a general name for freebooters from Northern Ireland, and in the fifth century these people set up a kingdom in Argyll. From this large bridgehead, they brought most of the country subsequently called Scotland under their sway, spreading their Goidelic language throughout the major part.

We may now consider the relationship between these colonial forms of Irish and the language of the homeland. Since we shall be referring to the modern period as well, it will be more appropriate to use the term Gaelic instead of Goidelic. All forms of Gaelic have sprung from Common (Irish) Gaelic and are often regarded merely as dialects of one single language. There is some practical philological justification for this, since naturally spoken Gaelic everywhere exists only in dialect form. At one time, before the anglicisation of the greatest part of the Gaelic-speaking area, the Gaelic dialects constituted a continuum from Cape Clear to Cape Wrath. Indeed, the old connections are still visible in the surviving dialects. A speaker of a northern Irish dialect has difficulty in understanding a man from Munster, but he has less difficulty in understanding a Scotsman from Argyll, who in his turn finds the dialect of Lewis or Sutherland almost a 'foreign language'. On the other hand, Ireland, Scotland and even Man have evolved independent literary forms of Gaelic. Although in practice they exert little or no influence on the ordinarily spoken word, it still seems more appropriate to think in terms of three separate languages. The basic fact is that the terms 'language' and 'dialect' are themselves imprecise concepts, which often require qualifying definition. There is no doubt, of course, that had Irish, Scottish and Manx Gaelic been able to develop as modern national languages, supported by all the paraphernalia of the present-day state, they would have been much more uniform within themselves and therefore more distinctively Irish, Scottish or Manx than they are today. They would have stood in the same relationship to each other as do, let us say, Danish, Norwegian and Swedish.

Irish Gaelic

The earliest Irish, that of the Ogam inscriptions, may be termed Goidelic or, better, Ogam Irish. The literary period proper begins with manuscripts written in the seventh and eighth centuries. These are, in the main, extensive glosses on biblical texts preserved in libraries on the Continent—a reminder of the missionary zeal of the Irish from the sixth to the eighth century when Ireland was the most important centre of learning in Western Europe. A few word forms in the glosses show that some of them were compiled as early as the sixth century. The remarkably uniform character of the language indicates that a high degree of standardisation had been reached, at least in the written language. The language of such texts before 900 is called Old Irish. The bulk of the vast corpus of traditional literature, the pride of Gaelic Ireland, dates from the Middle and Early Modern period, from 900 to 1650. Many texts, however, are copies of earlier originals embodying features proper to the oldest period; this is notably the case with the law tracts, which were composed before the glosses. The Modern Irish period has generally been one of decline caused by the neglect, not to say outright persecution, of the Irish language as a consequence of alien rule from 1603 to 1921. Since Ireland gained Home Rule, Gaelic as the national language has become official and may be used for all purposes.

The Golden Age came to an abrupt end with the Viking attacks which began in 795. The men of Lochlann settled in various places, notably in Dublin, and were not finally assimilated until the twelfth or thirteenth centuries. The Anglo-Normans became a power in the land in 1169, when Dublin and its immediate vicinity, later known as the Pale, were occupied by the invaders. The Normans who dispersed over the countryside soon went over to Gaelic, but English gained a foothold in the Pale. In the second half of the sixteenth century, England set out in earnest to reduce the whole of Ireland and the defeat of the Gaelic chiefs at Kinsale in 1601 marks the formal end of Gaelic Ireland. Large numbers of English colonists were given Irish land, especially under Cromwell, which soon radically altered the linguistic situation. A wide area around Dublin was now predominantly English and the plantation of Ulster introduced a second large enclave centred on Belfast. English was the sole official language and soon spread out over most of the eastern half of the country. But the economically more backward western districts generally remained chiefly Irish-speaking. In 1600 virtually the whole of the population had been Irish-speaking, by 1800 quite one-half of an estimated total of four millions will have been English-speaking. English continued to make great headway, but the rapid rise in numbers to eight millions at the 1841 census probably meant that Irish was then being used by as many as three millions. They did, however, represent the poorer section of the people. Their tongue was despised, not only by the English-speaking section, but also by the leaders of the Irish-speaking peasantry themselves, who regarded Irish as a hindrance to progress. Then came the famine years of the forties which carried off upwards of a million Gaels, while the survivors saw their main hope of salvation in America. The land was depopulated on a scale without parallel in Europe. Thus the Famine struck the Gaelic language in Ireland its death blow. By the end of the century, it was found only in rapidly shrinking enclaves in the far west.

Only then did a reaction set in. In keeping with trends abroad, a number of intellectuals began to see in the Irish language the hallmark of the nation they wished to emancipate. In 1893, the Gaelic League was formed with the task of restoring the Irish language. But the patriotic idealism of the restorers could make little progress in the face of the overwhelming difficulties. The 1851 census returns had given 1,524,000 Irish speakers, of whom 320,000 had no English. But when the Gaelic League began its work, there were not half as many, and most of those belonged to the oldest generation. Since independence, Irish has been widely taught in most schools. It is the normal medium of instruction in the Gaeltacht and this is also the position in many schools outside the Gaelic-speaking parts. It is true that school-teaching has imparted to many a certain knowledge of the national language, but it has not turned them into habitual speakers of Irish nor has it prevented the continued decline of Irish in the Gaelic-speaking areas proper, though it has undoubtedly done something to slow down this decline. Today not more than 40,000 (if as many) habitually use Irish today, at the most one per cent of the population, though perhaps as many more are native speakers who have a good or fair command of the language. Irish lingers on in Munster in a handful of villages and hamlets. The principal Irish-speaking areas today are West-Central Donegal and Connemara in Connaught.

Irish is still often printed in a decorative variety of the Latin alphabet based on a medieval manuscript form (semi-uncial), but the use of Roman type has recently become common.

Scottish Gaelic

As we saw above, this form of Gaelic was introduced via Argyll in the fifth century. By the end of the tenth century, the new language had conquered the Western Isles and most of the Mainland, replacing Pictish and British. But the English-speaking Merse was not affected. Gaelic suffered some temporary reverses owing to Norse penetration, especially in the Hebrides when, in the ninth century, Viking immigrants turned these islands into predominantly Norse-speaking colonies. How long Norse maintained itself here is unknown. Norway renounced her rights to the territory in 1266, by which time Gaelic appears to have become the usual medium again, though the place names remain very largely Scandinavian and the modern dialects are replete with loan words from Norse. As it pushed northward through Pictland, Gaelic also came into contact with Norse established in strength particularly in Sutherland and Caithness since the ninth century. This area was eventually gaelicised, except for the north-eastern part of Caithness.

Gaelic in Scotland attained its greatest extent in the eleventh century, but precisely then the first serious challenge came from the south. Large numbers of Saxon refugees fleeing from the Norman invaders of England poured into the Scottish Lowlands and their leading families were well received at court in English-speaking Edinburgh. The following centuries witness the gradual spread of English at the expense of Gaelic. By the sixteenth century, English had reached the Clyde and was about to drive Gaelic out of Galloway. It had pushed up the east coast, forcing Gaelic back to the Highland Line. Then the Scottish Reformation (1560) brought the pro-English faction to power and inaugurated the era of inspired attacks on Gaeldom. On the one side stood the Lowland Protestant English-speaker, on the other the Highland Catholic Gael.

Despite official sanctions on their language, the population of the Highlands and Islands generally remained monoglot Gaels. But after the defeat of the Stuart Pretender in 1745, the systematic destruction of Gaelic society began. During the Highland clearances from 1782 to 1853 large numbers of Gaels were evicted from what had been their clan-lands. Others left of their own accord to find employment in the English-speaking Lowland towns or in the colonies. As a consequence, the percentage of Gaelic speakers in Scotland rapidly declined. It had been 50 per cent or 150,000 Gaels in the sixteenth century, by 1801 it was 20 per cent or 335,000 Gaels, by 1861 it was down to 10 per cent or 300,000 Gaels (estimated figures). Towards the end of the last century, the remaining Gaels had in most cases become bilingual. Official policy is no longer openly hostile to the language and culture of the Highlands, but it is entirely indifferent. Meanwhile the number of Gaelic speakers has shrunk to about $1\frac{1}{2}$ per cent of the population. In 1931, 137,000 were returned as Gaelic-speaking, in 1951 the figure was 87,000. Apart from a few localities on the western seaboard, Gaelic is now predominantly spoken only in the Hebrides.

Emigration from the Highlands led to the loss of Gaelic except on Cape Breton Island, Nova Scotia, where a compact settlement of Gaels took place. Immigration began in 1773, reaching its maximum between 1790 and 1830. Many of the settlers knew only Gaelic and the language was widely spoken in the rural districts until quite recently, though English alone was the official language. In 1931, some 30,000 could use Gaelic, mostly people of the oldest generation, the younger ones having generally gone over to English. Twenty years later the number of speakers had fallen drastically to 6,789, so that Gaelic is now rapidly disappearing as a living idiom in Nova Scotia.

Scottish Gaelic plays hardly any part in education; most Gaelic speakers are in consequence illiterate in their native tongue. The written standard, based on the Bible of 1801, has thus had no appreciable influence on the spoken form. As in Ireland, broad dialect is the rule in Gaelic Scotland and every parish has its shibboleth. Dialect differences can be quite considerable, so much so that speakers from the north have difficulty in understanding the southerners, at least at first. For these the koine is English.

In the Middle Ages, learned Scottish Gaels, aware of their Irish ancestry, strove to write Irish Gaelic. There is therefore no medieval literature in Scottish Gaelic, but an oral folk literature, second to none, has been recorded in modern times. The first considerable document in Scottish Gaelic proper is an early sixteenth-century collection of poems. Here a break was also made with the traditional Irish orthography, but this new departure was not generally followed, though in Scotland only Latin letters are used.

Until fairly recently, Scottish (or Scots) Gaelic commonly went under the name of Erse, which is simply a development of the Lowlanders' form of the word 'Irish' (early Sc. dial. *Erische*). Sometimes this term was used for Irish Gaelic—though much to the disapproval of the men of Erin.

Manx Gaelic

Manx Gaelic, or simply Manx, is very close to Scottish Gaelic. The oldest monument of the language is a translation of the Book of Common Prayer made between 1606 and 1610. A number of religious publications followed and in more recent times folktales and the like have appeared. Unlike other Gaelic, Manx spelling is modelled on English. By tradition, the laws of the Isle of Man are promulgated in Manx as well as in English, though Manx has recently become extinct.

Until about 1700, or a little later, Manx was spoken by all the native inhabitants of the island, most of whom had no English. But in the eighteenth century the influence of Lancashire began to make itself felt. From the beginning of the nineteenth century, the decline of Manx was rapid and hastened by the exclusive use of English in school. Children born after 1870 did not usually acquire Manx, so that from this time Manx was certainly doomed. By 1901 it was known to only 4,657 persons, mostly of the oldest generation, and all but 59 were bilingual. In the course of the next two decades nearly all these Manx speakers died, so that by 1920 the language was scarcely heard anywhere. A careful enquiry just after the last war showed that only a score of native speakers were left: all aged persons who had learnt Manx in their childhood, though they had not used it for many a long year—except when prompted by some philological enquirer. Ten years later, and these last guardians of the tongue of Ellan Vannin were no more.

THE STRUCTURE OF CELTIC

Only the Celtic developed in the British Isles is fully known but it may be reasonably supposed that at least some of its peculiar features were first acquired in these islands as a result of the fusion of the

immigrant Celts with the pre-Celtic population. One such striking
feature is the use of periphrastic tenses consisting of the verb 'to be'
and a verbal noun, e.g., Welsh *yr wyf yn dyfod* 'I come', lit. 'I am a-
coming'. What makes this particularly interesting is the fact that
English, in its turn, has copied this strange construction, but has
given it a special semantic content not found in Welsh. Side by side
with the inherited Germanic verbal form *I come*, we have the exotic
construction '*I am (a-)coming*' which sets the pattern for our very
un-Germanic continuous tenses.

Despite such unusual features, the IE origin of Celtic is evident
enough. It is rather close to Italic. Though often obscured by phonetic
changes, declensions and conjugations reveal a great number of
correspondences well known from other languages. Some of these
will be apparent from the paradigms below. The following lexical
equations give some idea of the IE character of a large part of the
Celtic vocabulary.

Ir. *roth*, W. *rhod* 'wheel': Lat. *rota*, Ger. *Rad;* cf. Skt. *ráthas*
'chariot', lit. 'wheeled'

Ir. *cú*, W. *ci* 'dog': Lat. *canis*, Gk. *kúōn*, Lith. *šuõ*, gen. *šuñs*, Eng.
hound

Ir. *fear*, W. *gŵr* 'man': Lat. *vir*, Lith. *výras*, Eng. *wer-* in *werwolf*

Ir. *tanaí*, W. *tanau* 'thin': Skt. *tanás*, Lat. *tenuis*, Eng. *thin*

Ir. *canadh*, W. *canu* 'singing': Lat. *canō* '(I) sing', Gk. *ēikanós* lit.
'early singer', Goth. *hana* lit. 'singer', both meaning 'cock'

Ir. *athair* 'father': Gk. *patḗr*, Lat. *pater*, Skt. *pitár-*, Eng. *father*,
Armen. *hayr*

Ir. *lán*, W. *llawn* 'full': Skt. *pūrṇás*, Lat. *plēnus*, Lith. *pìlnas*, Russ.
pólon, Eng. *full*

We have already drawn attention to the two main divisions of
Insular Celtic, namely Brittonic and Goidelic; the former division
may be expanded as Gallo-Brittonic. These two divisions frequently
go under the names of P-Celtic and Q-Celtic respectively, terms due
to a phonetic innovation in the former. In Gallo-Brittonic, Primitive
Celtic *kw* becomes *p*, but remains in Goidelic, though only in the
oldest inscriptions, and is transliterated *Q*. Subsequently, the sound
was reduced to [k] and appears as such (written *c*) in the literary texts.
Examples: Gaul. *petor-* 'four', W. *pedwar*, Ir. *ceathair*, cf. Lat.
quattuor; Gaul. *Epo-*, Ir. *each* 'horse', W. *ebol* (diminutive) 'colt',
where Ir. *ch* and W. *b* are regular secondary developments of earlier
c and *p*, cf. Lat. *equus*. We note, however, that occasional examples
suggest that not all the dialects of Gaul had changed to *p*. Puzzling,
for instance, is the river name *Sēquana*, now *Seine*.

Since the two main forms of Celtic are considerably differentiated,
it will be convenient to treat them in more detail separately.

P-CELTIC

The best attested P-Celtic language is Welsh. The remains of the earliest period show that sweeping changes were taking place, but since the beginning of the literary period proper in the twelfth century, the written language at any rate has remained rather conservative. We may take our examples from modern literary Welsh which may be regarded, more or less, as representative of the earlier literary period as well.

WELSH

Phonetics

The following spelling conventions may be noted:

    c is like Eng. 'k'
    ch is like Scot. 'ch' in 'loch'
    dd is like Eng. 'th' in 'that'
    f is like Eng. 'v', *ff* is like Eng. 'f'
    ng is like Eng. 'ng' in 'sing'
    ngh is like Eng. 'ng' in 'sing' followed by 'h'
    u is like Eng. 'i'
    ll is voiceless 'l', *rh* is voiceless 'r' followed by 'h'
    w may have the value of 'u' in 'put': *cwm* 'valley, combe'
    wy is often like Eng. 'we'
    y when stressed is like 'er' in 'father', also in the particles *y, yr*. In final unstressed syllables it is pronounced like English short 'i'. In monosyllables it may be pronounced like 'ee' in 'seen'.

The stress falls on the penultimate.

Mutations

A remarkable and characteristic feature of the Insular Celtic languages are the so-called mutations. The P-Celtic mutations arose in the Brittonic period when a number of initial consonants were mutated, i.e., modified by the final sound of the preceding word in the sentence. For instance, any word beginning with [k] before a vowel became [g] whenever it was preceded by a word ending in a vowel. In like manner [p, t] became [b, d]. This change was part of a general sound law according to which the voiceless plosives became voiced in the intervocalic position, cf. *ebol* 'colt', but Gaul. *Epo-* 'horse' (p. 80). Subsequently, the final vowels which had caused the mutations disappeared, but the mutations themselves remained. At this point, analogical changes began to reshape the system and since the mutations were so common, they soon became grammaticalised.

Let us consider the mutations of a word beginning with the sound [k] and let the word be *ci* m. 'dog'. This, the radical form, can be mutated to any of the following according to its position in the sentence: *gi, chi, nghi*; these are known as the soft, spirant and nasal mutations respectively. The radical form (of a masculine noun) will be found, for instance, after the definite article: *y ci* 'the dog'; it will likewise be found after the verbal noun: *yr wyf yn caru ci* 'I love a dog' lit. '(I) am in loving (of) dog', there being no indefinite article in Welsh and *ci* genitive by position. But should this word occur after a synthetic tense, it appears with the soft mutation: *gwelais gi* 'I saw a dog'. The soft mutation will likewise appear in compounds: *corgi* lit. 'dwarf dog'. On the other hand, if we wish to say 'with a dog' we need the spirant mutation: *gyda chi*. Lastly, a few words govern the nasal mutation, e.g., *fy nghi* 'my dog'. The mutations sometimes affect the sense. The words *ei* 'his, her' and *eu* 'their' are pronounced alike, but if standing before a mutable consonant they cannot be confused semantically as they are each followed by a different consonant *ei gi* 'his dog', *ei chi* 'her dog', *eu ci* 'their dog'.

Any word in the language commencing with a mutable consonant will, in general, be affected in this way. But there are differences of detail. For example, a feminine noun preceded by the article is softened: *cath* f. 'cat', *y gath*. An adjective used attributively usually follows its noun and in this position retains a radical consonant except when the noun is fem.sg., in which case it takes the soft mutation: *y ci cadarn* 'the strong dog', but *y gath gadarn*.

TABLE OF WELSH MUTATIONS

Radical	Soft	Nasal	Spirant
c	g	nhg	ch
t	d	nh	th
p	b	mh	ph
g	(disappears)	ng	
d	dd	n	
b	f	m	
m	f		
ll	l		
rh	r		

Accidence

It can be postulated that the inherited IE case system survived to a large extent in British (as in Gaulish), but broke down completely before the literary period. Welsh has no case endings. Nouns have two numbers. The rules for the formation of the plural in Welsh are extremely complicated. We give a few typical examples: *eisteddfod* f. lit. 'session', pl. *eisteddfodau*; *corgi* m. lit. 'dwarf dog', pl. *corgwn*; *craig* f. 'rock, crag', pl. *creigiau*; *afon* f. 'river' (cf. the name *Avon*), pl. *afonydd*; *broch* m. 'badger, brock', pl. *brochion* or *brochod*; *bardd* m. 'bard', pl. *beirdd*; *Methodist* m., pl. *Methodistiaid*; *cwm* m. 'valley, combe', pl. *cymoedd*; *Cymro* 'Welshman', pl. *Cymry*; *Cymraes* 'Welshwoman', pl. *Cymraesau* or *Cymraesi*; *plentyn* m. 'child', pl. *plant; nyrs* f. 'nurse', pl. *nyrsys*.

Most adjectives are invariable, but a number have plural forms: *glas* 'blue', pl. *gleision*, while others distinguish (in the singular) between masculine and feminine as well: *gwyn* 'white', fem. *gwen*, pl. *gwynion*. In practice, the feminine form nearly always appears as *wen* in accordance with the laws of mutation. The neuter gender has been lost in Welsh.

The verb has four synthetic tenses in the indicative active (pres., imperf., pret., pluperf.) and two tenses in the subjunctive (pres., imperf., though in most verbs only the pres. has endings different from the indicative). Invariable impersonal forms have functions often corresponding to the English passive and, indeed, these forms are. historically speaking, true passives. The Celtic languages have no infinitive, but make great play of the verbal noun, especially to form periphrastic tenses. Sample paradigms:

Verbal noun *caru* 'love, loving'

Pres.sg.1	*caraf*	Imperf.sg.1	*carwn*	Pret.sg.1	*cerais*
2	*ceri*	2	*carit*	2	*ceraist*
3	*câr*	3	*carai*	3	*carodd*
pl.1	*carwn*	pl.1	*carem*	pl.1	*carasom*
2	*cerwch*	2	*carech*	2	*carasoch*
3	*carant*	3	*carent*	3	*carasant*
impers.	*cerir*	impers.	*cerid*	impers.	*carwyd*

Pluperf.sg.1	*caraswn*	(Subjunctive) Pres.sg.1	*carwyf*
2	*carasit*	2	*cerych*
3	*carasai*	3	*caro*
pl.1	*carasem*	pl.1	*carom*
2	*carasech*	2	*caroch*
3	*carasent*	3	*caront*
impers.	*carasid*	impers.	*carer*

Imperative sg.2 *câr*, 3 *cared*, pl.1 *carwn*, 2 *cerwch*, 3 *carent*

Examples of periphrastic tenses (verb 'to be' and verbal noun): pres. *yr wyf yn caru* lit. 'I am in loving', fut. *y byddaf yn caru*, imperf. *yr oeddwn yn caru*, pret. *yr wyf wedi caru* lit. 'I am after loving', pluperf. *yr oeddwn wedi caru*. The verb 'to be' naturally conjugates, e.g., in the present: sg.1 *yr wyf*, 2 *yr wyt*, 3 *y mae*, pl.1 *yr ydym*, 2 *yr ydych*, 3 *y maent* (*y*, *yr* is a meaningless particle which commonly accompanies the substantive verb; it may likewise accompany other verbs: *y caraf* etc.).

Vocabulary

A good deal of the Welsh vocabulary can be etymologised and a few examples of lexical equations showing its fundamental Indo-European affinities have been mentioned above. British borrowed a large number of words from Latin during the Roman occupation as may be seen from the hundreds of Latin loan words in Welsh, e.g., *braich* 'arm', *cadwyn* 'chain', *esgyn* 'ascend', *saeth* 'arrow' from Lat. *bracchium*, *catēna*, *ascendō*, *sagitta*. After the Conquest, Norman French words entered Welsh, in some cases directly, in other cases via English, which has supplied Welsh with its largest contingent of loan words.

Numbers: 1 *un*, 2 *dau*, 3 *tri*, 4 *pedwar*, 5 *pump*, 6 *chwech*, 7 *saith*, 8 *wyth*, 9 *nau*, 10 *deg*, 100 *cant*

Texts

J. E. Lloyd, *Trydydd Llyfr Hanes* ('Third History Book')
Carnarvon, 1900, p. 40

Yr oedd y   barwn Normanaidd, Rhobert o Ruddlan, yn
was   the baron Norman   Robert of Rhuddlan in

cymeryd cyntun yn ei gastell yn Neganwy
taking   sleep   in his castle in Deganwy

ganol hafddydd   yn nechrau mis
middle summer's day in beginning month

Gorffenaf pan ddaeth y newydd fod   llonaid tair
July   when came the news   being fullness of-three

llong   o wŷr Gruffydd wedi glanio dan
ship (i.e. three shiploads) of men of-Griffith after landing under

Ben y Gogarth   ac yn dwyn   ymaith
Pen y Gogarth (the Great Orme's Head) and in carrying away

ei dda a'i   ddynion. Rhedodd ar unwaith i ben y
his cattle and his men   ran   at once   to head of-the

mynydd   heb   aros   i roi ei lurig   amdano, ac yno
mountain without waiting to put his cuirass on-him   and there

dan   gesail y   clogwyn gwelai'r Cymry wrthi yn llusgo   ei
under hollow of-the cliff   saw the Welsh at-it in dragging his

eiddo   i'w   llongau. Er   nad oedd ei filwyr   eto wedi
property to their ships   although not was his soldiers yet after

cyrraedd y fan, methodd â   dâl   yr
reaching the place failed   with bearing (i.e. couldn't bear) the

olygfa, rhuthrodd ar   y Cymry, yn anarfog fel yr oedd, ond buan
sight   rushed   upon the Welsh unarmed as was   but soon

y syrthiodd dan   gawod o waewffyn.
fell   under shower of spears

(Mutations: *Ruddlan* radical *Rhuddlan, gastell* r. *castell, Neganwy* r.
Deganwy, ganol r. *canol, nechrau* r. *dechrau, ddaeth* r. *daeth, fod* r. *bod,
wŷr* r. *gwŷr, dan* r. *tan, Ben* r. *Pen, dda* r. *da, ddynion* r. *dynion, roi* r.
rhoi, lurig r. *llurig, gesail* r. *cesail, filwyr* r. *milwyr, fan* r. *man, olygfa*
r. *golygfa, gawod* r. *cawod, waewffyn* r. *gwaewffyn*)

Matthew vi.9–13

Ein Tad   yr hwn   wyt yn y   nefoedd; sancteiddier dy enw.
our Father the which art in the heavens be-hallowed thy name

Deled dy deyrnas. Gwneler dy ewyllys, megis yn y nef,   felly
come thy kingdom be-done thy will   as   in the heaven so

ar y ddaear hefyd. Dyro i ni heddiw ein bara beunyddiol. A
on the earth also   give to us today our bread daily   and

maddau i ni ein dyledion, fel y maddeuwn ninnau i'n   dyledwyr.
forgive to us our *debtors* as forgive   we   to our debtors

Ac nac arwain ni i brofedigaeth, eithr gwared ni rhag drwg. Canys
and not lead   us to temptation   but   deliver us from evil   for

eiddot ti yw'r deyrnas a'r   nerth a'r   gogoniant yn oes
thine is the kingdom and the power and the glory   in age

oesoedd.
of-ages
4

(Mutations: *deyrnas* r. *teyrnas*, *ddaear* r. *daear*, *brofedigaeth* r. *profedigaeth*)

Cornish

The Cornish Lord's Prayer has been handed down in variant forms. On these the following version in revived (Middle) Cornish is based.

9   *Agan Tas-ny, us yn nef: benygys re bo dha hanow.*
10 *Re dheffo dha wlascor. Dha voth re bo gwres, y'n nor kepar hag y'n nef.*
11 *Ro dhyn-ny hedhyu agan bara pup deth-oll.*
12 *Ha gaf dhyn agan camwyth, kepar del aven-nyny dhe'n re-na us ow camwul er agan pyn-ny.*
13 *Ha na wra agan gorra yn temptasyon, mes delyrf ny dyworth drok. Rag dhyso-jy yu an wlascor ha'n gallos ha'n gordhyans bys vyken ha bynary.*

Breton

9   *Hon Tad, a zo en neñv: ra vo santelaet da anv.*
10 *Ra zeuio da rouantelezh. Ra vo graet da youl war an douar evel en neñv.*
11 *Ro dimp hiziv hon bara pemdeziek.*
12 *Distaol dimp hon dle evel ma tistaolomp d'hon dleourien.*
13 *Ha n'hon laka ket da vezañ tentet, met hon dieub diouzh an droug. Rak dit-te eo ar rouantelezh hag ar galloud hag ar gloar da virviken.*

Q-CELTIC

The oldest literary form of Q-Celtic, Old Irish, differs greatly from the succeeding Middle Irish and from the modern Gaelic languages which are, in many ways, relatively close to Middle Irish. We append some notes on Old and Modern Irish as representative of the two main stages in the recorded evolution of Q-Celtic.

OLD IRISH

Phonetics
Mutations pretty well analogous to those of Welsh also occur in Irish. Old Irish has initial stress with consequent weakening or less of old final syllables.

Accidence

The three IE genders are preserved. Nouns may have a dual form (they are then accompanied by the numeral 'two'), but adjectives have distinct forms only for singular and plural. There are five cases, but fewer inflexions, though the former presence of endings is traceable in the varying quality of the (now) final consonant.

IE *ekwos* 'horse' in OIr.:

Sg.nom.	ech	Pl.	eich	Du.	ech
voc.	eich		eochu		ech
acc.	ech n-		eochu		ech
gen.	eich		ech n-		ech
dat.	eoch		echaib		echaib

n- is the relic of a lost ending which appears as the initial consonant of the word following.

The Old Irish verb has five tenses in the indicative (pres., imperf., pret., fut., secondary fut. or conditional) and two in the subjunctive (pres., pret.), active and passive. The passive has, however, distinctive forms only for the 3rd person, the other persons being expressed by the 3rd sg. plus the appropriate infixed pronoun. Deponent inflexion is found, but as a reduced and disappearing category.

Partly as a result of far-reaching phonological developments, the formation of the verb is exceptionally irregular. Several tenses have two sets of forms: absolute, e.g., *berid* '(he) bears', and conjunct (as when compounded), e.g., *níbeir* 'doesn't bear' or *dobeir* 'bears to, brings'. Should the conjunct form be enclitic, modifications may occur, e.g., *nítabir* 'doesn't bring'. Sample paradigms:

Verbal noun *breth* or *brith* 'bear, bearing'

		Absolute	Conjunct	
			(Stressed)	(Enclitic)
Pres.sg.1		biru	-biur	-bur
	2	biri	-bir	-bir
	3	berid	-beir	-bir
pl.1		bermi	-beram	-brem
	2	berthe	-berid	-brid
	3	berit	-berat	-bret

In addition, the extensive use of preverbs has led to the incorporation into the verbal unit of pronouns and various particles (negative, relative), all of which may bring about further phonetic changes. All in all, the Old Irish verb is so complex that one must wonder how the human mind managed to evolve and manipulate it. We append some typical examples of verbal forms:

robcarsi 'has loved you': *ro-* perfective preverb, *-b-* 'you', *-car* 'loved', *-si* 'you' (emphatic)

nimcharatsa '(they) love me not': *ni-* 'not', *-m-* 'me', *-charat* mutated from *-carat* '(they) love', *-sa* 'me' (emphatic)

amal asindbiursa 'as I say it': *amal* 'as', *as-* . . . *-biur* 'out . . . (I) bear' i.e. '(I) say', *-ind-* regular development of *-n-* plus *-id-* where *-n-* is a relative particle following *amal* and *-id-* 'it', *-sa* 'I' (emphatic)

amal rongabussa 'as I have taken it': *amal* 'as', *ro-n-gabus-sa* for **ro-n-d-gabus-sa* with suppression of *-d-* 'it' (cf. *-id-* above) where *ro-* is perfective preverb, *-n-* negative particle, *-gabus-* '(I) took', *-sa* 'I' (emphatic)

Vocabulary

Examples of the IE connections of Irish have been quoted above. In the preliterary period Irish borrowed extensively from British, e.g., OIr. *cáin* 'beautiful', *foilenn* 'seagull', *cland* 'children (descendants, 'clan')', cf. W. *cain*, *gŵylan*, *plant* (original *p* appearing as *c* in early loans), the last itself a borrowing from Lat. *planta* 'plant'.

Numbers: 1 *oín*, 2 *da*, 3 *tri*, 4 *cethir*, 5 *cóig*, 6 *sé*, 7 *secht n-*, 8 *ocht n-*, 9 *noí n-*, 10 *deich n-*, 100 *cét*

Texts

Eighth century Glosses (R. Thurneysen, *Old Irish Reader*, Dublin, 1949, pp. 43, 50–1):

ar atá brithem and cenutsu
for is judge in-it without-thee

i.e., for there is a judge apart from thee

is é side dano as éola and
is he-this moreover who-is skilled in-it

i.e., he is moreover skilled therein

ní cumme acus thussu
not-is like and thou

i.e., he is not the same as thou

doairchet a lláa mbrithemnachte sin
has-been-foretold the day of-judgement that

i.e., that day of judgement has been foretold

dobérat   uili a   coibsena   isind   láo sin
shall-give all their confessions on-the day that

i.e., all shall give their confessions on that day

taiccéra   cách dará   chenn fessin
shall-plead each for-his head own

i.e., each one shall plead for himself

Ninth-century monastic poem (G. Murphy, *Early Irish Lyrics*,
Oxford, 1956, p. 5):

Clocán   binn
little-bell melodious

benar   i   n-aidchi gaíthe
ringing on night   of-wind

ba   ferr   lim   dul   ina   dáil
it-be better to-me going to-its trysting

indás i   ndáil   mná   baíthe.
than to trysting of-woman foolish

MODERN IRISH

While languages enjoying full national status, such as English or
French, were evolving literary standards, and where the spoken styles
were becoming more and more uniform, the fate of Irish was entirely
the opposite. The literary language, disinherited, lay moribund, while
the spoken language, in so far as it managed to survive, continued to
exist solely as broad dialect. Today the Irish of Munster, which within
itself is considerably diversified, is appreciably different from that of
Connaught, while both are so far removed from the dialects of
Donegal in phonetics, accidence, vocabulary and syntax that mutual
comprehension is not always spontaneous and often difficult. The
problems involved in developing a language in this condition for use
as the national state language require no elaboration. Finally, in
1958, a standard grammar was prescribed for official purposes,
including school teaching; the material given below complies with
this standard.

Phonetics

Irish is a phonetically very complex language. Consonants have two qualities: neutral and palatal. The spelling rules for Irish were evolved in the Middle Ages. This traditional orthography, is still in use; it is, however, in spite of considerable simplifications introduced in 1948, not always a good guide, even to a native speaker, see 'Texts' below. Now that a standard grammar exists, it would be, of course, quite possible to prescribe a standard pronunciation.

Accidence

Since the Middle Irish period, only masculine and feminine genders are distinguished. The predicative adjective is uninflected. Sample paradigm:

Sg.nom.	*each* 'horse'	Pl.	*eacha*	Du.	*each*
voc.	*eich*		*eacha*		*each*
acc.	*each*		*eacha*		*each*
gen.	*eich*		*each*		*each*
dat.	*each*		*eacha*		

The Modern Irish verb preserves the moods and tenses of the older language, but is structurally very much simpler. The difference between absolute and conjunct inflexion has been eliminated and the baffling phonological irregularities reduced to manageable proportions. The preverbs have largely disappeared and with them the intricate system of infixed pronouns and the like. The traditional endings are in part preserved, but a system of analytical forms based on the 3rd sg. with an independent personal pronoun grew up alongside the synthetic forms and the two have become variously confused. The passive has become an invariable impersonal, somewhat similar in function to the analogous form in Welsh. Here are the paradigms of the indicative:

Verbal noun *breith* 'bear, bearing; giving birth, laying (eggs)'

Pres.sg.1	*beirim*	Imperf.sg.1	*bheirinn*
2	*beireann tú*	2	*bheirteá*
3	*beireann sé* ('he'), *sí* ('she')	3	*bheireadh sé, sí*
pl.1	*beirimid*	pl.1	*bheirimis*
2	*beireann sibh*	2	*bheireadh sibh*
3	*beireann siad*	3	*bheiridís*
impers.	*beirtear*	impers.	*bheirtí*

Fut.sg.1	*béarfaidh mé*	Conditional sg.1	*bhéarfainn*
2	*béarfaidh tú*	2	*bhéarfá*
3	*béarfaidh sé, sí*	3	*bhéarfadh sé, sí*
pl.1	*béarfaimid*	pl.1	*bhéarfaimis*
2	*béarfaidh sibh*	2	*bhéarfadh sibh*
3	*béarfaidh siad*	3	*bhéarfaidís*
impers.	*béarfar*	impers.	*bhéarfaí*

Pret.sg.1	*rug mé*	
2	*rug tú*	
3	*rug sé, sí*	The preterite of this verb is formed, exceptionally, from another stem; regular forms would be **bheir mé* etc., **bheiremar, *beireadh.*
pl.1	*rugamar*	
2	*rug sibh*	
3	*rug siad*	
impers.	*rugadh*	

Imperative sg.1 *beirim*, 2 *beir*, 3 *beiriadh* (*sé, sí*), pl.1 *beirimis*, 2 *beirigí*, 3 *beiridís*

Irish, like Welsh, has a series of periphrastic tenses (verb 'to be' and verbal noun), e.g., pres. *tá mé ag breith* lit. 'I am at bearing', pres. habitual *bím ag breith* cf. Anglo-Irish 'I do be', fut. *beidh mé ag breith*, imperf. *bhínn ag breith*, pret. *bhí mé ag breith*, perf. *tá mé tar éis breith* lit. 'I am after bearing'. The verb 'to be' is naturally conjugated, e.g., pres.sg.1 *tá mé*, 2 *tá tú*, 3 *tá sé, sí*, pl.1 *táimid*, 2 *tá sibh*, 3 *tá siad*.

Vocabulary

The Modern Irish lexicon preserves a large proportion of traditional Gaelic vocabulary. The later language contains loan words from Norse, Norman French and especially from English. Taken together, this extraneous element is very considerable.

Numbers: 1 *aon*, 2 *dó*, 3 *trí*, 4 *ceathair*, 5 *cúig*, 6 *sé*, 7 *seacht*, 8 *ocht*, 9 *naoi*, 10 *deich*, 100 *céad*

Texts

(The phonetics, in broad transcription, give an idea of the pronunciation of Connemara, the largest Irish-speaking district. This dialect generally preserves initial stress. Accents on consonants denote palatalisation.)

Matthew vi.9–13

Ár	*n-Athair, atá*	*ar neamh: go naofar*	*d'ainm.*	*Go dtaga do*
[ɑ:r	nɑhiŕ	əlta: ef ńæ:w gə ni:fər	dæńiḿ	gə dagə də]
our	father	who-is on heaven be-hallowed	thy name	come thy

ríocht.   Go ndéantar do thoil ar an talamh mar dhéantar ar neamh
[riəχt   gə ńi:ntər də hil′ eŕ ə talə   mar ji:ntər eŕ ńæ:w]
kingdom be-done   thy will on the earth as is-done on heaven

Ár n-arán laethúil tabhair dúinn inniu. Agus maith   dúinn ár
[a:r nəˈra:n læhu:l′ to:ŕ   du:ń əˈńu əgəs ma   du:ń a:r]
our bread   daily   give us   today and forgive us   our

bhfiacha, mar mhaithimid dár   bhféichiúna féin. Agus ná lig
[víəχə   mar wahiḿid′ da:r ve:hu:nə   he:ń əgəs na: l′iǵ]
debts   as   we-forgive to-our debtors   own and not allow

sinn i   gcathú.   ach saor sinn ó   olc. Óir is leat   féin
[ʃiń ə   gahu: aχ si:r   ʃiń o: olk o:ŕ əs l′æt   he:ń]
us into temptation but deliver us   from evil for is to-thee self

an ríocht   agus an chumhacht agus an ghlóir go síoraí.
[ə riəχt   əgəs ə χu:χt   əgəs ə ɣlo:ŕ gə ʃiəri:]
the kingdom and the power   and the glory everlastingly

(Mutations: *n-Athair* radical *Athair, dtaga* r. *taga, ndéantar* r.
déantar, thoil r. *toil, dhéantar* r. *déantar, n-arán* r. *arán, bhfiacha* r.
fiacha, mhaithimid r. *maithimid, bhféichiúna* r. *féichiúna, gcathú* r.
cathú, chumhacht r. *cumhacht, ghlóir* r. *glóir*)

Scottish Gaelic

9 *Ar n-Athair a tha air nèamh: gu naomhaichear d'ainm.*
10 *Thigeadh do rìoghachd. Deanar do thoil air an talamh mar a
    nithear air nèamh.*
11 *Tabhair dhuinn an diugh ar n-aran lathail.*
12 *Agus maith dhuinn ar fiachan, amhuil mar a mhaitheas sinne d'ar
    luchd-fiach.*
13 *Agus na leig 'am buaireadh sinn, ach saor sinn o olc. Oir is leatsa
    an rìoghachd agus an cumhachd agus a' ghlòir gu sìorruidh.*

Manx Gaelic

9 *Ayr ain, t'ayns niau: casherick dy row dty ennym.*
10 *Dy jig dty reeriaght. Dty aigney dy row jeant er y thalloo, myr te
    ayns niau.*
11 *Cur dooin nyn arran jiu as gagh laa.*
12 *As leih dooin nyn loghtyn, myr ta shin leih dauesyn ta jannoo
    loghtyn nyn 'oï.*

13   *As ny leeid shin ayns miolagh, agh livrey shin veih olk. Son lhiat's*
     y reeriaght as y phooar as y ghloyr son dy bragh as dy bragh.

APPENDIX

A NOTE ON PICTISH

The first historical notice of the Picts is found in a panegyric by
Eumenius, dated A.D. 297. Here *Picti* are associated with *Hiberni* as
enemies of the *Britanni*. A few years later they are again mentioned,
this time as similar to, or as part of, the *Caledones*. From A.D. 360
onwards, *Picti* are often in the news, notorious as fierce raiders attack-
ing the Roman province of Britain, usually in company with *Scotti*.
These latter were undoubtedly Irishmen, but who were the *Picti*?
Their name continues in use for centuries. The country north of the
Forth and Clyde was called Pictland and ruled over by a Pictish royal
house until 843 or thereabouts. The Picts were certainly not Irish,
because we are told by Adamnan in his *Life of St Columba* that the
saint used an interpreter in his dealings with them. Nor were they
Britons as is made clear by the impugnable testimony of Bede who
reports in his Ecclesiastical History that five languages were used in
Britain in his day, namely 'Book Latin' and the native languages of
the *Bretti, Scotti, Picti* and *Angli*. If Pictish was neither Irish nor
British, what could it be?
    The ancient place names of Pictland fall into two groups: those in
the east frequently show traces of Brittonic, obviously a legacy of
North British settlements. But the rest cannot be explained at all.
The names of a good many Pictish kings are preserved in a list known
as the Pictish Chronicle and in Irish annals. Among these are British
and Gaelic names, but a good number, especially the older ones, defy
interpretation. Lastly, there are some two dozen inscriptions in the
Pictish language. Two are engraved in Latin letters, the rest in the
Ogam alphabet. Most of them date from the eighth and ninth centuries, i.e., from the last period of Pictish independence. The inscriptions contain a certain number of Celtic names, but otherwise make a
most exotic impression, e.g., on a stone from Shetland *ettycuhetts*
ahehhttannn hccvvevv nehhtonn, even though the arbitrary (?) doubling
of letters is a feature of Ogam. The last word in the inscription must
be the Celtic name often attested in Gaelic as *Nechtan*, also *Nechton*;
it appears in Bede as *Naiton*, in Old Welsh as *Neithon*. But no one can
make anything of the rest of the inscription.
    The evidence points in one direction. The Picts were an independent
people, descendants of the mountaineers known to the earliest writers
as Caledonians, and this name, too, must have survived for a long

time as it occurs in later place names, e.g. *Dunkeld* which is Gaelic for 'Fort (*dún*) of the Caledonians'. They had been subject to British influence from the first century B.C. at least, when British Celts penetrated far into Scotland. Later they came under the influence of the Irish of Argyll who subsequently extended their sway over Pict-land. Such influences explain the presence of Celtic names in the Pictish records. But there remains an irreducible core of exotic material. We can scarcely now avoid the conclusion first put forward by Rhys in 1892 that Pictish (or Caledonian) was a pre-Celtic, non-IE language. In its mountain fastness and on the remote Orkneys and Shetlands, the language managed to survive into the Middle Ages. It would disappear from the islands during the ninth century and yield ground on the mainland opposite as a consequence of Viking immigra-tion. The Pictish royal house became extinct about 843. Nothing now stood in the way of the northward advance of the already aggressive Gael. Thus, in the end, Pictish succumbed to Gaelic and Norse. It was, we suppose, most likely defunct by the close of the first millen-nium.

7

GERMANIC

At the time when Celtic dominated in Western and Central Europe and was making its impact on Mediterranean countries, Germanic was still effectively isolated in its northern home and scarcely noticed by the classical world until the closing years of the second century B.C. It was then that the migrating Cimbri and Teutones made their warlike appearances in Cisalpine Gaul. All the same, Germanic tribesmen had been in touch with Mediterranean civilisation before this. A helmet from Negau in Steiermark bears, in North Italian letters, an inscription dated to the third century B.C. with the Germanic name *Harigasti* '(belonging to) Army-Guest'.

The earliest known home of Germanic was South Scandinavia and North Germany. But at the beginning of the historical period, it was already decidedly expansive. In the first century B.C., the Suevi are seen to have moved southwards and to have crossed to the left bank of the Rhine. To the east, other tribes were taking possession of land in Central and South Germany and in Bohemia. All these gains were, it is believed, on territory previously in the hands of Celts. Meanwhile, North-West Germany was also being germanised. It has been commonly assumed that Celtic was displaced in this area, too, but recent toponymical and historical studies supported by accumulating archaeological evidence suggest that the population north of the Taunus and west of the Aller cannot have been Celtic, so that Germanic will have advanced over the major part of present-day North-West Germany at the expense of an unknown, and so far unnamed, language.

Germanic expansion was temporarily brought to a halt by the Romans on the Rhine and Danube. But further east, no such obstacles prevented the migration of Germanic tribesmen. They had, in fact, for some time been moving southward as far as the Black Sea. As early as 182 B.C., Bastarnae are mentioned as negotiating with Greeks. The Bastarnae are generally considered to have been Germanic.

From about the second century B.C., a North Italian alphabet (not that represented at Negau) was borrowed and developed as the Germanic national script. It was at first used only for magical and religious purposes, hence its name Runic, i.e., 'Secret, Occult'. Later it became a monumental script and as such survived in Scandinavia into modern times. For ordinary literary purposes, however, the Latin alphabet was eventually adopted by all the Germanic peoples except the Goths who used a script of their own, as explained below.

Gothic and related dialects

The best known Germanic people living in Eastern Europe were the Goths. According to their own tradition, they had emigrated from Southern Sweden. Archaeologists place the beginnings of this migration in the first century B.C., when Gothic remains have been traced between the Oder and Vistula. By the middle of the third century A.D., they had moved to the area of the Black Sea between the Don and the Roman province of Dacia. Here their subjects were the Iranian-speaking Sarmatians. The Goths now appear in two large sections: to the east of the Dniestr were the Ostrogoths, to the west the Visigoths. In 348, a christianised group of the latter took refuge from religious persecution by crossing the frontier of the Empire to make a home in Moesia, now Northern Bulgaria. Here, about this time, was made a Gothic translation of the Bible, considerable fragments of which survive. As by far the most extensive document in Gothic and as the oldest text of any length in a Germanic language, it is of inestimable philological value. Gothic is reported by Strabo to have still been in use in Moesia in the ninth century. On the Black Sea coast, however, it lasted much longer. Between 1560 and 1562, a Flemish diplomat, Busbecq, ambassador to Turkey, noted down nearly a hundred words of Gothic still spoken in his day in the Crimea. Crimean Gothic was also spoken across the Strait of Kerch on the Taman Peninsula. It appears to have been in use until the eighteenth century.

Gothic rule in the Ukraine crumbled in 383 under the onslaught of the Huns (p. 146), who swept in from the east. Some of the Goths became subject to the newcomers and early in the next century moved with them into the Central European Plain, but others escaped Hunnish suzerainty by migrating to the west where they began a memorable series of conquests. The Visigoths seized Gaul as far as the Loire and overran the Iberian Peninsula. The Ostrogoths became masters of Italy and made strenuous efforts to maintain their ethnic distinction by forbidding intermarriage with Italians. Visigothic hegemony in Gaul was broken by the Franks in 507, but continued in the Iberian Peninsula until the invasion of the Moors in 711. Ostrogothic power in Italy was shattered by Justinian in 562. Since the Goths formed only a small fraction of the total population of the countries they ruled over, the destruction of their power led at once to the rapid assimilation of the survivors. In Spain, indeed, assimilation appears to have taken place before the collapse in 711. The Goths were traditionally Arian Christians, but in 589 the Iberian Visigoths embraced Catholicism. From this time onwards, romanisation must have been a matter of course. By the end of the seventh century, Gothic was doubtless a forgotten language everywhere in the west. But the former presence of the language can be traced, especially in Spain and Portugal, in personal names and in loan words in the modern languages. Although Gothic in the west flourished for but a short time, it is known to have been carefully cultivated, at least in Italy. It was here that the extant Gothic manuscripts were produced. They are written in a peculiar alphabet derived mainly from the Greek, but with some admixture of the native Runic alphabet; it was invented by Wulfila, the translator of the Bible.

Associated with the Goths were the infamous Vandals, whose conquests took them as far as Carthage. Nothing is known of the Vandal dialect except a few personal names, and the Vandals them-selves disappear from history in the sixth century. Another East Germanic people, also early emigrants from Scandinavia, were the Burgundians. These, however, remained in the territory between the Oder and Vistula until the beginning of the fifth century. Perhaps as a consequence of increasing Slavonic pressure, the Burgundians began their trek westwards via Thuringia and the Middle Rhine, eventually setting up a kingdom in Gaul. This kingdom, however, was over-thrown by the Franks in 534, an event which doubtless hastened the process of romanisation. Burgundian would be extinct by about the beginning of the seventh century; it is known only from personal names and from a handful of words in the French dialect of *Bourgogne* 'Burgundy'.

Early dialects of Germany and the Low Countries

From the end of the third century A.D., Germanic tribesmen repeatedly broke through the Roman fortifications on the Rhine and Danube, finally destroying them.

The Low Countries already held a Germanic population along the seaboard; these were the Frisians (p. 106). Further inland, the inhabi-tants were apparently romanised Celts, but now the Saxons and especially their neighbours to the south, the Franks, thoroughly germanised the area up to a line from Maastricht to Boulogne. With the final recall of the Roman garrisons in 402, this line was overrun and the Franks spread beyond Paris and even made settlements south of the Loire, as Germanic place names in the region prove. They gave Gaul its new name France.

Where the Frankish settlements were small or isolated, romanisation would begin almost at once. But in the areas of thicker settlement in the districts in touch with the Low Countries, Franconian speech must have persisted for a long time. It was from such areas that so many Germanic words found their way into French and no doubt Franconian influence is significant for the division of France into two great linguistic regions: *Langue d'Oc* in the south and *Langue d'Oïl* in the north. Yet none of the districts of Frankish settlement south of the Maastricht–Boulogne line could maintain its Germanic character permanently. When, about 1200, the linguistic frontier becomes clear from contemporary records, it is seen to be virtually as it is today (p. 104), apart from some losses to French in French Flanders.

South of the Low Countries, Germanic also moved forward on a broad front across the Rhine. Roman Trier and its partly Celtic hinterland (p. 64), including Luxembourg and most of Lorraine, became Franconian. The Alemanni colonised Swabia, Alsace and the major part of Switzerland. As a result of an advance across the Danube, Germanic Bavaria came into being. By the fifth century the Bavarians were possessing themselves of Austria and, before 650, were also established south of the Brenner. In pushing Germanic speech so far they absorbed or expelled the no doubt largely latinised Celts and Rhaetians, known to have lived in these Alpine areas in Roman times.

Other migrations continued into the Central European Plain. Here the Langobardi, later known as Lombards, were most prominent. In 568, this tribe moved into Italy. The main Lombard centres were in the north, in Lombardy, where the language is thought to have survived until about 1000.

While Germanic was thus progressing west and south, it was in general retreat on the eastern front, where Slavonic tribesmen had been on the move since the fifth century. By the middle of the next century, all territory east of the Elbe and Saale was lost to Germanic. Moreover, Slavs settled to a limited extent in places west of these rivers. At the same time, other Slavs were taking possession of Bohemia and advancing to occupy the Danube valley in present-day Austria. Further south, Slavs had reached Slovenia from the Central European Plain and had spread along the courses of the Drau and Mur to slavicise Carinthia and Styria.

From about 750, texts become available in these early Germanic dialects except in the case of Langobardic which is known only from some 200 words, mostly personal names. The dialects are seen to fall into two divisions: Saxon and Lower Franconian in the north are called Old Low German, while Upper Franconian in the centre and Alemannic, Bavarian and Langobardic in the south are classed as Old High German. These terms are applicable up to the twelfth century. The literary remains in OHG are much more extensive than in OLG, but the character of the literature is the same in both. The records, both prose and verse, are mainly of a theological nature, usually indebted to Latin models. There are a large number of glosses. The OLG documents are chiefly in the Saxon dialect, i.e., Old Saxon.

The Middle Period in Germany and the Low Countries

The old period, referred to above, is followed by a middle period variously considered as lasting until 1350 or 1500. Middle High German possesses a rich poetic literature, in standardised language, overshadowing the modest production of Middle Low German, again essentially Saxon. Low Franconian had by now developed to become the literary vernacular of the already prosperous and independent Low Countries. It may be termed Middle Dutch. Thus, by the end of the Middle Ages, there were in existence three literary forms of German (in the widest sense), all at a relatively advanced stage of standardisation.

During the middle period, German made great advances in the east. In the twelfth century, German armies overran Slavonic territory as far as the Oder and the delta of the Vistula. German peasants and artisans were brought into the conquered area in large numbers and, in view of the organised assault on Slavonic life and culture, German made rapid headway. From the same century dates the foundation of the first German-speaking enclaves in Eastern and Central Europe. At the same time German Jews began to emigrate to the east. Their speech developed in an exceptional way to become a separate language, see Yiddish. In the thirteenth century, German rapidly expanded along the Baltic coast as a result of the invasion of Prussia, which ultimately led to the extinction of the Prussian language. About this time, German settlements were made at various points on the east coast of the Baltic; Riga, for instance, was founded by Germans as early as 1201. The German used in the new eastern territories tended to have a composite character, as the colonists came from all parts of the country. On the Baltic coast, however, Low German, as the official language of the Hansa, was supreme.

Gains were also registered in the south-east. German advancing down the Danube valley was most likely becoming dominant in Lower Austria by the twelfth century, especially after the Babenbergs made Vienna their residence in 1156.

Modern German

The earlier modern period was characterised by the spread of New High German to the north and the loss of Low German (Plattdeutsch) as an official and literary language. The decline of the Hansa and the economic backwardness of the north left this area wide open to the influence of the High German centre and south. Furthermore, those towns and princes favourable to the Reformation encouraged the use of Luther's (High German) Bible—the last low German Bible was published in 1621. Berlin abandoned Low German in administration as early as 1504, the other North German cities following suit during the next hundred years or so. Then the upper classes went over to spoken High German, which eventually became common in the towns. Low German sank to the level of a patois which nevertheless survived widely, especially in the rural districts, down to the present century. It may still be heard locally, but is now receding.

Standard High German owes much to Luther, whose language had an eastern, colonial bias. In his day, the spoken HG dialects were very diverse, those of Switzerland being particularly aberrant. Had this country at the time been more influential, with a stronger regional tradition comparable, say, to that of the Low Countries, Luther's language would most likely not have been accepted. But as it was, after some hesitation, the German Swiss adopted standard HG as their written medium. When speaking among themselves, however, they normally use dialect to this day. HG dialects are still heard in Germany as well, more especially in Bavaria and Swabia, but all dialect is everywhere yielding to the standard form. The same is true of Austria. Dialect-speaking is common in Alsace and Lorraine, but here French is the official language. In Luxembourg not only German, but traditionally also French, are the official languages. The population, however, normally speaks a German dialect. Like the Swiss, the Luxembourgers regard their dialect as a hallmark of their individuality. Neither of these dialects—like many others—are immediately comprehensible to those who know only Standard German, though they can soon learn to follow them.

During the modern period, the replacement of Slavonic west of the Oder was completed, except for Lusatia (p. 157), and German consolidated its position east of that river. The frontier with Poland after World War I corresponded roughly to the linguistic frontier at the time, there being only a small Polish minority in Silesia. There were, however, at least a million German speakers who formed enclaves within the Polish-speaking area, chiefly in the districts of the Corridor. The population of East Prussia with Danzig and the Memelland was 95 per cent German. Elsewhere, too, German continued to make gains. Czech was now facing German on three sides. Moreover, Germans had settled in the towns throughout Bohemia and Moravia, where they for long constituted the most influential class. Indeed, German enjoyed such prestige that, until the nineteenth century at any rate, it seemed that Czech might eventually die out.

In the west, the linguistic frontier was more stable, but German lost some ground in Lorraine. But here and in Alsace, German is in an inferior position since French is the sole official language and also the medium of instruction in schools. From 1871 to 1918 and from 1940 to 1945 German was official. It is evident that France wishes to gallicise these provinces and a knowledge of French is certainly widespread. In the south, the linguistic frontier also remained fairly constant until recent times. In 1919, South Tirol with 250,000 German speakers in its northern part was allotted to Italy. Fascist policy aimed at absorbing these German speakers and government-sponsored industrialisation brought large numbers of Italians into the region. Post-war governments have not been so intolerant, but German is nevertheless yielding to Italian. In the north, German has advanced slowly at the expense of Danish and in the same way has almost driven (North) Frisian out of use.

Finally, new enclaves were established in Eastern Europe and the Balkans, and German was carried overseas by emigrants to the New World. Beginning in 1683, German speakers from the Rhenish Palatinate and Switzerland established a compact settlement in East Pennsylvania. Their dialects fused to give a new, exclusively colonial dialect, locally called Pennsylvania Dutch, which is still used by some 300,000 speakers. Pennsylvanian has become the vehicle of a typical folk literature, but the official language is English. The Pennsylvania Germans had all become bilingual by the beginning of the present century and their patois is now declining.

Recent losses. Before 1945, the area occupied by German was considerably greater than it is now. As a result of World War II, the Oder–Neisse line became the frontier with Poland and Germans east of this line, about seven millions in 1939, were deported. When Czechoslovakia was formed after World War I, its frontiers took in over three million Germans who had been established in this border-land since the Middle Ages. Nearly all these, together with another quarter of a million from the various enclaves far inside the country, were moved out in 1945, so that the state boundary with Germany and Austria became the linguistic one as well. The enclaves in Hungary and Yugoslavia, with about a million Germans, have likewise virtually ceased to be. Only in Rumanian Transsylvania are the old colonies more or less intact; here live 400,000 German speakers. The war also affected the position in the Baltic countries and in Russia. The German

Balts were transferred to the *Reich* in 1939–40. In view of the Hitlerite advance into Russia, the Volga German Republic, established after the Revolution, was dissolved and its one and a quarter million Germans resettled in various places, notably in Kazakhstan, so that the former cohesion has been broken and russification is proceeding apace.

Statistics. With the colonial settlements mentioned above German is the mother tongue of over 94 m. Figures for the central area are: German Federal Republic 59 m., German Democratic Republic 16 m., West Berlin 2.3 m., East Berlin 1.1 m., Austria 7.3 m., South Tirol 200,000, Switzerland 4.1 m., Liechtenstein 15,000, Alsace and Lorraine 1.5 m., Luxembourg 325,000, Eupen and Malmédy (Belgium) 150,000, Denmark (Danish Slesvig) 30,000.

Script. German has been printed in Gothic type more than any other European language. But in this century the use of Roman became common, though a revival of Gothic was a feature of the National Socialist period. It has been unusual since 1945, though Bibles are still often printed in this way. The corresponding handwriting may occasionally be used today by older persons; young people are generally no longer able to read it.

Yiddish

Yiddish, sometimes called Judeo-German, originated about the end of the first millennium when Jews, apparently from France, settled in the towns on the Middle Rhine. The newcomers at once acquired German, but when talking among themselves they retained a few words of their old Romance dialect and also used numbers of words of Hebrew or Aramaic origin; these were particularly words relating to Jewish folkways. About the end of the eleventh century, there began a drift of German Jews eastwards into Slavonic lands, chiefly Poland, a movement which reached its climax following the massacres after the Black Death in 1348 and 1349. Migrations continued for quite two centuries. Two main streams, one from Central, the other from South-East Germany, met together in the East and the fusion of their dialects led to a new colonial dialect, spoken only by Jews and containing, as we have mentioned, a Hebrew-Aramaic element. Inevitably this vernacular at once fell under the influence of surrounding Slavonic languages, and soon Eastern Yiddish became considerably differentiated from the older Western Yiddish which remained in direct contact with German.

As a consequence of emancipation in the latter half of the eighteenth century, the traditional life of Western Jewry largely dissolved and Western Yiddish declined. Within Germany it disappeared altogether, only in peripheral areas have Western Yiddish dialects maintained themselves, the most notable being that of Alsace. But in the east the old orthodox mode of Jewish life persisted into the second half of the last century. The Jews, though generally able to speak the language of the country they lived in, were not assimilated. Hundreds, even thousands of families lived side by side in the Jewish quarters. In several large towns, the Jewish population constituted half the total number of inhabitants or more. Before World War I 50 per cent of the inhabitants of Warsaw were Yiddish-speaking Jews, in Minsk the figure was 55 per cent, in Odessa 57 per cent, in Berdichev 88 per cent. In many small townships, the population could be almost entirely Jewish. In these conditions, Jewish culture was very strong. Beginning in the 1880s, emigration to America and other places carried the Yiddish language all over the world. It is estimated that in 1939 between ten and twelve million people spoke the language, of whom more than two-thirds lived in Eastern Europe. But after the catastrophe that overwhelmed Eastern Jewry in World War II, these figures and the outlook for Yiddish have been radically changed. Of six millions done to death, a good majority were Yiddish speakers, and the survivors, apart from the Russian Jews, have mostly left Eastern Europe. Brought almost to the verge of extinction in the areas that nurtured it as the primary medium, Yiddish now faces rapid decline, for linguistic assimilation is today nearly everywhere the rule. In 1928 Biro-Bidjan, a sparsely inhabited area in the Soviet Far East, was designated as an autonomous territory with Yiddish as an official language. Apparently no more than a few thousand Yiddish speakers actually went there, and meantime the official use of the language has been discontinued. In Israel only Hebrew is recognised as the official language, so that Yiddish seems destined to disappear there as well in a couple of generations or so.

Yiddish literary records go back to about the thirteenth century. Like all Jewish languages, Yiddish is written in Hebrew characters read from right to left. While the Western Yiddish dialects were disappearing as their speakers became assimilated, Eastern Yiddish developed a rich literature in a highly standardised language. Though on all counts an independent language—no other language modified by Jewish communities has become so different from its source— Yiddish nevertheless remains in essentials rather close to its origin. Structurally it is more analytic than literary High German, in this respect having more in common with the German dialects.

Modern Dutch and Flemish

Dutch is spoken throughout the Netherlands, but in the province of Friesland the first language is often Frisian. Dutch is not limited to the Netherlands, but extends southward covering the northern part of Belgium and overspilling into the French *arrondissements* of Hazebrouck and Dunkirk. But here the language is called Flemish. The linguistic frontier with French (Walloon) runs roughly due west from a little south of Yprès to the tip of the Dutch province of Limburg. Brussels, just north of this line, has a mixed population, where the Flemings tend to be bilingual, the Walloons monoglot; one therefore addresses strangers in French. The Flemish areas have been much subject to French influence, especially from 1830 onwards when the state of Belgium came into being with French as the sole official language. Only in 1932, after a long and acrimonious struggle, did legislation guarantee the Flemish language precedence in the Flemish districts and equality with French in state matters. Brussels was declared bilingual.

Whereas in the Netherlands most people normally speak Standard Dutch, except in some country areas, dialect speech is still quite common in Flanders. But a change is under way. The official use of the language and Flemish-medium education, a modern press and the radio have ushered in a new era, familiarising the people with the standard literary language which is identical with that of the Netherlands. In French Flanders, however, where the language is not officially recognised, Flemish has still the status of a patois.

Many Flemings crossed over to Great Britain with William of Normandy in 1066—in those days the Flemish-speaking area extended further east, reaching the coast south of Boulogne—and some of these found a home in the Gower and South Pembrokeshire. Flemish immigration, especially into the latter, continued during the next century and the language seems to have survived there until entirely replaced by English about 1300.

Dutch colonial enterprise spread the language overseas. New York was founded as New Amsterdam and Dutch remained in use there until the end of the eighteenth century. Just outside, in New Jersey State, 'Jersey Dutch' was still known to a few hundred old people at the end of the last century. Dutch is, of course, the official language of Dutch Guyana and the Dutch Antilles, where it is widely known as a second language. It was the chief official medium of the Dutch East Indies until replaced by Bahasa Indonesian in 1945.

Dutch is the mother tongue of at least seventeen million persons; of these some twelve millions live in the Netherlands, about five millions in Belgium and a further 150,000 in French Flanders.

Creole Dutch, Afrikaans

In three places Dutch was creolised. Firstly, in the former Dutch East Indies, as the so-called Language of the Sinyos and Nonahs 'gentlemen and ladies' (words from Malayo-Portuguese, another creole language of the area). Now that the Dutch administration has left, the language is unlikely to maintain itself; its speakers will go over to the various Indonesian languages. Secondly, a creolised Dutch was the language of the coloured population of the former Danish Antilles, the European colonists here being mainly Dutchmen. In 1917, these islands were sold to the USA. Since then, English has become general and the so-called Negro Dutch faces extinction in the near future. But far greater things were in store for Dutch in South Africa, where a creole form of the language was adopted by the Dutch settlers themselves. This creole, now known as Afrikaans, has become an official language in every sphere and in the fullest sense of the word. It is thus the only creole language anywhere in the world to have achieved such status.

Afrikaans arose as follows. In 1652, a party of Dutch landed at the Cape of Good Hope to found a refreshment station for the Dutch East India Company. Here, pidgin Dutch developed rapidly as a medium for dealing with the many non-Europeans employed in Capetown. Children born in the town, regardless of race, at once became habitual speakers of this pidgin, thus completing its transformation into a creole unique in that it was the primary medium of Europeans as well as non-Europeans, the ancestors of the parties known today as 'Whites' and 'Coloureds'. The new vernacular was then spread far and wide as settlers moved inland, but Dutch remained their written language.

The linguistic situation was complicated by the establishment in 1806 of an English colony at the Cape which inaugurated a period of anglicisation (p. 111). English became the official language and the language of polite society. In 1820, English settlers arrived in the Eastern Province. But Afrikaans, in spite of disabilities, generally remained the language of the home for both 'Whites' and 'Coloureds'. In particular the Boers, who in the 1830s trekked northward to found the republics of the Orange Free State and the Transvaal, escaped anglicisation altogether.

In the 1870s the question of the vernacular came to the fore as part of the political activity of the Afrikaners. Cut off for so long from Holland, they could now rarely speak or even write Dutch correctly, and the idea grew that Afrikaans, i.e., 'African', as the vernacular now began to be called, was the language of the future in South Africa. A start was made in publishing in Afrikaans.

In 1902, the Boer Republics lost their independence and became part of the British Empire. But the Boers opposed the anglicisation of these territories and in the Act of Union of 1910 it was laid down that Dutch as well as English was to be official for all purposes. At the same time, however, the inadequacy of Dutch was becoming ever more obvious. The movement for the recognition of Afrikaans, gained strength and soon, for official purposes, 'Dutch' was being interpreted as 'Afrikaans'. By 1926, the latter had won the day, so that henceforth the official languages in South Africa were English and Afrikaans.

Afrikaans is the home language of some 60 per cent of the country's European population of rather more than three and a half millions. Some 90 per cent of the nearly two million 'Coloureds', and a very much smaller number of 'Natives' also speak Afrikaans as their mother tongue. It is thus the primary medium of four millions out of South Africa's total population of eighteen millions. Most of the 550,000 Indians in the country speak English, making it the first language of about two millions, the rest speak various African, mainly Bantu, languages, of whom an unknown number are able to express themselves, more or less, in Afrikaans and/or English.

Afrikaners today generally have a good knowledge of English, but it is less usual for the English speakers to know Afrikaans well. The English speakers occupy a disproportionate number of the influential positions in the Union and there is considerable rivalry between the two official languages. English has the enormous prestige of a world language, but Afrikaans, as a uniquely African language, has a strong patriotic appeal. Political trends are confirming and strengthening its position.

Frisian

According to the testimony of classical writers, the territory of the *Frisii* stretched from the Rhine Delta to the Ems. Unlike other Germanic tribes, the Frisians did not move in a body at the time of the Migrations of the Peoples but remained in their old haunts. Later, however, they became expansive. They colonised the North Frisian islands and the strip of coast opposite, perhaps sometime between A.D. 700 and 1000 (see below). Heligoland also became Frisian. In the twelfth century, settlers spread eastward across the Jade so that Frisian now extended along the coastal belt from the north-east corner of the Zuyder Zee to Cuxhaven. But since the beginning of the modern period, and especially since the seventeenth century, the Frisian-speaking area has been contracting.

The oldest Frisian sources are almost exclusively legal writings dating from the tenth to the sixteenth centuries. Up to 1400, the language is termed Old Frisian, its conservative structure suggesting comparison with Old Low German or Old High German. Middle Frisian is used for the language between 1400 and 1600. Medieval Frisian falls into two slightly divergent dialects, East and West, the boundary being the river Lauwers. There are no medieval records in North Frisian.

Frisian has maintained itself best in the west. It is spoken in most rural areas in the province of Friesland, but in the larger towns a compromise language, half-Dutch and half-Frisian, the so-called Town Frisian, is commonly used. Altogether between 250,000 and 300,000 speak West Frisian. Since the first half of the sixteenth century, however, the official language of Friesland has been Dutch. There is nevertheless considerable literary activity in Frisian, which has reached a high degree of standardisation, and recently Frisian has become the medium of instruction during the first two years of primary school in many districts. Frisian speakers, apart from small children, all know Dutch as well. The languages are structurally very similar and, especially in the modern period, Dutch has greatly influenced the minority language.

Frisian speech has now disappeared from the traditional East Frisian area. It survived until the 1920s on the small island of Wangeroog and in the colony from this island, Neu-Wangeroog, near Varel, where the last speakers died in the 1930s. Sometime during the Middle Ages, perhaps in the thirteenth century, a colony of East Frisians was established south of the linguistic border in a remote part of Saterland. This enclave of East Frisian, though much diminished, has not yet entirely succumbed to the German which surrounds it. But since this dialect is not used by more than a thousand souls, it is doomed to disappear in the near future.

Linguistic evidence suggests that North Frisia was colonised from East Frisia. The North Frisian dialects, however, are so diverse that mutual comprehension is not always easy. Moreover, profound differences between the dialects of the islands and those of the mainland suggest two waves of colonisation, the former being reached first, perhaps about A.D. 700, the second beginning in the ninth century, if not somewhat later. In its northern environment, Frisian came into intimate contact with Danish and has been greatly influenced by this language. It is the Danish element in North Frisian which makes it so different from East or West Frisian. It never developed a literary standard, hence all writing in North Frisian is of necessity dialect writing. The language enjoys neither official recognition nor encouragement and is now rapidly receding. At present, indeed, not more than 5,000 people know North Frisian. It is strongest on the island of Föhr and on the mainland just south of Niebüll. Its speakers are naturally bilingual, German being their major language.

English in Britain
Hengest and Horsa, so runs the entry in the Anglo-Saxon Chronicle for the year A.D. 449, *gesohton Brytene on þām stæþe þe is genemned*

Ypwines fléot 'attacked the Britons at the place which is named Ebbsfleet'. So began the Germanic invasion which was to transform entirely the linguistic configuration in these islands. By 600, the newcomers were established everywhere south of the Cheviots, except in Devon and Cornwall, Wales and the mountainous parts of the northwest; north of the Cheviots they were in possession of the Merse. Such of the native Celtic inhabitants as survived within the area of conquest appear to have been quickly assimilated. After the beginning of the seventh century, the period of mass migrations was virtually over, but Celtic continued to retreat, as described in the previous chapter.

The country early became known as *Englaland* 'Land of the Angles' and Alfred refers to his native language as *Englisc*. Bede, however, a century and a half before, employed the expression *Angli sive Saxones* 'Angles or Saxons', implying that the terms were synonymous. In this connection we note that the Celts adopted the latter term, as Welsh *Sais* 'Englishman', *Saesneg* 'English'. Nowadays the language is often called Anglo-Saxon, a term coined in the eighteenth century, but recently Old English has tended to be the name preferred.

The first records of English are names of persons and places contained in charters from the end of the seventh century. Continuous texts appear somewhat later, but do not become frequent until the tenth century. Three main dialect areas are distinguished, named after old tribal divisions: Kentish in the chief area of Jutish settlement, Saxon over the rest of the South, Anglian in the Centre and North. The last is subdivided into Mercian, south of the Humber, and Northumbrian. The bulk of the literature was written in West Saxon, a variety of the Saxon dialect, following the usage of Winchester, at the time the most influential centre.

It is seen that English is most closely related to the Germanic dialects spoken in the Low Countries and North Germany. Indeed, Saxon is still the name of a Low German dialect spoken in Holland and North Germany. A district in Schleswig is known to this day as Angeln, and Jutland is, of course, a familiar name, though this area has long been Danish-speaking (p. 121). Until recently, it was thought that English and Frisian were particularly close, but it has now been shown that what were once held to be Anglo-Frisian peculiarities are, in fact, also present in the Low German dialects in the area.

Old English was but little affected by Celtic, though the beginnings of the English continuous tenses, which were inspired by Celtic, go back to this period. But a new element was about to be introduced from Scandinavian. Viking raids began in the late eighth century. This activity was greatly increased after 855, leading to permanent settlement in England from 876 onwards. In many districts the newcomers constituted a majority of the population and maintained their language for generations. It was during this time that large numbers of Scandinavian words passed into English. Norse and English had much in common, and a mutually intelligible pidgin would quickly develop wherever speakers of the two languages were in contact. Such a development doubtless hastened the break-down of the inflexional system of spoken Old English.

It was the Norman Conquest which was to be of the greatest consequence for the history of English. The language of the new rulers and their entourage was French, and French became the leading literary medium, maintaining its position until the fourteenth century. In these circumstances, the cultivation of English was neglected, the Old English literary tradition petered out in the twelfth century and with it the Old English literary vocabulary. The artisans and peasants continued to talk English, of course, though they would be happy to interlard their speech with French words whenever they could—it was the classic situation of the menial cribbing his master. When, in the thirteenth century, English again came to be written extensively, it is seen to contain a sizeable and growing Gallic element. The inflexional system of Old English had by now collapsed and the un-Germanic continuous tenses were developing apace. Especially since the Renaissance, English has borrowed an enormous number of words from Latin and Greek, often via French, with the result that the Germanic component of the modern English lexicon has shrunk to, say, a tenth of the total. On the other hand, this tenth includes most of the commonest words.

The linguistic influence of London has been most significant since the fourteenth century. It has exercised a strongly standardising influence, so that today the local dialects of England have been brought to the verge of extinction. Only in the Scottish Lowlands is dialect speech still an important reality, hence the use of Lallands as an occasional literary medium.

During the Middle English period, variously regarded as lasting from about the end of the eleventh to the beginning of the fifteenth or sixteenth centuries, English continued to encroach slowly on Celtic. It was introduced into Ireland in 1169. From the beginning of the seventeenth century the rate of expansion within the British Isles quickened, see 'Celtic' *passim*. The Norn-speaking Orkneys and Shetlands became completely English-speaking (p. 126). The anglicisation of the Channel Islands began in the early nineteenth century. Before this, French was universally spoken and the language of government, even though English influence had been dominant since the reign of John. French remains in use to a limited extent, but is likely to die out before the end of this century.

English is the native tongue of nearly 54 millions living in Great Britain and Northern Ireland and of 2.9 millions in Éire.

English overseas

America. By the beginning of the seventeenth century, English had become an important European language, spoken by some five millions, and was moreover preparing to spread to the New World. Already in Elizabethan times Raleigh and Gilbert had attempted settlements in North America, but unsuccessfully. However, in the next reign, a permanent 'plantation' was started in Virginia in 1607, followed by the landing of the Pilgrim Fathers at Cape Cod in 1620.

About this time other European nations had gained a foothold in North America, namely the Dutch, French and Spanish, but Britain became the dominant colonial power and thus assured the triumph of the English language. The United States, declared independent in 1776, has never recognised as official any language other than English. Nevertheless, a traditional enclave of French in Louisiana— and also a much younger German one in Pennsylvania—have survived until today, though they are in the long run bound to succumb. This observation is equally valid for the various Amerindian languages which have managed to maintain themselves. There are about 400,000 speakers of these languages in the United States, and a further 100,000 or so in Canada (see 'A note on indigenous North American languages' below). The population of the United States and Canada is 196 millions and 20 millions respectively; of the latter some 6.5 millions speak French as their native tongue. It will be remembered, of course, that for many millions of immigrants, English is an acquired tongue. Indeed, the figures for other European languages given elsewhere in this work could be variously increased if one were to include native speakers now domiciled in America (and elsewhere overseas). Certain groups of immigrants have handed down their language to the second and even third generation, but for those born in the country, English is invariably the best-known medium.

The linguistic legacy of British enterprise in the New World is further seen in the Bermudas (pop. 50,000), the settlement of these previously uninhabited islands going back to 1609. English is well to the fore in the Caribbean. The Bahamas, Columbus' first landfall, were depopulated by the Spaniards, the British occupying the deserted islands in 1629; today the inhabitants number 150,000. The largest English-speaking island is Jamaica with 1.8 million; it became British in 1655 when the small Spanish community was expelled. English is further the language of the 175,000 Leeward Islanders between Porto Rico and Guadeloupe, including the few under Dutch or

French rule. English is official in Dominica and St Lucia, British since 1805 and 1814, and with populations of 70,000 and 100,000 respectively. Here the language is gaining ground as the first medium, but Creole French is still strong, especially in the countryside. St Vincent (pop. 80,000), British since 1783, is now purely English-speaking, and Barbados (pop. 250,000) has been so since 1627 when British settlers landed after the island had been depopulated a century before. Grenada, pop. 75,000, British since 1763, and Trinidad and Tobago, pop. 1 million, British since 1802 and 1814 respectively, are to all intents and purposes English in speech, the little remaining Creole French being moribund. On the adjacent mainland, the formal occupation of Guyana, previously British Guiana, once held by the Dutch, took place in 1803. Carib dialects are spoken by a few thousand tribesmen, but for the rest of the heterogeneous population of 650,000 English is generally the primary medium. Here, as in Trinidad, a minority of the large East Indian component is not yet entirely assimilated. English is further the official language of British Honduras, for long a sphere of British influence. It is the native speech of 60,000 of the colony's 110,000 inhabitants, a good half of the remainder speaking Spanish, the rest Maya or Island Carib. The total number of native speakers of English in the Caribbean area will be not less than four millions. They are mainly of African descent and their spoken style generally contains a greater or lesser number of creole features, see below.

Lastly, far in the South Atlantic, off the coast of Argentina, lie the English-speaking Falkland Islands. Between 1766 and 1832 there was some Spanish settlement here, but in the latter year the British seized the archipelago and introduced a new population which has grown to 2,500 today.

Africa. Britain built up an immense Empire in Africa. She early had bridgeheads on the west coast (Gambia 1783, Sierra Leone 1787). But progress inland was easier in the South. In 1806 a British colony was established at the Cape, to the consternation of the Dutch already present, with results described on p. 105. From this advantageous position, British influence spread northwards as the century drew to a close. There are now over 200,000 native speakers of English in Southern Rhodesia, where it is the official language. In the Union of South Africa and in South-West Africa, Afrikaans is official as well as English. Here about two million people speak English as their primary medium, while perhaps as many again use it effectively as a second language.

Considerable numbers of British settlers arrived in East Africa, chiefly in this century, and now number considerably more than 100,000. West Africa was not so attractive for white settlement. All the same, native English has established itself in two places, this time as the language of Africans: firstly in Sierra Leone albeit in a creolised form (see below) and secondly in Liberia, a state created in 1822 by freed slaves returning from America. Their descendants, some 25,000 in number, constitute the ruling class and speak Standard English as their native language. They are found chiefly in the capital Monrovia. The vast majority of the population, however, speak autochthonous languages as the first, often only medium.

Beginning in 1956 with the Anglo-Egyptian Sudan, now the Republic of the Sudan, followed in 1957 by the Gold Coast, now Ghana, the various British-controlled African territories have nearly all become independent. In the case of the Sudan, English has been replaced by Arabic, but otherwise—with one exception—the official use of English has continued. This is not surprising since the local languages are often spoken by small numbers and have generally not been cultivated fully for modern purposes. The former British Cameroons are part of the present Federal Republic of the Cameroons, where both English and French are official. In Tanzania, Swahili has gained full official status beside English. But English has disappeared from what was British Somaliland. This area is now a district of the Republic of Somalia where only Arabic is official.

When, in the foregoing, we have spoken of English as the official language, this is to be understood as 'chief official language'. A large number of indigenous languages, especially the more widespread, have played, and continue to play, an important part, officially, in local administration. Similarly, a considerable number of local languages were employed in primary education during the period of British rule. This policy is being continued in the succession states, though with a tendency to place more emphasis on the local languages as elementary education expands. The position in the territories with French or Portuguese connections is, however, very different. Here the metropolitan languages have played an absolutely dominant role and government-aided education has been conducted exclusively in these languages—much to the disadvantage of the recipients. The Portuguese, indeed, have consistently opposed the recognition of an indigenous language for any purpose.

St Helena (pop. 5,000), has been English-speaking since Britain took possession in 1657.

Australasia. The arrival of the convict ships at Sydney Cove in 1788 was the first step towards the anglicisation of the continent of Australia, at the time inhabited by aboriginals, perhaps 300,000 in all. This indigenous population has since declined catastrophically. Today no more than 50,000 preserve their native dialects; many have no knowledge of English. The Europeans in Australia now number

$11\frac{1}{2}$ millions, predominantly of Anglo-Saxon stock. New Zealand was colonised from Australia, the first settlers landing in 1814. The Maori inhabitants, of Polynesian origin, were much more advanced than the primitives of Australia, but the often violent contact with the white man reduced their numbers. They survive today mainly in the North Island. Their language has no official standing, even in Maori schools the medium of instruction is English, so that New Zealand Polynesian is purely a patois doomed to extinction. But meanwhile some 60,000 use it as the language of the home. Otherwise New Zealand's 2,700,000 inhabitants are purely English-speaking.

The official use of English has spread from Australia and New Zealand to various places in the Pacific. Australia has the custody of Papua and the territory of New Guinea. Here, however, Standard English remains essentially a white man's language, but this is the most significant area of Pidgin English today (see Neo-Melanesian). New Zealand administers certain Pacific territories, notably Western Samoa, where English is well known as a second language.

India and Further India. The British East India Company set up business in Madras in 1639. After the defeat of the French in 1757, Britain was in a position to reduce the whole sub-continent, an aim achieved by the middle of the next century. Already in 1835 it had been laid down that English should become the language of higher education. This proved to be an almost mortal blow to Sanskrit, the great classical tongue of India. It also lead to the disuse of Persian which had been widely employed at Muslim courts. Henceforward the Indian intelligentsia adopted English as the second medium. As such, English has exercised a unifying influence over the whole country as no language had previously done. Indifferent to creed or caste, it has become the vehicle of a Pan-Indian literature. When India became independent in 1947, Hindi and its Muslim counterpart Urdu became the state languages of India (Bharat) and Pakistan respectively, but English remains in official use as well. It is without question the dominant medium in business, publishing and higher education and in spite of continuing indianisation is likely to retain this position for a long time to come. But English has rarely become the first medium of Indians living in India. It is estimated that about 300,000 persons resident in India (in the wider sense) use English as their first language; many of these are Anglo-Indians.

Ceylon, first in Portuguese, then in Dutch hands, passed to Britain in 1802. Gaining independence in 1947, Ceylon at first continued the official use of English, but in 1961 declared Sinhalese the official language of the Republic. But, as elsewhere under analogous circumstances, English continues to play an important role. The Maldives, which became a British protectorate in 1887, achieved independence in 1966. Maldivian, of Sinhalese origin, is now the official language.

In the nineteenth century, British influence developed strongly in Further India. Singapore was occupied in 1823 as a prelude to expansion in the Malayan Peninsula and Borneo. In the succession states, Malaysia and Singapore, English remains an official language, but Malay is regarded as the national language and is also official for all purposes. Burma, which had become British in 1886, proclaimed its independence in 1947 with Burmese as the official state language.

Other areas. English has been the official language of Gibraltar since 1704, but the permanent inhabitants speak Spanish, though they mostly know English as well. Malta became British in 1800. At that time Italian was the language of prestige in Malta, and Italian could be used officially until 1934, when it was replaced by Maltese. English was, of course, all along the language of government and also became largely the language of education. Most Maltese today can speak English which has now ousted Italian as the islanders' second language. Malta became independent in 1964 with Maltese and English as its official languages.

Britain occupied Egypt in 1882. The country gained a degree of independence in 1922 and more in 1936, but Britain retained rights in the country until the nationalisation of the Suez Canal in 1956. After World War I, British influence in Palestine, Jordan, Iraq and the Arabian Peninsula was also paramount for a time, and English acquired official standing in various territories. But political changes culminating in the withdrawal of Britain from Aden in 1967 led to the discontinuation of official English. Today Arabic is the official medium of the whole area, except of course for Israel, where Hebrew is the state language. Kurdish has recently acquired some local recognition in Iraq. English was used officially in Cyprus during the period of British rule from 1878 to 1960. Today Greek and Turkish are the official media, but knowledge of English remains common.

English is the sole official language of the Seychelles and the chief official language (beside French) of Mauritius. Education is conducted mainly in English, but in both places the vernacular is Creole French (p. 32). English is likewise official in Fiji and the British Pacific Islands, where it is known to a considerable extent as a second language, but the native languages, in Fiji also Hindustani, continue in use as the naturally spoken media of the local people.

The United States has played a part in the transplantation of English. It was officially introduced in the Philippines in 1898 when the US effectively took over the territory from the Spaniards. Both English and Spanish were now official, but the former was naturally the more influential, so that the native intelligentsia henceforward tended to adopt English as their second language instead of Spanish. In 1936, the country became a republic. But Philippine nationalism found its linguistic expression in Tagalog, the language of South Luzon with the capital Manila. Tagalog acquired official standing in 1940, becoming the state language after Independence in 1946. But Tagalog suffers from regional connotations and in 1955 Pilipino, an artificially constructed purist form of Tagalog, was declared to be the state language. Tagalog/Pilipino is making great headway as the lingua franca of the whole country, a not surprising development seeing that it is of Indonesian stock like all the other hundred-odd indigenous languages of this linguistically diversified archipelago. It is taught in schools, but English remains the chief educational medium. Both English and Spanish may also be used officially. There is a modern Philippine literature in English.

Guam passed from Spanish into American hands in 1898; it is now an Incorporated Territory. As the official language, English is widely known in the territory, but native-born Guamanians speak Chamorro as their first language (p. 36). American Samoa is also an Incorporated Territory where English has official status and is well known, but Samoan remains in everyday use.

English has virtually ousted the native Polynesian language of Hawaii. The archipelago was discovered in 1778, and in 1820 English-speaking missionaries arrived. By a treaty of 1876, Hawaii was drawn close to the United States and finally annexed in 1898. The native population declined rapidly, but a unique medley of immigrants arrived to supply a labour force for economic development. For these newcomers, English was the common language which was more and more adopted by the indigenous minority as well. Today only a few of the older people remember the Hawaiian language which before the arrival of the Europeans was the sole medium of at least 300,000 persons. Hawaii became an American state in 1950.

English is an official language in the Panama Canal Zone and also in Puerto Rico, now a US Commonwealth, but the ordinary language of these areas, and also an official language, is Spanish.

A note on indigenous North American languages

America is noted for the extreme heterogeneity of its indigenous languages. We will suppose that the total population of North America at the time of its discovery by Europeans may have been between three and four millions speaking something like two hundred different languages. This population is today about one-third of this estimate, and of these hardly more than half a million employ Amerindian languages, of which over a hundred survive. Most of those who continue to speak indigenous languages live in reservations.

The great majority also know English and families leaving the reservations tend to abandon the native language. None of the native languages play any mentionable part in schooling, much less do they have any official standing, except in Greenland. This country is, however, politically united to Denmark. Its population consists of 35,000 Eskimo and 3,000 Danes, though the latter do not usually make permanent homes there. Elementary education is provided through the medium of the native language and all Greenlanders are literate, about 10 per cent also knowing Danish. Greenland Eskimo has official status locally, beside Danish. It is said that colonial policy here has been altogether more enlightened than elsewhere in America.

The usual factors have caused the decline in the indigenous population: the white man's policies and his diseases. Many smaller groups have disappeared entirely; once powerful tribes are sometimes barely discernible. In 1497 Cabot is said to have encountered the Beothuks, the aboriginal inhabitants of Newfoundland. They were but few in number and unable to compete with the intruding Indians from the mainland, chiefly Micmacs, and with the Europeans settling around the coast. All trace of this people vanishes about 1830. Virtually nothing is known of their language whose affinities remain undetermined. The Hurons, once lords of the St Lawrence Valley from the Great Lakes to the estuary and some 50,000 strong at the beginning of the seventeenth century, were the largest Indian people at the time. Today, less than 2,000 survive: one group found a refuge in distant Oklahoma, the other still remaining in its native haunts near Quebec, though having abandoned the Huron language in favour of French. Only in modern times, in certain favourable circumstances, has this trend been reversed. The most striking example is that of the Navaho, who at present are the largest North American tribe with numbers approaching 100,000—ten times as many as a century ago. About 90 per cent are estimated to employ the Navaho language.

The tundra zone of the Arctic north from Alaska to Labrador is the domain of Eskimo (30,000 speakers). The (remotely) related Aleutian is spoken by some 6,000 in the Aleutian Islands and on the Alaskan Peninsula. Both Eskimo and Aleutian are used by miniscule groups on the north-east tip of Siberia. There are further 35,000 Eskimo in Greenland (see above). Over the remainder of North America one tentatively distinguishes a dozen or so major linguistic families, a score of minor families and quite as many isolated single languages. It is possible that there is more fundamental unity in this bewildering diversity that can yet be demonstrated scientifically on the basis of the material available and so far studied. The languages themselves are, of course, known solely from modern times and in many cases the documentation is far from adequate.

Among the major families is Athapascan stretching from the Churchill River to Alaska, with an offshoot as far away as the south-west of the USA, chiefly in Arizona and New Mexico, which includes Navaho, now the numerically most significant native language with some 90,000 adherents. All the other languages in this family are spoken by diminutive numbers, none by more than a couple of thousand, several by groups with less than a hundred speakers. To the south lies the Algonquian family, whose traditional territory extended down the Atlantic coast to Cape Hatteras, then turned inland to the Mississippi, along that river to its headwaters, thence eastward to follow the upper reaches of the Missouri as far as the Rockies. The biggest languages in this family are Chippewa (USA) or Ojibwa (Canada) with 35,000 speakers, Cree (20,000), Blackfoot (8,000), Potawatomi (5,000), further the languages of the Micmac (3,000) and Delaware (2,000). Algonquian languages are also spoken in a con-siderable enclave west of the Missouri. The main Algonquian area, however, encloses the territory of another family, the Iroquoian, spoken principally in a triangle from near Cape Hatteras almost to the southern shore of Lake Michigan, whence along the southern banks of Lake Huron to the St Lawrence in the neighbourhood of Quebec. Among the languages of this family is, first and foremost, Cherokee with its 55,000 speakers, and then the languages of several historically well-known tribes, as Seneca (5,000), Mohawk (2,000), Huron (under 1,000), Mohican (extinct in this century, the few hundred survivors being now anglicised). The plains between the Mississippi and the Missouri were occupied by the Siouan family, of which the most significant today are Dakota (45,000) and Omaha (10,000). Oklahoma is the centre of the Muskogean family, whose main representatives are Choctaw (25,000) and Creek (12,000). Further west lie the languages of the Uto-Aztecan family with Pima (12,000), Shoshone (6,000) and Ute (5,000). This great family extends far into Mexico where it includes Nahuatl, the major indigenous tongue of that country (p. 35). The other multifarious families and isolates of North America are found partly in enclaves within the above mentioned, but chiefly outside these areas, especially along the Pacific coast from California to Alaska.

English as a world language

We calculate that 287 millions speak English as their first language or, in the case of immigrants, as the ordinary language of their environ-ment. The expansion of English across the face of the globe has given it an unparalleled pre-eminence as the world language *par excellence*. In this respect, it is in a class by itself and daily strengthens its unique position. Nor is there a competitor in sight. French and Spanish may have international character, but no comparable extension of territory or influence. Russian is hopelessly land-bound. From the point of view of international intercourse, Hindi is inarticulate, Chinese might as well not exist in spite of the stupendous number of its speakers. The same applies to Japanese or Bahasa Indonesia, each the official medium of more than a hundred million souls. It is mainly to English that these people turn in business matters outside their own countries. Hence the intense interest in English found everywhere in the world today. Hence, too, the influence which this truly global language is exerting on other languages. Post-1945 German is replete with anglicisms; a Frenchman has written a book entitled *Parlez-vous franglais*? It will be remembered, of course, that North America contains by far the largest concentration of English speakers whose usage radiates throughout the rest of the English-speaking world, and beyond.

Creole English

Pidgin English is considered to have come into existence on the west coast of Africa in the second half of the sixteenth century. It was used as a lingua franca by slaves transported to America and here it developed into a Creole language as it became the basis of the native speech of the generation born in the New World. But particularly after the abolition of slavery, more standard forms of English were progressively acquired, so that the old Creole speech has now generally disappeared. However, a highly creolised form of English, known as the Gullah dialect, is still in use among some thousands of negroes in the Sea Islands off Charleston, South Carolina. An equally aberrant speech is the so-called Bongo Talk used by a few people in out-of-the-way places in Jamaica. To be sure, the unaffected colloquial of many negro speakers in the southern states of America and particularly in the Caribbean area retains, in varying degrees, Creole features, but Creole English in the fullest sense of the term survives in the New World today only in Surinam. Here assimilation to Standard English could not take place as the official language has been Dutch since 1667.

Creole English in Surinam (Dutch Guiana) consists of two distinct, mutually incomprehensible languages. The first in Sranan, in full Sranan Tongo 'Surinam Tongue' or popularly Taki-Taki 'Talkie-Talkie', the second is Saramaccan, so called from the Saramacca river. Africans were brought to Surinam in the sixteenth century. The greater part of their descendants, well over 100,000 today, constitute the chief element in the capital Paramaribo and environs. Their speech is Sranan. It was committed to writing in the last century by the German Herrenhut mission, and since the forties of this century a secular literature has begun to develop. Latterly, a knowledge of the official language of the province has spread among the Sranan speakers thanks to Dutch-medium education. The second Creole language in Surinam separated from the first as follows. Escape into the interior was always a possibility and absconded slaves lived there from the earliest times. These were reinforced, after a successful revolt in 1730, by large numbers of runaway slaves who likewise placed themselves out of reach of the central administration. The situation in this respect is not very different today. These independent Bush Negroes, estimated to number 30,000, speak Saramaccan. They are essentially monoglot, their dialects purely an oral medium. The early history of these languages is, as often in such cases, still quite obscure, but it is apparent that a Creole Portuguese element is present. Saramaccan is undoubtedly more archaic than the Sranan known to us.

It is not easy to forecast linguistic developments in Surinam. The European Dutch do not exceed 2,000. The numerically significant groups besides the Creoles are about 100,000 East Indians, mainly Hindustani-speaking, and 60,000 Indonesians who also maintain their traditional languages. But both use Sranan as a lingua franca. Presumably one day the various elements will be culturally united to form a Surinam nation. One wonders whether assimilation will come through Dutch, the chief written language, or through Sranan, the most influential spoken medium. On the other hand, large-scale immigration to this underpopulated land could add new complicating factors.

Creole English has also developed in West Africa. Krio 'Creole', centred on Freetown, Sierra Leone, is of complex origin. The colony was founded in 1787 as a home for liberated slaves. The earliest of these arrived in three batches. The first two had had plenty of contact with Standard English, the third, coming from Jamaica, very little. From 1811, new elements were introduced as the British Navy landed the cargoes of captured slave ships. The rapidly developing patois was now strongly influenced by Yoruba, which became the predominant African element. Krio is the mother tongue of some 25,000 persons, of whom only an educated minority are familiar with Standard English. It is rapidly spreading as the lingua franca of Sierra Leone's linguistically multifarious population. A modest beginning has recently been made in the writing of Krio. It may be that Standard English, the official language, will in the long run prove too strong for Krio. On the other hand, Sierra Leone nationalism may come to favour its use as a symbol of nationhood.

West Coast Pidgin English was formerly widespread in the British-controlled territories as an oral medium between speakers of different linguistic groups, and penetrated inland as far as the Hausa-dominated area. Today, Pidgin is being rapidly replaced by more standard forms thanks to the spread of English-medium education. In the former British Cameroons, however, more retarded conditions have favoured the preservation of Pidgin. It is very widely used as a lingua franca and plays a part in elementary education, as a prelude to instruction in Standard English.

Entirely distinct from the foregoing Creoles of African origin is an important language used in the South Seas, technically known as Neo-Melanesian, but more popularly as Beach-la-Mar. This curious term is a corruption of an equally curious Seychelles French *bêche de mer* 'tripang' lit. 'sea spade', which in turn stands for *bicho de mar* lit. 'sea worm', a Portuguese name for this exotic culinary delicacy. Beach-la-Mar came to denote the Pidgin English spoken between East Australian and Melanesian tripang fishermen. Its earliest beginnings are said to go back to the end of the eighteenth century. By the twenties or thirties of the next century it was spreading in New Guinea and neighbouring islands to become the lingua franca between white man and native as also between native and native in this linguistically most differentiated territory. Its use today is pretty well universal in Western Melanesia. It has been a medium of instruction in elementary education for over sixty years, the Roman Catholic mission initiating this development. After World War II, some of the youngest generation in certain places, for instance, Rabaul, were using Pidgin as their first language, thus beginning its transformation into a regular Creole. There seems no doubt that it has a considerable future. It could indeed become the national language of a future independent Melanesian state, much as Bahasa Indonesia 'Language of Indonesia', the official medium of the present Republic of Indonesia, has grown out of Bazar Malay, a pidginised language long used as a lingua franca. Neo-Melanesian is thus of obvious political importance. This may be the reason for the still general opposition in government circles to the use of Neo-Melanesian, especially to its development as a written medium. But when native participation in government affairs increases, prevailing attitudes may be modified in favour of the medium which is essentially the creation and possession of the Melanesians themselves. In any case Tok Waitman or Tok Boi, as the Pidgin is also called locally, is already quite indispensable to the administrator in these territories.

While Australian and Melanesian fishermen were making the first contacts in a newly devised Pidgin English that was to develop into Neo-Melanesian, in another part of the South Seas a Creole language was being born in most unique circumstances. In 1789, nine British mutineers were steering the 'Bounty' towards Pitcairn Island. With them were their Polynesian servants and consorts: six men, a dozen women and one baby. Neither party knew more than a few words of the other's language, and inevitably a Pidgin arose. Although the males had virtually eliminated each other within ten years, the linguistic influence of the British sailors proved decisive, for the Pidgin was English-based. The children of the first generation understood the Tahitian speech of their mothers, but adopted the Pidgin as their main medium, beginning its evolution into Pitcairnese Creole. Britain discovered this little colony in 1814. Shortly afterwards, spelling primers and religious books reached the island, so that contact with literary English was made almost at the outset. Nowadays, all Pitcairnese can use Standard English, but Creole is still the patois of the two hundred or so natives of the island.

During the last century the Pitcairn population was twice evacuated: firstly to Tahiti for some months in 1831, and secondly to Norfolk Island in 1856, then uninhabited. But in 1859, two families returned to Pitcairn, and others followed. But some remained on Norfolk and their descendants today, the so-called 'islanders', six hundred strong, retained their Pitcairn speech, locally known as 'Norfolk'. But the present population of the island includes about an equal number of 'mainlanders' speaking Standard English, so that Norfolkese is being more quickly decreolised than the language on Pitcairn.

Scandinavian before 1350

We have referred above to the Goths and others known to have emigrated from Scandinavia. We now turn to the peoples who remained in the North. Their language first appears, in strikingly archaic form, in Runic inscriptions from the third to the seventh centuries; it is termed Primitive or Proto-Norse. The amount of material from these sources is exiguous in the extreme, but still enough to indicate the nature of the phonology and accidence. After 700 the language, now termed Old Norse, is seen to be undergoing rapid change, doubtless the result of the restless movements of the Viking Age.

But even before the Viking Age, North Germanic was extending its geographical range. The population was all the time expanding northwards. The Åland Islands became Norse in the sixth century. To the south, the Danes moved into Jutland, which had held a different people—the original Jutes who took part in the Anglo-Saxon conquest of Britain. The Danes pushed down into Slesvig where in 811 the Danish–German frontier was established on the Eider. It is possible that some ground was early lost again, since the Frisian colonisation of part of the west coast of Slesvig may have been effected, wholly or in part, at the expense of Norse (p. 107).

About 800, Norse was carried overseas when Norwegian Vikings seized Orkney and Shetland, a prelude to their occupation of the adjacent parts on the mainland and of the Hebrides. The Viking era had already opened with the sacking of Lindisfarne in 793 and now massive attacks were launched particularly against Ireland, with Danish Vikings joining in about 830. The newcomers early formed bases at points on the Irish coast, notably at Dublin; from these arose the first towns in that country. The Isle of Man acquired a powerful Norse contingent. From 876, Danes settled extensively in Yorkshire, Lincolnshire and the East Midlands. Perhaps about the same time Norwegians from the Gaelic area occupied North-West England, then (according to the testimony of place names) still British speaking; from there they were spreading across North Yorkshire by the early tenth century. The Vikings also severely harried Northern France. They obtained land in 911, known as Normandy after them; it included the Channel Islands.

Meanwhile the Faroes had been discovered by the Norsemen, most likely in the early decades of the ninth century, and were subsequently settled. Iceland was located about 860, the first colonists arriving in 874. Men sailing from Iceland discovered Greenland in 981 and two colonies were planted there, the first in 985. In the East, the achievements of the Vikings were almost as impressive. The Swedes crossed to Estonia and Livonia and then moved inland. They set up a kingdom at Novgorod and another, more important still, at Kiev.

The linguistic effects of this lightning expansion were various. The Swedish kingdoms in Russia were entirely slavicised by the twelfth century. In the West, however, the language generally survived better. Norse obliterated the Pictish of Orkney and Shetland and hastened its demise on the mainland. Known locally as Norn, the language lived on there and across the Pentland Firth in Caithness until modern times. The evidence of place names shows that the Hebrides were predominantly Norse-speaking in the Viking Age, but how long the language lasted is not known. When historical records begin to appear about the middle of the thirteenth century, the islands seem to be purely Gaelic-speaking. Associated administratively with the Hebrides (Sodor) was the Isle of Man. Here Norse was in use perhaps as late as the thirteenth century before succumbing to the local Gaelic. And elsewhere in the British Isles, Norse died out in the Middle Ages. It will be remembered that the Norsemen in the British Isles were constantly reinforced by new immigrants until the eleventh century. In Ireland, however, Norse power suffered an irreparable reverse at Clontarf in 1014. Even so, the Norsemen preserved their identity much longer, for they still held the ports when the Anglo-Normans landed in 1169. Whether the language also survived is a moot point, but if it did it was fast declining, if not already moribund. In England the similarity between English and Norse would make for speedier assimilation even though the Scandinavian settlements were sometimes very large. There was no significant colonisation after the early decades of the tenth century and the Norman Conquest cut the last links with Scandinavia. It is thought that very little Anglo-Norse would survive as late as the twelfth century. Perhaps it continued longest in the North-West: two runic inscriptions from that area show that it was still in use about 1150. Franco-Norse seems to have barely survived into the eleventh century. At any rate, it had long passed out of use when Duke William set sail. The only permanent Norse colonisation was that in Faroe and Iceland. The Greenland colonies, however, maintained themselves until the end of the Middle Ages (see below).

After the close of the Viking Age, Norse once again extended its territory by conquest, this time at the expense of Finnish, when permanent colonies were established along the west and south coasts of Finland following the subjugation of that country shortly after 1250.

The term Old Norse is used of the language until about 1350. By 1000, two distinct dialect groupings are seen to have developed: East and West Norse. To the former belong Old Swedish and Old Danish, to the latter Old Norwegian with its colonial varieties. Old Swedish is represented by some two thousand runic inscriptions, mostly of the eleventh and twelfth centuries, and by literary texts since the thirteenth century. The contemporary dialect of the Baltic island of Gotland, Old Gutnish, attested chiefly in a mid-fourteenth century codex of local law and history, varies very considerably from other Swedish, and is sometimes spoken of as a separate language. Old Danish records are poorer than those of Old Swedish. Inscriptions are scanty, literary texts do not appear until about 1300. Some of the early material is written in the dialect of Skåne in South Sweden, at the time classified with Danish; among its surviving documents is a 200-page manuscript written in runes.

The West Norse tradition is much more extensive. The oldest literary records are poetic texts belonging linguistically to the ninth century. Prose follows in manuscripts of the twelfth century, the most original genre being the *saga*. Altogether Old Norse became the vehicle of an extraordinarily rich and varied literature inspired by the traditions and manners of the incomparable Viking Age. Most of the texts were produced in Iceland, hence this literature and its language may be specifically referred to as Old Icelandic. Medieval texts from the Norwegian mother country are common, too, notably legal documents.

Scandinavian after 1350

It is customary to extend the use of the terms Old Swedish (with Old
Gutnish) and Old Danish to cover the period up to the Reformation,
if necessary qualifying the language of the later period as Younger
Old Swedish, etc., but the West Norse languages of this epoch are
conventionally denoted as Middle Norwegian and Middle Icelandic
respectively. From this period, a few documents are also known from
Faroe, Shetland and Orkney. The Reformation marks the beginning
of the modern period and prepares the way for the contemporary
scene. By the sixteenth century, the continental languages are seen
to be participating in a fairly rapid, largely common, development.
The inflexional system is drastically reduced, e.g., nouns have now
only a basic form and a genitive derived from it instead of the four
traditional cases (see below). Thus the continental languages drew
closer together, evolving away from Insular Norse which remained
much more archaic, Modern Icelandic, indeed, is still structurely very
close to the old language. As far as the Continental Scandinavian of
today is concerned, Old Norse is a foreign tongue. For the Icelander,
however, it is merely an old-world form of his own daily speech. From
the point of view of the modern languages, the previous division
into East and West Norse has become solely a matter of history.
Furthermore, Continental Scandinavian borrowed excessively from
Middle Low German, the official language of the Hansa, particularly
in the fourteenth and fifteenth centuries. Today, speakers of the
continental languages can, in general, follow each other easily or, at
least, rapidly learn to do so. For this reason, a Dane does not feel
Swedish or Norwegian to be a foreign language, and vice versa.

The modern standard languages of Sweden and Denmark have
evolved out of forms based on the usage of their respective capital
cities and environs. But the situation in Norway is much different, for
historical reasons. In 1349 Norway was devastated by the Black Death,
suffering even more than its neighbours. The Old Norwegian literary
language broke down since most of those who could write it died in
the plague. Such Norwegian as was written afterwards, i.e., Middle
Norwegian, had a different character, the morphology in particular
being considerably simplified. The Norwegian royal house had died
out in 1319, and eventually the throne passed to the Danish king.
Under Danish government, Norway was gradually subordinated to
Denmark, and during the fifteenth century, Danish was widely used
in official documents. Norway had no printing press, and after the
Reformation (1537) the Bible and all other religious books were in
Danish. When later a native Norwegian literature reappeared, it was
composed in Danish. Eventually a large number of Danish usages

became established in spoken Norwegian, especially in Christiania (Oslo) and district. In 1814, the political union with Denmark was dissolved, connections with that country were no longer so close and writers now tended to introduce into their Danish specifically Norwegian usages. This style may be termed Dano-Norwegian. Simultaneously there grew up a movement for the written use of Norwegian as it was spoken in the purer and more conservative dialects of the western valleys. The prime mover was Ivar Aasen who termed this form of the language *Landsmål* 'National Language', which in 1885 won official recognition beside Dano-Norwegian, now known as *Riksmål* 'Language of the Realm'. In 1929, the two varieties were renamed *Nynorsk* 'New Norwegian' and *Bokmål* 'Book Language' respectively. In school teaching the former predominates in the rural districts of the west, the latter in the towns and in the east of the country generally. *Bokmål* is much the more commonly written form and urbanisation is strengthening its influence. But *Nynorsk* has a considerable idealistic appeal. Lexical purism is a feature of much literary *Nynorsk*, which naturally increases the difference between this sort of Norwegian and Swedish or Danish. It remains to be added that there is no little antagonism between the partisans of the two types of Norwegian. Eventually, no doubt, there will be an agreed amalgamation of these styles, which are so closely allied that mutual intelligibility is easy. It is noteworthy that the various reforms of *Riksmål-Bokmål* have been in the direction of making it more 'Norwegian', i.e. drawing it nearer to *Landsmål-Nynorsk*.

Developments in Bornholm have been rather exceptional. The speech of the islanders was close to the dialects of South Sweden, but the island came under Danish sway, temporarily in 1522, then permanently in 1660. Meanwhile Standard Danish has established itself and the local dialect is withering away. However, its influence will long remain in the pronunciation. The 50,000 native Bornholmers speak Danish with a strong Swedish accent.

The indigenous Lappish population of Northern Scandinavia has been partly assimilated, but some thousands, chiefly in Norway, retain the use of the Lappish language—it belongs to the Finno-Ugric family—particularly in the case of those who are still nomadic or semi-nomadic. Lapps are usually more or less bilingual these days, and their complete transformation into purely Norwegian or Swedish speakers will almost surely take place once they have become fully sedentary.

As a result of the conquest of Finland (above), Swedish became the usual written language of that country. Owing to this foreign domination, Finnish was slow to appear as a literary language. Apart from a few religious books, no literature appeared until 1835. Today, the use of Swedish is confined to the districts where the language is actually spoken. Swedish speakers, the so-called Finnlanders, constitute less than 8 per cent of the total population, but their tongue enjoys the same official rights as Finnish, the major language. Finnlanders do not usually trouble to acquire Finnish.

Against the territorial gains for Swedish must be placed the losses suffered by Danish in Sleswig. Though the Eider remained the political boundary from 811 to 1864, Low German had been encroaching on Danish since the Middle Ages. Indeed, German communities are found just north of the present state frontier (p. 102). Conversely, about 10,000 Danish speakers live south of the border. These minorities are bilingual and will presumably be gradually assimilated, though in both cases the languages have official standing locally.

As many as 5,000 Norse are believed to have lived in Greenland. But their communities declined, dying out by the middle of the fifteenth century. Report has it that the last survivors were killed by the Eskimos.

We have referred to the use of Danish in Norway. The former Norwegian dependencies, Iceland and Faroe, fell under Danish influence in the same way. But Icelandic, unlike Norwegian, continued to be cultivated, though Danish was also used officially. It has remained the Icelanders' first foreign language, but lost its official status with the proclamation of the Republic of Iceland in 1944. The Faroes are still under the Danish crown. Here Danish has exerted enormous influence. It was for centuries the sole official language, but now formally takes second place to Faroese (see below). Greenland, too, became a Danish possession at the same time as the other dependencies. Danish remains the official language, though Greenlandic, a speech of Eskimo stock, is locally important as only a minority of Greenlanders know Danish, though they are literate in their own tongue. The union with Denmark had no appreciable effect on the Norn used in Orkney and Shetland, for although they were dependencies of Norway until 1468, Scottish influence had begun somewhat earlier. All the same, Norn was still being written in the fifteenth century; it was close to contemporary Norwegian. Norn survived as the usual speech of the Orcadians until about 1600, finally dying out about the middle of the eighteenth century. Events took a similar course in the Shetlands, but the remoteness of these islands favoured the retention of Norn for about a century after it had disappeared from the Orkneys. Only the most meagre scraps of Modern Norn have survived. They are all corrupt, but a very large number of single words are known since the dialects of these places, especially Shetland, preserve many Norn expressions. Finally, a word about the Norn in Caithness. On the Scottish mainland generally, Norn was ousted by Gaelic during the Middle Ages, except in the North-East of Caithness where it appears to have lingered on until the sixteenth century, when it was replaced by Lowland Scottish advancing along the east coast.

Colonial West Norse survives today in Icelandic and Faroese. As we have noted, Modern Icelandic is an exceptionally archaic language, in fact no other Germanic language has remained so close to the ancestral form. Moreover, there is a strong tradition of purism in Icelandic, so that neologisms are most usually constructed of purely native elements, e.g., such terms as 'cigar, cigarette', commonplace in so many languages, are rendered *vindill*, *vindlingur*, based on *vinda* 'wind, twist'. Faroese has only come into relative prominence in modern times. It possesses a considerable literature, having been written for nearly two hundred years, since the 1840s in an etymologising orthography which gives it a distinctly Icelandic look. But structurally, Faroese is more analytic than Icelandic, corresponding rather to Middle Norwegian. Spoken Faroese and Icelandic are not mutually comprehensible, nor is Faroese understood by continental Scandinavians. Modern literary Faroese is considerably indebted to Icelandic purism. Only in this century has the native language broken the monopoly of Danish in the church, the schools, in administration and business. In 1947, Faroese was declared the 'chief language', but Danish retained official status. Even though Faroese is now used in every sphere and is by far the more commonly written medium, publishing in such a minor language is not without serious drawbacks. Children still acquire a good deal of their basic knowledge from Danish school books, while adults who read more than certain local newspapers, must do most of that reading in Danish. Nevertheless, the Faroese are proud of their language and its victories to date. It is one expression of their individuality and of the measure of local independence they have won for themselves.

Statistics. Danish is spoken by 4.6 millions, Norwegian by 3.7 millions, of whom perhaps as many as a quarter use *Nynorsk*. Swedish is the native language of 7.8 millions in Sweden and a further 350,000 in Finland. Icelandic is used by nearly 200,000, Faroese by rather more than 35,000.

THE STRUCTURE OF GERMANIC

The Indo-European affinities of Germanic are evident from the vocabulary:

Eng. *salt*, Ger. *Salz*: Lat. *sāl*, Gk. *háls*, Russ. *sol'*, Toch. A *sāle*, B *salyiye*, Armen. *al*, also *alt*, Ir. *solann*, Welsh *halen*

Eng. *mere*, Ger. *Meer* 'sea': Lat. *mare*, Russ. *móre*, Ir. *muir*
Eng. *is*, Ger. *ist*: Lat. *est*, Gk. *estí*, Skt. *ásti*, Russ. *jest'*

The affinities become much more apparent, however, when it is observed that Germanic has made sweeping changes in the inherited occlusive system. As part of this, the so-called Germanic sound shift, IE [p, t, k] appear as Gmc. [f, þ, χ often becoming h] while IE [b, d, g] become Gmc. [p, t, k]:

Eng. *foot*: Lat. *pēs, pedis*, Gk. *poús, podós*, Skt. *pát, padás*
Eng. *three*: Lat. *trēs*, Gk. *treîs*, Skt. *tráyas*, Ir. *trí*
Eng. *hound*: Lat. *canis*, Gk. *kúōn*, Ir. *cú*, pl. *cúnna*
Eng. *cow*: Skt. *gaús*, Latv. *gùovs*
Eng. *deep*: Lith. *dubùs*

(High) German has in many cases made a further, independent shift, hence beside *Hund* 'hound, dog' and *Kuh* 'cow' with the same occlusives as English, we find *Fuß* 'foot', *drei* 'three' and *tief* 'deep' with the German innovations, likewise *Salz* 'salt'.

At the time of the oldest records, the Germanic languages were still rather close to each other. We propose to illustrate the earliest recorded stages from Gothic and Old English, the former of course being the more archaic.

GOTHIC

Phonetics

The pronunciation of Gothic is not fully understood. It is likely that *ai* and *au* were open vowels [ε] and [ɔ], while *e* and *o* were the corresponding closed sounds. Nothing is known for certain about vowel length, but *ei* is conventionally pronounced [i:]. Intervocalic *b, d, g*, appear to have been spirants; *q* = [kw]. Doubled consonants were long (as in all Old Germanic languages), except *gg* which, following a Greek convention, was pronounced *ng*.

Accidence

There are three genders, two numbers and four cases, with traces of a vocative. Indo-European declensional classes are, in general, easily recognisable. The following paradigm shows endings corresponding to those of IE *ekwos*:

Sg.nom.	*stains* 'stone'	Pl.	*stainos*
voc.	*stain*		
acc.	*stain*		*stainans*
gen.	*stainis*		*staine*
dat.	*staina*		*stainum*

Adjectives have a strong (i.e. Indo-European) declension and, as a Germanic innovation, also a weak declension, semantically differentiated: *mikils stains* '(a) big stone', *mikila stains* 'the big stone'.

Verbs have only two tenses: present and past (indic. and subj.). There are two main types of conjugation: strong and weak. Strong verbs, continuing an Indo-European principle, form their tenses with different root vowels: *baira* '(I) bear', *bar* '(I) bore', *berum* '(we) bore'. In the case of weak verbs, the past is formed with a dental suffix, a purely Germanic development: *hailja* '(I) heal', *hailida* '(I) healed', *hailidedum* '(we) healed'. There are special dual forms for 1st and 2nd persons, and a present passive. Sample paradigm:

Infin. *bairan* 'bear'

	Present		Past	
	Indicative	Subjunctive	Indicative	Subjunctive
Sg.1	*baira*	*bairau*	*bar*	*berjau*
2	*bairis*	*bairais*	*bart*	*bereis*
3	*bairiþ*	*bairai*	*bar*	*beri*
Pl.1	*bairam*	*bairaima*	*berum*	*bereima*
2	*bairiþ*	*bairaiþ*	*beruþ*	*bereiþ*
3	*bairand*	*bairaina*	*berun*	*bereina*
Du.1	*bairos*	*bairaiwa*	*beru*	*bereiwa*
2	*bairats*	*bairaits*	*beruts*	*bereits*

Imperf.sg. *bair*, pl. *bairiþ*, du. *bairats*
Participles: *bairands* 'bearing', *baurans* 'borne'
Passive:

	Indicative	Subjunctive
Sg.1,3	*bairada*	*bairaidau*
2	*bairaza*	*bairaizau*
Pl.	*bairanda*	*bairaindau*
Du. (not attested)		

Numbers: 1 *ains*, 2 *twai*, 3 *þreis*, 4 *fidwor*, 5 *fimf*, 6 *saihs*, 7 *sibun*, 8 *ahtau*, 9 *niun*, 10 *taihun*, 100 *hund*

Text

Matthew vi.9–13

Atta unsar þu in himinam: weihnai namo þein. Qimai
father our thou in heavens be-hallowed name thy come

þiudinassus þeins. Wairþai wilja þeins, swe in himina jah ana
kingdom   thy   be-done will thy   as in heaven and on

airþai. Hlaif unsarana þana sinteinan gif uns himma daga. Jah
earth bread our   the daily   give us this   day   and

aflet uns þatei   skulans   sijaima, swaswe jah weis afletam
forgive us that-which owing (we) may-be so-as and we   forgive

þaim skulam unsaraim. Jah ni   briggais uns in fraistubnjai, ak
the debtors our.   and not bring   us in temptation but

lausei uns af   þamma ubilin. Unte þeina ist þiudangardi jah
deliver us from the   evil   for thine is kingdom   and

mahts jah wulþus in aiwins.
power and glory   in ages.

OLD ENGLISH

(The forms are those of 'Standard' Old English, i.e. West Saxon,
c. 1000)

Phonetics

g is a spirant pronounced [j] in palatal, [ɣ] in velar surroundings; *c* is
likewise [tʃ] or [k], and *h* (except when initial) [ç] or [χ]. *þ* equals
Mod. Engl. *th* (voiced or voiceless), *y* is pronounced [y].

Accidence

There are three genders, two numbers and four cases. Indo-European
origins are, in part at least, not hard to recognise. Sample paradigm:

Sg.nom.acc. *stān* 'stone', gen. *stānes*, dat. *stāne*; pl.nom.acc.
stānas, gen. *stāna*, dat. *stānum*

As in Gothic, adjectives may be strong or weak: *(ān) micel stān*
'(a) big stone', or weak: *(sē) micela stān* 'the big stone'.

The verb has only two inflected tenses, present and past, but
compound tenses were coming into use: *bere* '(I) bear', *bær* '(I) bore',
hæbbe geboren '(I) have borne', *hæle* '(I) heal', *hælde* '(I) healed',
hæbbe gehæled '(I) have healed'. Unlike Gothic, Old English has no
dual verbal forms and no synthetic passive. Sample paradigm:

Infin. *beran* 'bear'

	Present		Past	
	Indicative	Subjunctive	Indicative	Subjunctive
Sg.1	*bere*		*bær*	
2	*birest*	*bere*	*bǣre*	*bǣre*
3	*bireþ*		*bær*	
Pl.	*beraþ*	*beren*	*bǣron*	*bǣren*

Imperf.sg. *ber*, pl. *beraþ*
Participles: *berende* 'bearing', *geboren* 'borne'
Numbers: 1 *ān*, 2 *twā*, 3 *þrī*, 4 *fēower*, 5 *fīf*, 6 *siex*, 7 *seofon*, 8 *eahta*, 9 *nigon*, 10 *tīen*, 100 *hundred*

Texts

From Ælfric's *Colloquies*, c. 1000

Master: *Hwæt sægst þū, ierþling?   Hū begǣst   þū*
　　　　 what sayest thou ploughman how performest thou

þīn weorc?
thy work

Ploughman: *Ēalā! lēof hlāford,   þearle ic deorfe. Ic*
　　　　　　 alas   dear lord ('my Lord, Sir') hard I work I

gā ūt on dægrǣde   þȳwende oxan tō felde, and   geocie
go out on day-red ('dawn') driving oxen to field and (I) yoke

hī   tō syl.   Nis   hit swā stearc   winter þæt ic durre
them to plough not-is it so stark ('severe') winter that I dare

lūtian æt hāme for mīnes hlāfordes ege. Ac gegeocodum   oxum and
lurk   at home for of-my lord   fear but having-yoked oxen and

gefæstnodum sceare and cultre mid   þǣre syl,   ælce dæg ic
fastened   share and coulter with ('to') the plough each day I

sceal   erian fulne æcer oþþe māre.
shall ('am to') plough full acre or   more

Master: *Hæfst þū   ǣnigne gefēran?*
　　　　 hast thou any   mate

Ploughman: *Ic hæbbe sumne   cnapan þywende oxan mid*
          I have   some ('a') lad   driving   oxen with

gādīsene,   þe   ēac swilce nū   hās   is for cielde and hrēame.
goad-iron who also so   now hoarse is for cold and shouting

Master: *Hwæt māre dēst þū   on dæge?*
       what more dost thou on day ('in a day')

Ploughman: *Gewislice þænne māre ic dō. Ic sceal   fyllan*
          certainly yet   more I do I shall ('am to') fill

oxena   binna   mid hīeg, and wæterian hī,   and beran
of-oxen bins ('mangers') with hay and water   them and bear

ūt   heora scearn.
out their dung

Master: *Hig, hig, micel gedeorf is hit!*
       alas alas great labour is it

Ploughman: *Gēa, lēof,   micel gedeorf hit is, forþan ic*
          yea   dear ('Sir') great labour it is for   I

neom   frēo.
not-am free ('a free man')

Matthew vi.9–13 (West Saxon, end of tenth century)

Fæder ūre, þū   þe   eart on heofonum: sī þīn nama gehālgod.
father our thou which art on heavens   be thy name hallowed

Tōbecume þīn rīce.   Geweorþe þīn willa on eorþan swāswā on
come   thy kingdom be-done thy will on earth as   on

heofonum. Ūrne dæghwāmlican hlāf   sielle ūs tō dæge. And forgief
heavens   our daily   bread give us to-day and forgive

ūs ūre gyltas swāswā wē forgiefaþ ūrum gyltendum. And ne gelæd
us our debts as   we forgive our debtors   and not lead

þū   ūs on costnunge, ac ālīes   ūs of yfele. (No doxology)
thou us on temptation but deliver us of evil

MODERN GERMANIC LANGUAGES
(The Paternoster)

WEST GERMANIC

English

9   Our father, which art in heaven: hallowed be thy name.
10 Thy kingdom come. Thy will be done on earth as it is in heaven.
11 Give us this day our daily bread.
12 And forgive us our debts, as we forgive our debtors.
13 And lead us not into temptation, but deliver us from evil. For thine
    is the kingdom and the power and the glory for ever and ever.

German

9   Unser Vater in dem Himmel: dein Name werde geheiligt.
10 Dein Reich komme. Dein Wille geschehe auf Erden, wie im Himmel.
11 Unser täglich Brot gib uns heute.
12 Und vergib uns unsere Schulden, wie wir unsern Schuldigern
    vergeben.
13 Und führe uns nicht in Versuchung, sondern erlöse uns von dem Übel.
    Denn dein ist das Reich und die Kraft und die Herrlichkeit in
    Ewigkeit.

Yiddish

9   Undzer voter, vos bist in himl: geheylikt zol vern dayn nomen.
10 Zol kumen dayn malkhes. Zol dayn rotsn geton vern oyf der erd,
    azóy vi in himl.
11 Gib undz haynt undzer teglekh broyt.
12 Un zay undz moykhl undzere shuldikeytn, vi mir zenen oykh
    moykhl undzere bale-khoyves.
13 Un breng undz nit tsu keyn nisoyen, nayert zay undz matsil fun dem
    shlekhtn. Vorn dir gehert di melukhe un di gvure un der koved oyf
    eybik.

Dutch

9   Onze vader, die in de hemelen zijt: Uw naam worde geheiligd.
10 Uw koninkrijk kome. Uw wil geschiede, gelijk in den hemel,
    alzoo ook op de aarde.
11 Geef ons heden onze dagelijks brood.
12 En vergeef ons onze schulden, gelijk ook wij vergeven onzen
    schuldenaren.

13   *En leid ons niet in verzoeking, maar verlos ons van den booze.
Want Uw is het koninkrijk en de kracht en de heerlijkheid in der
eeuwigheid.*

Afrikaans

9   *Onse vader, wat in die hemele is: laat u naam geheilig word.*
10 *Laat u koninkryk kom. Laat y wil geskied, soos in die hemel net so
ook op die aarde.*
11 *Gee ons vandag ons daaglikse brood.*
12 *En vergeef ons ons skulde, soos ons ook ons skuldenaars vergewe.*
13 *En lei ons nie in versoeking nie, maar verlos ons van die bose. Want
aan U behoort die koninkryk en die krag en die heerlikheid tot in
ewigheid.*

North Frisian (Moring Dialect)

9   *Üüsen tääte önj e hamel: hili hülen wård dan noome.*
10 *Din rik kam. Dan wale rädj as önj e hamel sö ok aw e jard.*
11 *Jeew üs diling üüs däilik brüdj.*
12 *An ferjeew üs üüs shälj, sö as ok we da ferjeewe, wat üs shäli san.*
13 *Fäär üs ai in önj fersäking, naan, friliis üs fon et hiinjs. Dan din as
et rik an e måght an e härlikhäid önj eewihäid.*

West Frisian

9   *Us heit, dy't yn de himelen binne: jins namme wurde hillige.*
10 *Jins keninkryk homme. Jins wollen barre allyk yn 'e himel, sa ek
op ierde.*
11 *Jow ús hjoed ús deistich brea.*
12 *En forjow ús ús skulden, allyk ek wy forjowe ús skuldners.*
13 *En lied ús net yn forsiking, mar forlos ús fan 'e kweade. Hwant
Jowes is it keninkryk en de krêft en de hearlikheit oant yn ivichheit.*

SCANDINAVIAN
Icelandic

9   *Faðir vor, þú sem ert í himnunum: helgist nafn þitt.*
10 *Komi ríki þitt. Verði vilji þinn, svo á jörðu sem á himni.*
11 *Gef oss í dag vort daglegt brauð.*
12 *Og gef oss upp skuldir vorar, svo sem vér og höfum gefið upp
skuldunautum vorum.*
13 *Og leið oss ekki í freistni, heldur frelsa oss frá illu. Því þitt er
ríkið og mátturinn og dýrðin að eilífu.*

Faroese

9 *Faðir okkara, tú sum ert í himli: heilagt verði navn títt.*
10 *Komi ríki títt. Verði vilji tín, sum í himli, so á jørðini við.*
11 *Gev okkum í dag dagliga breyð okkara.*
12 *Og fyrigev okkum skuldir okkara, sum eisini vit fyrigeva skuldarum okkara.*
13 *Og leið okkum ikki í freistingar, men frels okkum frá illum. Tí títt er ríkið og valdið og heiðurin í allar ævir.*

Norwegian (Nynorsk)

9 *Fader vår, du som er i himmelen: lat namnet ditt helgast.*
10 *Lat riket ditt koma. Lat viljen din råda på jordi so som i himmelen.*
11 *Gjev oss i dag vårt daglege brød.*
12 *Og forlat oss vår skuld, som me og forlet våre skuldmenn.*
13 *Og før oss ikkje ut i freisting, men frels oss frå det vonde. For riket er ditt og makti og æra i all æva.*

Norwegian (Bokmål)

9 *Fader vår, du som er i himmelen: helliget vorde ditt navn.*
10 *Komme ditt rike. Skje din vilje, som i himmelen, så og på jorden.*
11 *Gi oss idag vårt daglige brød.*
12 *Og forlat oss vår skyld, som og vi forlater våre skyldnere.*
13 *Og led oss ikke inn i fristelse, men fri oss fra det onde. For ditt er riket og makten og æren i evighet.*

Danish

9 *Vor Fader, du som er i himlene: helliget vorde dit navn.*
10 *Komme dit rige. Ske din vilje, som i himmelen, således også på jorden.*
11 *Giv os i dag vort daglige brød.*
12 *Og forlad os vor skyld, som også vi forlader vore skyldnere.*
13 *Og led os ikke i fristelse, men fri os fra det onde. Thi dit er riget og magten og æren i evighed.*

Swedish

9 *Fader vår, som är i himmelen: helgat varde ditt namn.*
10 *Tillkomme ditt rike. Ske din vilja, såsom i himmelen, så ock på jorden.*
11 *Vårt dagliga bröd giv oss i dag.*

12 *Och förlåt oss våra skulder, såsom ock vi förlåta dem oss skyldiga äro.*

13 *Och inled oss icke i frestelse, utan fräls oss ifrån ondo. Ty riket är ditt och makten och härligheten i evighet.*

Norn (Orkney)

9 *Fa vor i ir i chimeri: helleut ir i nam thite.*

10 *Gilla cosdum thite cumma. Veya thine mota vara gort o yurn sinna gort i chimeri.*

11 *Ga vus da on da dalight brow vora.*

12 *Firgive vus sinna vora sin vee firgive sindara mutha vus.*

13 *Lyv vus ye i temtation, min delivra vus fro olt ilt.*

Norn (Shetland)

9 *Fy vor o er i chimeri: halaght vara nam dit.*

10 *La konungdum din cumma. La vill din vera guerde i vrildin sin da er i chimeri.*

11 *Gav us dagh u daglocht brau.*

12 *Forgive sindor wara sin vi forgiva gem ao sinda gainst wus.*

13 *Lia wus ikè o vera tempa, but delivra wus from adlu idlu. For do i ir konungdum u puri u glori.*

ENGLISH CREOLES

Neo-Melanesian

9 *Papa bilong mipela, yu i stap long heven: nem bilong yu i mas i stap holi.*

10 *Kingdom bilong yu i kam. Laik bilong yu ol i bihainim long heven, olsem ol i mas bihainim long graun tu.*

11 *Kaikai bilong mipela inap long de nau yu givim mipela.*

12 *Na yu lusim sin bilong mipela, olsem mipela tu i lusim pinis rong bilong ol ol i mekim long mipela.*

13 *Na yu no bringim mipela long samting bilong traiim mipela, tasol tekewe mipela long samting nogut. Kingdom na strong na glori bilong yu tasol oltaim oltaim.*

Krio

9 *Wi dadi we de na èvin: mek wi nò tek yu nem ple.*

10 *Mek yu kingdom kam. Mek yu wòd pas na dis wòl lèk au i de pas na èvin.*

11 *Gi wi wetin fò it tide.*

12 Èn nò fala we wèn wi ambòg yu lèk au wisèf nò fò fala dèn wan we
    ambòg wi.
13 Èn nò mek wi go da sai we wi go fil fò du bad, èn pul wi kòmòt na
    bad rod. Na yu na king, na yu gèt pawa èn prez tete dis wòl dòn.

Sranan

 9 Wi tata na hemel: joe nen moe de santa.
10 Joe kondre moe kon. Joe wani moe go doro na grontapoe, so leki
    na hemel.
11 Gi wi tide a nanjan foe wi.
12 Gi wi pardon foe den ogri di wi doe, so leki wi toe e gi pardon na
    den sma di doe wi ogri.
13 No meki wi kon na ini tesi, ma poeroe wi na a ogriwan. Bika a
    kownoekondre na foe joe, a tranga nanga a glori na foe joe, tego.

8

BALTIC

The Baltic branch of Indo-European falls into two divisions: western and eastern. The former is mainly represented by Old Prussian, the latter by Lithuanian and Latvian. The dialects of other Baltic tribes, known from personal and place names, have been either absorbed by the Baltic languages now surviving or else been replaced by encroaching German or Slavonic. The most tangible of these is Curonian, the East Baltic idiom of the historic province of Curonia, which became extinct about 1600, yielding in its southern part to Lithuanian, in the north to Latvian.

Early references to the Baltic peoples are sparse, for nowhere in Europe did prehistoric conditions last so long. Place names, however, confirm that Baltic once occupied latitudes similar to the present much farther east, in fact almost as far as Moscow. But here the Baltic dialects were early replaced by Slavonic expanding from its ancestral centre in the area of the present Polish–Russian frontier; nevertheless, a Baltic tribe, called in the Old Russian source *Goljadĭ*, is recorded as inhabiting the region of Mozhaisk as late as the twelfth century. In antiquity, Baltic was thus in touch with Finnic to the north and east, with Slavonic to the south and Germanic to the west.

There are particularly close connections between Baltic and Slavonic, covering both vocabulary and grammar. Indeed, it was usual at one time to regard the two as stemming from a single Balto-Slavonic entity. Nowadays it is thought that the significant similarities are more likely to have arisen as the result of exchanges which inevitably took place during the co-existence, through centuries untold, of two once more distinct branches of Indo-European. Even though known only from modern times, Baltic is remarkably archaic and consequently of special interest for comparative Indo-European studies.

Old Prussian

Baltic Prussians, or Borussians, occupied the coastal belt of the Baltic from the Vistula to the Memel. In 1230, the Knights of the German Order began the conquest of this territory which they finally subdued in 1283. Germanisation was rapid—the despoiled country was planted with German peasants—and when the rule of the Order came to an end in 1525, the Prussian language survived only in the Samland Peninsula. Here were peasants still unable to understand German, and for these a catechism, in Prussian and German, was twice printed in 1545, followed in 1561 by Luther's Catechism, also in a bilingual edition. Apart from two glossaries amounting to less than a thousand words, these catechisms—some thirty pages of text—are the chief remains of the Prussian language which is presumed to have become extinct by 1700. These records of the language, meagre and often corrupt though they be, are nevertheless sufficient to demonstrate the exceptional conservatism of Western Baltic.

Lithuanian

From the evidence of place names, it seems probable that the Lithuanians, like other East Baltic tribes, were not originally settled on the seaboard, but belonged to inland districts farther east. Slavonic pressure in the early centuries of the Christian era will then account for the appearance of such tribes in the coastal zone.

Lithuania lay away from the mainstream of European civilisation and writing made its appearance there rather tardily. The earliest known document in Lithuanian is dated to about 1515, though it is certain that the language was being written in the previous century. It has not greatly changed since the first attestations, but forms now obsolete may be characterised as Old Lithuanian.

Two main dialects are distinguished: High and Low Lithuanian, the latter confined to the far west and north-west. The modern literary standard is based on a southern variety of High Lithuanian proper to the districts just west of Kaunas. But literary Lithuanian was late in developing. From the end of the fourteenth to the end of the eighteenth century Lithuania merged its identity with that of Poland in personal union. In 1795 it fell to Russia. Such historical circumstances were not conducive to the cultivation of the native language. However, the nationalist spirit of nineteenth-century Europe affected the Lithuanians, too, and encouraged the growth of a literature in the Lithuanian language in spite of the hostility of the Czarist regime to publishing in non-Russian languages, particularly during the repressive period from 1864 to 1905. After Independence in 1918, Lithuanian became the state language of the new Republic. The Lithuanians regarded Vilnius as their historic capital, though both the city and its

surroundings were largely polonised. In 1920 this territory was
awarded to Poland, but in 1939 most of it was returned to Lithuania,
the Polish population being subsequently transferred to Poland. In
1940, Lithuania became a Soviet Republic, with Russian as an official
language beside Lithuanian.

Lithuanian is spoken in its native land by about two and a half
million persons, accounting for over four-fifths of the population,
the minority being, in the main, Russians concentrated chiefly in the
towns. Perhaps as many as a half a million Lithuanian speakers live
abroad as émigrés, chiefly in the USA.

Lithuanian is written in the Latin character. There has been a
limited use of Cyrillic, especially in the difficult period 1864 to 1905.

Latvian

There is some truth in the characterisation of Latvian as Lithuanian
in the mouths of foreigners, in this case speakers of languages belonging to the Baltic division of Finnic (p. 152). The best known of the
languages concerned is Livonian which in the thirteenth century still
predominated in the area of the Gulf of Riga, i.e., in the historic
province of Livonia. It is not yet entirely extinct, being remembered
by some three or four hundred fisherfolk from hamlets along the coast
opposite the southern tip of the Estonian island of Saaremaa (Ösel).

The first attested writing in Latvian dates from the middle of the
sixteenth century. The literary standard has developed out of the
central dialect, closely associated with the speech of Riga, for centuries the great metropolis of the country. But since the thirteenth
century, the ruling class in Latvia had been German. In 1795, the
country was taken by the Russians and the subsequent history of
Latvia is similar to that of Lithuania. Such conditions were not propi-
tious for the development of a literary Latvian language, but nevertheless the nineteenth century witnessed a remarkable growth. In
1918, Latvian became the state language of the new Republic. When,
in 1940, Latvia was incorporated into the Soviet Union, Russian was
admitted as an official medium beside Latvian.

Latvian is spoken by about two million persons living mainly in
Latvia itself. The number of émigrés is not large, in no way comparable to the figure for Lithuanians. Continuing large-scale Russian
emigration into Latvia since the war has reduced the proportion of
Latvians in the Republic to about 65 per cent. The trend is most
marked in the urban centres; at least half the population of Riga is
now Russian, whereas in the twenty-two years of independent Latvia
it was well under 10 per cent. Such developments naturally constitute
a threat to the future of the Latvian language.

In older works especially, Latvian is often termed Lettish.

THE STRUCTURE OF BALTIC

LITHUANIAN

In certain details the extinct Old Prussian is more archaic than Lithuanian, but its records are meagre and sometimes corrupt. Lithuanian, on the other hand, has all the richness of a living language and is by far the best representative of the Baltic type.

Phonetics

Vowels with a subscript hook are long, having been formerly nasalised; *ė, ū, y*, are pronounced [e:, u:, i:], *č, š, ž, j* [tʃ, ʃ, ʒ, j].

Grave, circumflex and acute accents are used in philological works, the first denoting a short vowel, the others long vowels with rising or falling intonation respectively. The sonants (*m, n, l, r*) are marked with the circumflex when lengthened.

Accidence

Nouns retain only two genders, masculine and feminine, but have seven cases, important remains of the dual, and the general inflexional system of Indo-European is exceptionally well preserved. IE **ekwos* has not survived, cf. however *ašvà*, OLith *ešvà* 'mare' <IE **ekwā*, but the declension as such is amply attested, e.g., in *diẽvas* 'god', as follows:

Sg.nom.	*diẽvas*	Pl.	*dievaĩ*	Du.	*dievù*
voc.	*diẽve*		*dievaĩ*		—
acc.	*diẽvą*		*dievùs*		*dievù*
gen.	*diẽvo*		*dievũ*		—
dat.	*diẽvui*		*dieváms*		*dievám*
loc.	*dievè*		*dievousè*		—
inst.	*dievù*		*dievaĩs*		*dievam̃*

The adjectives have comparable declensional schemes, but may have a neuter in sg.nom.voc.acc., e.g., *naũjas* m. 'new', *naujà* f., *naũja* n.

The verb is much less conservative than the noun. All the same it has four synthetic tenses of the indicative active, other tenses and the passive being formed periphrastically with *būti* 'to be' and various participles. There is a synthetic present subjunctive and an imperative. The dual is in restricted use. The third person of all numbers is identical; it is historically a singular. Lith. *ber̃ti* 'to scatter' would appear to continue IE **bher-* with exceptional semantic change. Paradigms:

Indicative

	Present	Future	Imperfect	Preterite
Sg.1	beriù	beřsiu	beřdavau	bèriaũ
2	berì	beřsi	beřdavai	bèreĩ
Pl.1	bĕriame	beřsime	beřdavome	bĕrème
2	bĕriate	beřsite	beřdavote	bĕrète
Du.1	bĕriava	beřsiva	beřdavova	bĕrèva
2	bĕriata	beřsita	beřdavota	bĕrèta
3rd	bĕria	beřs	beřdavo	bĕrè

Subj. sg.1 beřčiau, 2 beřtum, pl.1 beřtume, 2 beřtute, du.1 beřtuva, 2 beřtuta, 3rd beřtų

Imperative: sg.2 beřk, pl.1 beřkime, 2 beřkite, du.1 beřkiva, 2 beřkita (k being an incorporated particle)

Participles include: pres.act. bĕriantis, pret.act. bĕręs, pres.pass. bĕriamas, perf.pass beřtas

Numbers: 1 víenas, 2 dù, 3 trỹs, 4 keturì, 5 penkì, 6 šešì, 7 septynì, 8 aštuonì, 9 devynì, 10 dẽšimt, 100 šim̃tas

Vocabulary

Typical elements include:

Lith. mirtìs 'death': Skt. mr̥tís, Lat. mors, gen. mortis, Czech mrt 'dead part', with semantic specialisation Eng. murder, further the compound OCS sŭmrĭtĭ (Russ. smert') 'death'

Lith. pàts, older patìs 'husband': Skt. pátis, also contained in Gk. despótēs 'master of the house', Goth. bruþfaþs 'bridegroom'

Lith. sáulė 'sun': Skt. sū́ryas, Gk. hḗlios, Lat. sōl, Ir. súil ('eye'), Welsh haul, Icel. sól

Lith. sūnùs 'son': Skt. sūnús, Russ. syn, Eng. son

Lith. sĕnas 'old': Skt. sánas, Gk. hénos, Ir. sean, Welsh hen, Armen. hin, further Skt. sanakás, Lat. senex, Goth. sineigs

Lith. áuga 'grows': Lat. auget, Goth aukiþ 'increases', Eng. ekes

Lith. gãri 'burns': Russ. gorít, Skt. ghr̥n̥óti ('glows'), Ir. gorann ('heats, hatches'), Welsh gawr ('broods')

Text

Matthew vi.9–13

Tève mūsų, kurs esi danguje: teesie šventas tavo   vardas.
father of-us who art in-heaven be   holy   of-thee name

Teateinie tavo   karalystė. *Teesie tavo   valia, kaip danguje,   taip*
come   of-thee kingdom be   of-thee will   as   in-heaven so

ir   ant žemės. Kasdienės mūsų duonos duok mums šiandien. Ir
and on earth daily   of-us bread give us   today and

atleisk mums mūsų kaltes, kaip ir   mes atleidžiame savo
forgive us   of-us debts as   and we forgive   of-selves

kaltininkams. Ir nevesk mus į   pagundą, bet gelbėk mus
debtors   and not-lead us into temptation but deliver us

nuo pikto. Nes tavo   yra karalystė ir   macis ir   garbė iki
from evil   for of-thee is   kingdom and power and glory for

amžių.
ever

OTHER BALTIC LANGUAGES
(The Paternoster)

Latvian

9 *Mūsu tēvs debesīs: svētīts lai top tavs vārds.*
10 *Lai nāk tava valstiba. Tavs prāts lai notiek kā debesīs, tā arī virs
   zemes.*
11 *Mūsu dienišku maizi dod mums šodien.*
12 *Un piedod mums mūsu parādus, kā arī mēs piedodam saviem
   parādniekiem.*
13 *Un neieved mūs kārdināšanā, bet atpesti mūs no ļauna. Jo tev
   pieder valstiba un spēks un gods mūžīgi.*

Old Prussian

9 *Tāwa noūson kas tu essei en dangon: swintints wīrst twais emnes.*
10 *Perēit twais rīks. Twais quāits audāsin kāigi en dangon, tīt dēigi
   no semien.*
11 *Noūson deinennin geitien dais noūmans schan deinan.*
12 *Bhe etwērpeis noūmas noūsons auschautins kai mes etwērpimai
   noūsons auschautenīkamans.*
13 *Bhe ni weddeis mans en perbandāsnan, schlāit isrankeis mans esse
   wargan (. . .)*

9

SLAVONIC

The earliest historical allusions to the Slavs date from the first and second centuries A.D., when their patrimony is seen to comprise the region from the Vistula to the Dnieper—or possibly to the Don—and from the Carpathians to the Narew. Neighbours to the north were the Balts, with whom they appear to have long been in close contact (p. 138). To the west lay the lands of Germanic tribes, to the south were Celts and perhaps also Thracians. Iranian nomads roamed over the plains to the south-east, while the primeval forests to the east concealed the sparse settlements of the non-Indo-European Finnic race. Celts and Thracians were soon to vanish, their haunts occupied by migrating East Germanic tribes, who in the third century set up a powerful kingdom in the steppe country close to Slavonic territory.

It is often considered that the heartland of Slavonic lay in Polesye, that desolate province dominated by the marsh lands of the Pripet system. In these isolated wastes, so it is argued, Slavonic speech evolved its characteristic forms and here its speakers remained until the early centuries of the present era. On the other hand, it is not impossible that increasing Germanic pressure, say towards the beginning of the Christian era, had obliged the Slavs to take refuge in less attractive surroundings.

Early Slavonic expansion

The Slavs are first seen to have become expansive about the beginning of the fifth century, moving into territory apparently deserted by Germanic tribes. The expansion becomes more marked after the disintegration of the Hunnish state following Attila's death in 453 for the end of Hunnish power relieved the containing pressure on the Slavs. By the beginning of the next century, they are seen to be moving forcefully west and south, inaugurating migrations which were to continue until the tenth century and permanently alter the linguistic configuration of central Europe and the Balkans. At the same time, scarcely noticed, Slavonic was expanding eastwards into the vast, but almost empty tracts of Russia.

By the middle of the sixth century, the once purely Germanic lands east of the Elbe and Saale had been entirely slavicised. Moravia and Bohemia were similarly affected, Slavonic expansion reaching the valley of the Austrian Danube. The Slavs also advanced to the Pannonian Plain, whence they spread westward to take possession of Slovenia, and from here Styria and Carinthia were occupied. About 570, or a little later, the leadership of the Pannonian Slavs passed into the hands of the Turkic Avars (p. 146). Avar and Slav then together undertook raids into the Balkans, reaching Mainland Greece in 587, then on to Crete and islands in the Aegean. These assaults led to Slavonic settlement in South-East Europe, in essentials probably the work of the next century. Although the newcomers became the dominant ethnic element, earlier populations remained in varying strength, witness Greek, Rumanian and Albanian today. Indeed, it is known that all these recovered some of the territory taken from them in the first onslaughts of the Slavs. It may be mentioned, too, that by arrangement with the Byzantine authorities large numbers of Slavs were settled across the Bosphorus on the Anatolian side, where however they were in due course hellenised.

The Slavs suffered a set-back when the Hungarians seized the principality of Pannonia in 896. Furthermore, the Germans soon regained control of much of the Danube Valley in Austria, and here Slavonic began to retreat, though it was not until about half-way through the twelfth century that German joined up with Hungarian on the Leitha, thus completing the geographical isolation of the Balkan Slavs from the rest of the Slavonic world.

Contemporary Slavonic advances in other directions were also impressive, if less spectacular, and in the long run even more momentous. Colonists progressed down the Dnieper and about 600 founded Kiev in an area which became known as the Ukraine 'Borderland'. But elsewhere, these Eastern Slavs made great headway, partly at the expense of Baltic, but chiefly replacing Finnic. To the north, the Slavs were certainly established at Novgorod by the ninth century. In the east, tenth-century traditions speak of the Slavonic population as having reached the headwaters of the Volga. To such advances through thinly populated forest there can have been no serious resistance. Nor was there indeed in this part of the world any human force capable of staying, to any appreciable degree, the further movement of Slavonic in subsequent centuries. Only in the south-east, on the open steppe, was the way blocked by the Turkic nomads who, following the Huns, had dominated these plains since the fifth century, and would continue to do so until the sixteenth.

Notes on Hunnish, Avar and Hungarian

The Central European Plain, the ancient province of Pannonia, has several times witnessed the incursions of nomads from the East; the earliest known to us were Iranians (p. 233). These were succeeded by the Huns, a Mongol people, but almost certainly including a considerable Turkic component. The Huns had subdued the Ukrainian Goths in 383 and, reinforced from the ranks of their new subjects, they advanced early in the next century into Central Europe to assume the leadership of the local Germanic tribes, by then the chief inhabitants of the Plain. After Attila's death in 453, the power of the Hunnish aristocracy collapsed, the Huns themselves—a small minority—either departed or were rapidly assimilated. Next came the Turkic Avars, believed to have also been a mixed horde, but in this case chiefly Turkic, and the new arrivals established themselves as lords of the Plain early in the second half of the sixth century. Their subjects were the Pannonian Slavs who at the time were replacing the earlier Germanic population. It was the arrival of the Avars which caused the Germanic Langobardi to emigrate to Italy (p. 98). From their strongholds on the Danube the Avars, like the Huns before them, terrorised the West until finally checked in 803. After this set-back, the survivors completely merged with the Slavs.

The next incursion, however, was to have a much more durable character. The Magyars, of the same linguistic stock as the Ostyak and Vogul speakers of Western Siberia (p. 152), had in the first centuries of the Christian era migrated from the Middle Volga to occupy steppe country north of the Caucasus and the Black Sea. Strengthened by Turkic allies, these nomads next moved westward. In 896, they crossed the Carpathians and came upon the congenial Plain. They speedily took over possession from the Slavs they found there, at the same time breaking the power of Moravia. Though decisively defeated by the Germans on the Lech in 955, their essential conquests remained unimpaired. Indeed, in succeeding centuries, their Hungarian language spread to a considerable extent into the mountainous districts surrounding the Plain, particularly into Transsylvania.

Hungarian is the most influential member of the Uralic family; it is spoken by upwards of twelve and a half million persons living in Central Europe. Of the ten million citizens of the Hungarian Republic, nine and a half speak Hungarian as their mother tongue. A large Hungarian minority (1,750,000) lives in Rumania in widespread settlements from the state boundary to Eastern Transsylvania. Hungarians are also found in the frontier areas of the other neighbouring states: USSR (Carpatho-Ukraine) with over 150,000, Czechoslovakia (over 400,000), Yugoslavia (over 500,000), Austria (about 15,000). Except for the last, all these minorities use Hungarian officially for local purposes and in education.

The first Hungarian text dates from about 1200. The language contains numerous loans from the language of the dispossessed Pannonian Slavs, the last survivors being totally assimilated by about the twelfth century. Magyar is the native name for the language.

Church Slavonic

According to traditional accounts, Slavonic was first employed as a written medium in the seventh decade of the ninth century in the following circumstances. Rostislav of Moravia, anxious to strengthen his position against his German Catholic neighbours, turned to Byzantium and the Orthodox Church. As a result of these moves two brothers, Cyril and Methodius, arrived to organise Eastern Christianity in Moravia. These 'apostles of the Slavs' were Greeks from Salonika who had acquired Slavonic, then the common language of the city and its Macedonian hinterland. In preparation for their mission, the brothers are said to have translated religious material, including the liturgy and New Testament, into Slavonic. They began their labours about 863, but political changes subsequently undermined their position. The Roman Church rose to ascendancy in Moravia and the Orthodox mission was obliged to withdraw in 885, transfering its activities to Macedonia. The brothers termed their language 'Slavonic' and it is noteworthy that at this time the dialects of Moravia and Macedonia were still close enough to share the same literary form. Neither can have been far removed from Common Slavonic.

This tradition of the origin of literary Slavonic is, however, not without puzzling features: the date, for instance. The Slavs had certainly been in close contact with the eminently cultured Greeks since the late sixth century. Many of them had become Byzantine citizens and Christians. Others were at an equally early date in touch with Latin civilisation. One may therefore be surprised that there was apparently no call for written Slavonic before 860. But strangest of all, the allegedly brand-new literary tongue appears from the start in two entirely different alphabets (see 'Script' below). One inclines to think that writing in Slavonic was, in fact, older than the Moravian mission, but that pious legend has obliterated a truer record.

In view of the evidently high degree of linguistic homogeneity in the Slavonic world at the time, it was only natural that the language employed by Cyril and Methodius should become the literary medium in those lands owing allegiance to the Orthodox Church, namely Bulgaria, Serbia and Russia. In its oldest form, the language may be termed Old Slavonic or, more precisely, Old Church Slavonic. It remained in use down to modern times, but was more and more influenced by the living, evolving languages, so that one distinguishes Bulgarian, Serbian and Russian varieties. The use of such media hampered the development of the local languages for literary purposes and when they do appear the first attempts are usually in an artificially mixed style. Even in their standard modern forms they all contain large numbers of Old Church Slavonic forms particularly, though not exclusively, to express abstract concepts. In other words, these modern Slavonic tongues have enriched themselves from Church Slavonic much as the Romance languages have turned to the ancestral Latin for a good deal of their literary vocabulary. Although orientated to the west and Catholic, Croatia also produced a medieval literature in Church Slavonic.

Church Slavonic made one conquest. It set itself up as the literary language of the Rumanians and continued as such until the mid-seventeenth century when it yielded to the native tongue.

Scripts

Strange to say, the earliest Slavonic is written in two distinct alphabets: Cyrillic and Glagolitic. The first was so called since it was attributed to Cyril, one of the missionary brothers, and is an adaptation of the Greek alphabet. The second, bizarre and cumbersome, but more commonly used, is of unexplained origin. Its name is no help; it simply derives from *glagolŭ* 'word', a term often occurring in biblical texts, but which became unusual in current speech. There is no way of establishing the age of these scripts.

By the eleventh century, Cyrillic had become general wherever the Orthodox Church was established, i.e., in Bulgaria, Serbia and Russia, in which countries frequently reformed and acquiring local variations it remains to this day. It was adopted by the Rumanians for their own language until the change to Latin script in the second half of the last century. Since the late 1930s, the employment of Cyrillic has spread to most non-Slavonic languages spoken in the USSR. Glagolitic survived only in Croatia, on the Adriatic coast, where in a modified form it remained general throughout the Middle Ages. From the beginning of modern times, it was progressively supplanted by the Latin alphabet, but its use in the religious sphere continued into the nineteenth century. It is sometimes argued that Glagolitic arose in the west as a highly stylised offshoot of Latin script.

According to an early (9th or 10th-cent.) account, the heathen Slavs could count and prophesy from marks and notches. This sounds perhaps like runes, which the Slavs could be expected to have borrowed from their Germanic neighbours.

THE LIVING SLAVONIC LANGUAGES

Prior to the arrival of the Hungarians in Pannonia at the end of the ninth century the Slavonic tribes, in spite of their immense geographical range, remained essentially contiguous, and their dialects, as yet but little differentiated, formed a vast Slavonic continuum. The complete separation of the Balkan Slavs from those of Central and Eastern Europe which later followed was naturally a cause of subsequent linguistic divergence between the two parts of the Slavonic world, but each remained a continuum unto itself. Only with the growth of national states did there arise anything like linguistic boundaries between Slavonic peoples. Even where different standard languages faced each other over a boundary fence, frontier dialects continued to merge into each other as they had always done before there were any such frontiers. Generally speaking, this is still the case. Only where exceptional factors have supervened does one find more clear-cut linguistic boundaries, as for example on the frontier between Poland and the Kaliningrad Region of the RSFSR, formerly German, but planted with Russians after 1945. Similarly on Poland's eastern frontier with the USSR, population movements taking place at the same time disturbed the older settlements and with them the transitional nature of the frontier dialects. On the other hand, it is undeniable that the general decline in dialect speaking in this modern age will indeed lead to much sharper linguistic delimitations along all political frontiers in the future.

One distinguishes eastern, western and southern divisions of Slavonic. These divisions will now be treated in turn.

EAST SLAVONIC

East Slavonic, the most uniform of the three divisions of Slavonic, consists of Russian, technically called Great Russian, and the closely connected Belorussian and Ukrainian. The latter were for long regarded as mere dialects of the former, but as they now possess recognised literary norms in full official use they have clearly attained the status of independent languages.

Literary language in Russia

Slavonic literature in Russia dates back to the early eleventh century; the medium was of course Old Church Slavonic, doubtless introduced from Bulgaria. This book language, progressively russified with the passing of the centuries, remained the written style until recent times. By the eighteenth century, however, the native East Slavonic element was coming strongly to the fore in what had, in fact, turned into a

6

thoroughly mixed language. Accelerating development in this direction led to the establishment of modern literary (Great) Russian in the Age of Pushkin in the twenties and thirties of the last century. The new standard was essentially the spoken idiom of the central European area with Moscow as its dominating focus, but with an indispensable, integrated Church Slavonic element also. In Belorussia and the Ukraine, analogous varieties of East Slavonic were coming into being more or less contemporaneously.

Belorussian

Belorussian, or literally White Russian, is the official language of the Republic of the same name and spoken by some nine million persons. A large part of its territory was once Baltic-speaking and a Baltic substratum conceivably played some part in the genesis of a Belorussian linguistic identity. The area was for long under Polish control and the language has been considerably influenced from that quarter. After the partitions of Poland, Russian power became dominant and many speakers of Belorussian appear to regard the quite familiar Great Russian as their natural literary tongue. Until relatively recently, various mixed types of Church Slavonic were in use as written media. The present, now substantially standardised literary form—it is based on the dialects of the south-west—is the product of nineteenth-century nationalism, in this case perhaps especially romantic. The language is today normally written in Cyrillic, but has often appeared in Latin letters, too, a reflexion of Polish example. Very occasionally, Belorussian has been transcribed in Arabic characters by local Muslims, the slavicised descendants of erstwhile Tartar invaders. The new Poland of 1918 still included a large Belorussian minority, but boundary changes from 1939 have reduced the number to 175,000.

The origin of the term 'White Russia', in use since late medieval times, is unexplained.

Ukrainian

Ukrainian is the official language of the Ukrainian SSR and spoken by 42 million persons. The language developed in an area stretching from west of Lviv (Lemberg) to east of Kiev, the course of the Pripet formally separating it from Belorussian, the other westerly division of East Slavonic. The two languages are particularly close and both have been influenced by Polish before coming into the Great Russian orbit. Ukrainian became expansive in the latter part of the sixteenth century following the collapse of Tartar power in the steppe country south-east of Kiev. The term Ukraine henceforth included the vast spaces north of the Black Sea which now received Slavonic colonisers, in their van the cossacks, the fighting cowboys of that age. These Slavs broke away from Poland and placed themselves under Russian protection in 1648. Relations between the Ukrainians and the Russian Czars eventually deteriorated and the language suffered the usual penalties during the repressive period 1864 to 1905. The most westerly portion of the Ukrainian-speaking area, however, lay within the boundaries of Austro-Hungary, where more liberal policies prevailed. The Lviv district, with its many Polish speakers, became part of post-1918 Poland, but frontier revisions after 1939 have now incorporated virtually all Ukrainian-speakers in the present Republic. A minority of 200,000 remains on Polish soil.

The oldest literature in Russia is associated with the ancient capital of Kiev and Church Slavonic in various styles dominated in the Ukraine, as elsewhere, until quite recent times. The modern literary standard, based on the usage of Kiev, was established at the very end of the eighteenth century. Ukrainian has usually been written in Cyrillic, but there was formerly some publishing in Latin script in Poland.

Since the later Middle Ages the Ukraine has often been called Little Russia in evident contrast to Great Russia, i.e., Greater Russia, that far larger part of the East Slavonic world which, unlike the Ukraine, had always lain outside the sphere of Polish influence. Hence the term Little Russian formerly applied to the language. The Ukrainians of Eastern Galicia, whose territory came to form part of the Austro-Hungarian monarchy, were known as Ruthenians and their speech accordingly referred to as Ruthenian.

Great Russian

Great Russian, or simply Russian, is the native language of some 128 million persons. Its historic centre was Muscovy, which rose to prominence in the thirteenth century, delivered the Slavs from the Tartar yoke, and whose rulers became Czars of all the Russias. In consequence, the language has spread over an immense area and possesses tremendous potential, see 'Russian in contact with other languages' below. It is used freely in Belorussia and the Ukraine, where it is too close to the local tongues to be regarded as foreign in any true sense. It is becoming more and more the acquired medium of all the non-Slavonic peoples of the USSR and is the state language of 232 million persons. (See further 'Literary language in Russia' above).

Russian in contact with other languages

The momentous expansion of Slavonic naturally led to the extinction of many languages once spoken in the areas colonised by the Slavs.

This is particularly true in the east, where the most spectacular gains have been made. In the following, we consider Russian in relation to the various linguistic families with which it has come into contact.

Uralic. Among the earliest victims of Slavonic expansion were a number of Baltic tribes (see p. 138), about which time languages belonging to the Finnic division of the Uralic family also began to be absorbed. The process continued as Russian advanced north and east. However, on the periphery of the area of expansion, several Finnic languages remain to this day distributed in a half circle from Estonia to the Middle Volga. The chief ones are Estonian (1 m., Estonian SSR), Karelian (over 100,000, Karelian ASSR—this hardly more than an eastern dialect of Finnish proper; it is normally unwritten, Finnish being the usual literary language), Zyryene (375,000, Komi ASSR), Votyak (500,000, Udmurt ASSR), Cheremiss (500,000, Mari ASSR), Mordvin (1 m., Mordva ASSR), East of the Zyryene-speaking area, in Siberia, lie Ostyak and Vogul which with Hungarian form the Ugric division of Uralic; the Siberian languages are spoken by some 14,000 and 4,000 souls respectively. To the north of these lies the more distantly related Samoyedic division, the dialects of which are spoken by a small population of not more than a few thousands ranging over an immense tract of Arctic coast. But none of these languages holds exclusive sway in their respective homelands as they did in the Middle Ages. Russian has broken through in many places and frequently established itself inside the districts where Uralic speech still predominates. In the region of the Middle Volga the linguistic situation is further complicated by the presence of various Turkic languages.

Turkic. The centre of diffusion of the languages of this family is believed to have lain east of Lake Baikal. Turkic speakers were almost certainly present in the horde led by their Mongol neighbours, the Huns, though the Slavs would get to know them better with the arrival of the Avars, who early in the second half of the sixth century assumed the leadership of the Pannonian Slavs (pp. 145f.). Another Turkic tribe, the Bolgars, penetrated south-west as far as the Balkans, overcoming the Slavs south of the Danube about 680 (p. 163). Others moved in a contrary direction from the steppes north of the Black Sea to found a powerful state on the Middle Volga in the eighth century; it flourished until destroyed by other Turkic invaders, the Tartars, in 1236. The Volga-Bolgars established themselves on what was at the time Finnic territory; their language survives as Chuvash (1,500,000, Chuvash ASSR and neighbouring republics), situated between Cheremiss to the north and Mordvin to the south.

By the seventh century, Slavs were settling around Kiev, but the country to the east was in the hands of the Turkic Kazars. By the ninth century, it was the Pechenegs who contested the Slavonic advance in this area until finally defeated in 1036. These Turks were, however, at once succeeded by the powerful Cumans, who began to despoil the Slavs of their recent gains. The next, and most serious blow came from the Tartars who fell upon Russia in the second decade of the thirteenth century. Not until the capture of their main centre at Kazan in 1552 was their political power broken. But their language remains to this day, spoken by some four and a half millions. Its speakers constitute nearly a third of the Tartar ASSR and are also scattered widely throughout the region of the Middle and Lower Volga, in the Urals and in Asia. Very closely allied to Tartar (or Tatar) is Bashkir (1 m., Bashkir ASSR). Tartar was formerly the chief language of the Crimean Khanate. It began to recede after the Russian conquest in 1783, the more so as during the next century many of its speakers emigrated to Turkey. The remnant were deported to Uzbekistan in 1945. Another relic of the Tartar period is Nogay, the language of an allied people, today less than 50,000 in number, lingering on at various places in the North Caucasian foreland. The speakers of Kumyk in the North-East Caucasus and of Karachay-Balkar in the North-West, each with at least 125,000 adherents, are survivors of earlier Turkic invaders, the languages deriving essentially from the dialect of the Cumans.

The capture of Kazan was followed in 1566 by the annexation of Astrakhan, the second Tartar stronghold. Henceforward Slavonic expansion was rapid. The steppe country south-east of Kiev now acquired a predominantly Ukrainian population (pp. 150f.). The path beyond the Urals lay wide open, and by the 1580s settlements were being effected there after overcoming feeble resistance. The drive across Siberia, vast but almost empty of human beings, brought the Russians to the Pacific by the middle of the next century. Colonists, however, were not numerous until the middle of the nineteenth century, at which time Russia was becoming politically very active in the East. China ceded large tracts on the left bank of the Amur in 1858 and on the right bank in 1860, at the tip of which Vladivostok ('Ruler of the East') became a symbol of Russian prowess. Meanwhile the Turkic Khanates of Central Asia were being attacked and progressively annexed, the present frontier with Iran, Afghanistan, etc., being reached in 1891. In the Far East, the Russians had reached the Bering Strait as early as 1725. They crossed over into Alaska in 1741, but Russian had a very short lease of life in the New World as the territory was sold to the United States in 1867.

In Asia, Russian has come into contact with many indigenous languages, but here, even more than in Europe, the Turkic languages are the most significant. The following are today in regular literary use: Turkmen (1 m., Turkmen SSR and adjoining republics), Kara-kalpak (175,000, Karakalpak ASSR), Uzbek (over 6 m., Uzbek SSR and adjoining republics), Kazakh (3,750,000, Kazakh SSR and adjoining republics), Uigur (number unknown: 1959 census gave 95,000 in districts bordering on Sinkiang, but many are said to have recently crossed over from that province where the bulk of the Uigur population lives, numbering 3,640,000 according to the Chinese census of 1953), Kirghiz (1 m., Kirghiz SSR and adjoining republics), Altai (40,000, Gorno-Altai Autonomous Region), Khakass (50,000, Khakass Autonomous Region), Tuva (100,000, Tuva ASSR), Yakut (nearly 250,000, Yakut ASSR).

We refer, in conclusion, to one other pocket of Turkic speech in European Russia, known as Gagauzi, and used by some 125,000 persons living in the southern part of the Moldavian SSR and eastwards into the Ukraine near Odessa. This language was brought here in the years around 1800 from Bulgaria, to which country it had apparently been introduced from Turkey. Meanwhile it has become appreciably different from other Turkish and must now be regarded as a separate language especially as it has, in this century, become the vehicle of a modest literature.

Members of other linguistic families. Smaller families than Turkic are Mongol and Manchurian. The former is represented in Soviet Asia by one member only, Buryat (250,000, Buryat ASSR), but a second Mongol language is found in Europe, namely Kalmyk (125,000, Kalmyk ASSR), an enclave of comparatively recent origin, representing in fact the last incursion into Europe of nomads from Asia. Migrating from Dzungaria, this Mongol people crossed the Emba in 1636 to take possession of the steppe country north of the Caspian. They accepted Russian suzerainty in 1646. In 1771, the tribes living east of the Volga returned to China, leaving the present enclave. It is appropriate to mention here that Russian is particularly influential in the Mongolian Republic, where the official language, Mongolian, has since 1941 been commonly written in Cyrillic instead of the traditional, but cumbersome Uigur-Mongol script, of Sogdian origin (p. 236).

The Manchurian languages are dispersed over an immense tract of the Soviet Far East, but the total number of speakers does not exceed 45,000, the chief language being Evenki (25,000, Evenki National Area). An even smaller linguistic family is Chukotic, spoken from Chukotka to Kamchatka by under 20,000 souls, the chief representative being Chukcha (10,000, Chukcha National Area). Lastly, there are isolated languages spoken by diminutive populations. These are Gilyak (under 5,000, North Sakhalin and Lower Amur Valley) and, with a thousand speakers each, or less: Ainu (South

Sakhalin), Yukagir (Yukagir National Area), Ket (Central Siberia, along Yenisei); also miniscule Eskimo and Aleutian (extreme NE), see p. 116.

South of the Central Asiatic band of Turkic languages, the Indo-European family is represented by Tajiki and several other Iranian languages of long standing, also by recent Yiddish and German.

Caucasian. During the second half of the eighteenth century, Czarist expansion reached the North Caucasus, and from 1801 onwards districts belonging to the State of Georgia were annexed one after another. By 1865 Georgia had entirely lost the independence she had enjoyed from time immemorial. She regained it briefly in 1918, but became an integral part of the USSR in 1921. The northern half of Azerbaijan also fell to the Czar.

Knowledge of Russian spread rapidly in the towns in the newly acquired territory, in particular in Baku where a rising industry attracted Russian employees as well as masters. But generally speaking, the earlier populations have continued their traditional languages, especially in the countryside. But losses there have been. A minor language, Ubykh, has disappeared, most of its speakers having emigrated to Turkey. Altogether about a million North Caucasians, mainly speakers of Circassian, and Moslems like the Crimean Tartars, took the same course. But thanks to Soviet policies, no less than twelve indigenous languages of the area are today in regular literary use. Caucasian languages fall into two main divisions: northern and southern. There are similarities between the two, but also great differences. It is not yet possible to state whether the two divisions represent two distinct linguistic families drawn together through contact during millennia, or whether they are the divergent progeny of a single parent type. They are spoken by about five million people.

Georgian (2,750,000, Georgian SSR) with texts going back to the end of the fifth century is the chief representative of South Caucasian and serves as the literary language for speakers of the other, very minor, South Caucasian tongues. North Caucasian embraces two very distinct sections: eastern and western. The most significant language of the latter is Circassian (nearly 250,000, Karachay-Cherkess Autonomous Region and Kabardin-Balkar ASSR). To the former belong Chechen and Ingush (with over 400,000 and over 100,000 speakers respectively, (Chechen-Ingush ASSR) together with not less than twenty-seven other languages, twenty-six of them found in Daghestan, the numerically most important being Avar (nearly 250,000), Dargin (160,000) and Lezgin (110,000).

Other languages. Other tongues heard in the Caucasus belong to the Turkic family (see above), to which is to be added Azerì or Azerbaijani (3 m., Azerbaijan SSR), a language close to Turkmen; its speakers reached their present territory via Persia (see further p. 238). Indo-European other than Russian is represented in the Caucasus by Armenian and the Iranian languages Ossetic, Kurdish, Tati and Talishi. Lastly, Semitic is present in isolated pockets of Syrian, introduced by immigrants in the last century and spoken today by about 20,000 of their descendants.

Russification

The literary use of the multifarious languages referred to above has been, in the main, an achievement of the post-revolutionary era. Their official recognition by the Soviet government was a reaction against the repressive policies of Czarism and led to an unprecedented development of the languages concerned. Nevertheless, russification is continuing apace. Russian is, above all, the language of prestige. It plays a leading part in education in the non-Russian areas, where the intelligentsia at least is now bilingual. Although all the numerically significant non-Russian languages are fully recognised media in their respective localities, they are not exclusive, Russian being also official for all purposes. Where Russian immigration is considerable, the position of the regional language is de facto compromised. This is strikingly the case at the moment in Central Asia, whose under-populated areas have for some time been the scene of large-scale settlement from European Russia (see also p. 239).

Before the Revolution several languages had, under the influence of Islam, been written in Arabic script, but this was abolished in a flourish of romanisation. Many languages which had previously had no written form were similarly provided with a Latin alphabet. From the late thirties, however, Latin was replaced by Cyrillic. The only notable languages of the USSR not employing Cyrillic today are Armenian and Georgian, each with traditional alphabets of their own, and the languages of the Baltic republics, Lithuanian, Latvian and Estonian, also Finnish in Karelia, which keep the Latin alphabet.

Recent gains in the west

As a consequence of World War II the territory covered by Russian was very appreciably augmented in the west. The whole frontier from the Arctic to the Black Sea was advanced westward, the areas so gained being generally occupied by Russian speakers and the older populations resettled west of the new frontier. The annexation of the Baltic republics in 1940 prepared the way for the considerable Russian influx which has taken place since the end of the war. The same applies to Bessarabia and other smaller areas incorporated at the same time. We may add that, since 1945, Russian has become the chief foreign language to be taught in schools in a number of countries within the

Soviet orbit, as Poland, German Democratic Republic, Czechoslovakia, Hungary and Bulgaria.

WEST SLAVONIC

We have already seen how, by the middle of the sixth century, the Slavs had advanced to the Saale and Elbe. Disregarding minor Slavonic gains in the border zone, and deep but only temporary German inroads in the tenth century, the courses of these rivers marked the linguistic boundary until the second quarter of the twelfth century. The Slavonic tribes east of this line were known to the Germans collectively as Wends. These Wends became a sea power, too, and most likely in the eleventh or early twelfth centuries seized small areas on the southern coasts of Denmark, as a number of places called Vindeby, 'Wends' Village', conclusively proves. Nevertheless, from 1125 onwards, Wendish independence crumbled before the advancing Germans who, before the century was out, had reached the Oder and the delta of the Vistula. Germanisation of the conquered lands was thorough and, by the end of the Middle Ages, Slavonic had disappeared unrecorded from most of this territory.

All West Slavonic languages use the Latin alphabet; on the use of diacritics, see under 'Czech'.

Polabian

A diminutive islet of Elbe Slavonic or Polabian (*po* 'on', *Laba* 'Elbe') lingered on into the first decades of the eighteenth century. It was situated just west of the Elbe in the Lüneburg Wendland north of Salzwedel, comprising several villages along the Jeetze river. A modest number of texts and glossaries were taken by antiquarians from the end of the seventeenth century until the final extinction of the dialect. As these Polabians—they called themselves Wends—were concentrated in the stretch of country known as Drawähn, their dialect may be particularised as Dravaenic.

Upper and Lower Sorbian

Not surprisingly, Slavonic in Germany maintained itself better further east where indeed it is still found in an enclave in Lusatia, a province which, we may add, belonged to the Bohemian Crown from the fourteenth to the seventeenth centuries. The territory of the Lusatian Wends, or Sorbs as they are now officially called, occupies the major portion of the central part of the province. The towns in the area—Bautzen in the southern, Cottbus in the northern half—are German-speaking, Slavonic being confined to rural areas, but even here many villages are germanised or partly so.

Slavonic in Lusatia—it may be termed Sorbian or Lusatian as well as (Lusatian) Wendish—falls into two divergent dialect groups, southern and northern, a division as old as the period of settlement. Out of these have arisen two independent literary languages, Upper and Lower Sorbian, centring on Bautzen and Cottbus respectively. The earliest, very brief written record is a legal formula in Upper Sorbian from the beginning of the sixteenth century, the first literary attestation proper is a (manuscript) New Testament from 1548 in Lower Sorbian. Productions were broadly dialectal at first, but approximate standards for both varieties evolved in the eighteenth century. A modest literature, most of it religious, developed and continued fairly well at least in the Upper Sorbian area until 1937, when all publishing in Sorbian was prohibited. After the war, a policy without precedent in Germany has attempted to preserve the languages threatened with extinction. Legislation ended discrimination and Sorbian, in its two forms, became fully official. Sorbian-medium education, secondary as well as elementary, has led to an unparalleled output of printed material of all kinds.

The first census taken, in 1832, returned 130,000 Sorbian speakers. The number rose to 170,000 in the 1860s, but has declined since. It is at present probably considerably under 70,000, rather more than half using the southern form. Historically, Sorbian abutted onto the domains of Polish and Czech, but the connection had already been severed by the beginning of modern times. As one would expect, Sorbian has been excessively affected by the encompassing German.

Kashubian

Indigenous Slavonic has also survived in Further Pomerania, the former German province on the Baltic coast between the Oder and Vistula. The present territory of these Pomeranian Slavs, Kashubs as they call themselves, comprises no more than the north-eastern tip from Lake Leba to the southern outskirts of Gdynja (Gdingen). Its southern border is ill-defined, being followed by a broad band of transitional dialects, basically Kashubian, but already highly polonised. Due west of the present Kashubian area lies the district of Slupsk (Stolp), where autochthonous Slavonic survived until the end of the last century, when it was entirely supplanted by German; here the dialects were locally termed Slovinzian.

German has of course been the main enemy of Kashubian, and its survival for so long will be in part due to the fact that the area was often under Polish control, e.g., from 1466–1772. It formed part of the Polish Corridor between the Wars, and after 1945 again became Polish. Such events slowed down and in the end prevented total germanisation, though they encouraged polonisation and it is now clear that Kashubian will finally succumb to Polish. This language had, in fact, long been infiltrating from the south, intermingling with and sometimes replacing the German which to some extent had interposed itself between the two Slavonic languages at this point. The evacuations after the last war have removed the Germans from the entire area, so that Kashubian is now completely surrounded by Polish, which is of course the normal literary language of the Kashubian population also.

Essentially a patois, Kashubian never became a literary medium in the full sense of the word. However here, as elsewhere, the spirit of the Reformation prompted members of the clergy to express themselves in writing in the local language and a small amount of (noticeably polonised) Kashubian was composed in the sixteenth and seventeenth centuries, though most of it remained in manuscript. Only after the middle of the last century has any mentionable amount of publishing taken place, but even this has remained within a very limited compass. No improvement can be expected, rather the reverse, since Kashubian has no official standing. In the nature of the case, it is difficult to estimate the number of those who could be described as speaking Kashubian. We suggest 100,000 at the outside; a count at the turn of the century showed twice as many.

Polish

As early as the middle of the tenth century the Poles had developed a strong central authority which laid the basis for their state and with it their state language, now the native medium of 31 out of the $31\frac{1}{2}$ million inhabitants of the country. The present republic is the most linguistically homogeneous Polish state ever to have existed, but its territory is not entirely historical. This applies to the areas taken from Germany, most of which had never in any real sense been Polish. In these parts the German population, in so far as it had not already left, was removed and the land resettled by Poles, many of whom were themselves deportees from eastern districts ceded to the Soviet republics of the Ukraine, Belorussia and Lithuania.

Literature in Polish developed relatively late, the first known documents being sermons from the second half of the fourteenth century or a little before. In its formative period, Polish owed something to Czech which had developed a viable literary language somewhat earlier. The centre of Polish power was at first in the west, likely in Gniezno (Gnesen), later in Cracow, afterwards in Warsaw. The literary standard evolved essentially in Cracow, but was influenced by forms brought from the west. As a language within the Catholic cultural orbit, Polish had to contend with Latin, in the early period the only written medium.

Czech and Slovak

The Czechoslovak linguistic type constitutes a grouping within West Slavonic comparable to Sorbian or Polish. As early as the thirteenth century literary Czech had begun to develop on the basis of the Central Bohemian dialect of Prague, and in consequence the language was often termed Bohemian. The first texts are translations, especially of the psalter, but by the next century a fairly comprehensive secular literature had also come into existence. This literary language was quite independent of the Church Slavonic introduced into Moravia in the ninth century, for after the events of 885, Latin soon established itself as the language of the medieval Bohemian church and dominated in state affairs as it did in other western countries at the time.

Czech served equally as a literary medium for Slovakia also. Then, in the eighteenth century, the use of Czech seriously declined in favour of German. In Slovakia there was in any case competition from Hungarian as well—the country had formed part of the Kingdom of Hungary almost continuously since 1028—to say nothing of the considerable role that Latin played in the administration of that multilingual kingdom down to the first half of the last century. So it came about that from 1750 onwards publications in one or other of the Slovak dialects themselves first made their appearance. By the end of the century the idea of a Slovak literary language as opposed to Czech had been mooted and, borne along by the spirit of modern nationalism, quickly found widespread acceptance. By the middle of the last century, a literary Slovak, based on central dialects, was set up as a model for a future standard. In the prevailing circumstances, production in Slovak remained very limited, but the position changed radically in 1918. The constitution of the new republic declared the official language to be 'Czechoslovak', a term with no linguistic reality in the contemporary situation, and perforce interpreted as Czech in Bohemia and Moravia, but as Slovak in Slovakia. The latter now developed rapidly as a modern medium and standardisation has come much nearer. Proposals made between the Wars to merge Czech and Slovak came to nothing and the two languages continue to go their separate, though parallel ways, for the pressure is on keeping them as close together as possible. Thus there exists a kind of collaboration, in which Slovak is much the junior partner. It is occasionally pointed out, however, that the Slovaks are multiplying very much faster than the Czechs. Present figures are $9\frac{1}{2}$ million for Czech and 4 million for Slovak, compared with e.g. $8\frac{1}{2}$ million against 3 million twenty years ago.

The practice of adding diacritics ('accents') to existing Latin letters was invented by John Hus (1367–1415) to create a phonetic alphabet for Czech. He thus set a fashion destined to be widely copied. Czech has been greatly influenced by German. Even though the words themselves be pure Slavonic, loan translations and loan formations abound; and the general mode of expression is strikingly reminiscent of German.

SOUTH SLAVONIC

The Southern Slavs are those living in the Balkans; they are separated from their linguistic brethren to the north and east by German, Hungarian and Rumanian populations. They have developed four literary languages, as follows.

Slovene

Slovene is the official language of the Constituent Republic of Slovenia and spoken by considerably more than one and a half million persons. After World War I, 40 per cent of Slovenes found themselves in areas awarded to Italy, but frontier adjustments in 1945 united virtually all Slovene speakers in the present republic. The language is used as a patois by some few thousands across the Austrian border in Styria and Carinthia. Here Slovene has been in retreat both during and since the Middle Ages and seems doomed to extinction within a generation or two. The same will most likely apply to the small amount of Slovene still remaining on Italian soil.

Exceptional good fortune has preserved in the Freising Leaves—a few pages of religious matter—a unique record of Slovene as old as the eleventh century. A small number of religious texts are known from the Middle Ages, but not until the Reformation was there any notable cultivation of the language as a written medium. Secular literature developed from modest beginnings in the second half of the eighteenth century. Slovene employs the Latin alphabet. The language is germanised in much the same way as Czech.

Serbo-Croatian

Serbo-Croatian, the chief and state language of Yugoslavia 'South Slavia' nowadays sometimes popularly, but quite inaccurately called 'Yugoslav', is the native tongue of some fourteen and a half million persons. The creation of Yugoslavia in 1918 gave speakers of Serbo-Croatian their own state for the first time in history. Only a small minority remained outside the new frontiers, mostly on territory held by Italy. However, boundary changes (Istria, Dalmatian coast) to Yugoslavia's advantage in 1945 have altered this situation.

There are numerous dialects; they merge in the north-west into Slovene, in the south-east into Macedonian-Bulgarian. Out of forms spoken in the central area, a unified Serbo-Croatian language was created in the first half of the last century. Previously, regional types, in particular that of Dubrovnik (Ragusa), had been in use since the end of the fifteenth century; see further under 'Church Slavonic'. But the new standard was at once affected by provincial peculiarities, morphological as well as lexical, associated with the two rival cultural centres, Belgrade and Zagreb (Agram). As a consequence, two somewhat differentiated forms of the literary language are found today, Serbian and Croatian. Speakers will normally declare themselves to be using one or the other of these, the collective Serbo-Croatian being more of a linguist's term than a popular name. The distinction between the two styles is further underlined by the scripts, Serbian being written in Cyrillic, Croatian in Latin letters. The former is usual in Serbia and Montenegro, the latter in Croatia, while in Bosnia and Herzegovina both alphabets are common. It is difficult to quote figures for habitual users of Serbian as opposed to Croatian, but one may think in terms of about two to one in favour of the former. As a curiosity it may be mentioned that the language has occasionally been written in Arabic script—there are about a million Muslims in Yugoslavia.

It goes without saying that Serbo-Croatian, is widely employed as a second language, not only by the related Slavs in Yugoslavia, i.e., Slovenes and Macedonians, but also by the other national minorities, chief among whom are the Albanians and Hungarians.

Macedonian

The historic province of Macedonia seems to have always been a frontier zone, even in antiquity, as we saw in the discussion of the ancient Macedonian language (p. 6). In modern times the province has acquired a very mixed population. Beside the dominant Slavs, whose dialects are therefore properly called Macedonian, there were large non-Slavonic populations: Greeks, Arumanians (Vlachs), Albanians, Turks.

The Macedonian dialects are essentially Bulgarian, sharing with them the striking loss of case inflexion. Had all Macedonia been reunited with Bulgaria after the withdrawal of the Turks in 1913, then Standard Bulgarian would certainly have served the Macedonians as well. As it was, most of the province was divided between Serbia (later incorporated into Yugoslavia) and Greece. The territory falling to the latter included over 100,000 Slavonic speakers, but large numbers of these were subsequently able to join their fellow Slavs north of the border. In the meantime Greek Macedonia has been largely hellenised; the census of 1951 gave only 41,000 Slavs, doubtless a dwindling minority. The greatest concentration of Macedonian speakers was found in that part of the province which passed to Serbia. In 1945, this area became the Macedonian Constituent Republic of Yugoslavia with Macedonian as its official language. The number of speakers exceeds one million.

Macedonia was the cradle of literary Slavonic (see 'Church Slavonic'), and the language flourished in that province, then part of Bulgaria, from the end of the ninth century. The earliest record of the modern tongue is a glossary from 1764. There followed a small amount of literature published in various dialects, and often written in Greek letters. Literary activity increased greatly in the present century, the use of Cyrillic now becoming general. The official language follows a standard previously codified on the basis of the central dialects spoken around Prilep and Veles. It is close to Standard Bulgarian. The Republic of Macedonia still has significant linguistic minorities, especially Albanians and Turks, who may use Macedonian as a second language.

Bulgarian

About 680, the Bolgars or Bulgars, of mixed Turkic origin, crossed the Lower Danube and gained the leadership of the Slavonic population between that river and the Balkan Range, but were themselves eventually slavicised much as the Avars who assumed command of the Pannonian Slavs a century before. But the name of the Bulgars lived on. By the ninth century, Bulgarian power is seen to have expanded to incorporate much of the historic province of Macedonia, by this time predominantly Slavonic. However, the Bulgarian state proved unstable. Its territories were often seized by more powerful neighbours, and finally, by 1376, all had passed under the Turkish yoke, destined to last until 1878. But in the drawing and redrawing of frontiers that followed, Bulgaria never received more than a small part of Macedonia, with linguistic consequences described under 'Macedonian'.

We have already seen that Old Church Slavonic was founded on the usage of the Macedonian Slavs. During the period of prosperity from the end of the ninth to the beginning of the eleventh century, this language became the vehicle of a substantial religious literature in Bulgaria and may properly be called Old Bulgarian. The writing of Old Bulgarian continued for centuries afterwards, but in a corrupt and artificial form, see 'Church Slavonic'. Only towards the end of the eighteenth century did the living Bulgarian language appear again as a literary medium. Writing was of necessity dialectal at first, with Macedonians taking the lead. Finally a compromise form with elements from both east and west became the accepted standard.

Some seven and a half millions or 91 per cent of the population of Bulgaria speak the state language as their native tongue. It is of course also widely used by the national minorities, chiefly Turks and Gipsies.

Bulgarian (in the wider sense, including Macedonian) is unique among Slavonic languages in having, since the Middle Ages, lost its case inflexions.

THE STRUCTURE OF SLAVONIC

OLD CHURCH SLAVONIC

Phonetics

Vowels with a subscript hook are nasal; *ĭ, ŭ* are reduced vowels which may be pronounced as very short *i, u; y* is a sound between *i* and *u; e* is [ɛ], *i* is [ji] after vowels; *c, ch, j, c, š, ž* are pronounced [ts, χ, j, tʃ, ʃ, ʒ]. The accent is not marked, but was certainly movable as in some of the descendent languages, e.g., Russian.

Accidence

There are three genders and numbers and seven cases of nouns. No trace is found of IE **ekwos* 'horse', but the declensional type as such is clearly identifiable in spite of secondary changes, as follows:

Sg.nom.	*gradŭ* 'town'	Pl.	*gradi*	Du.	*grada*
voc.	*grade*		*gradi*		*grada*
acc.	*gradŭ*		*grady*		*grada*
gen.	*grada*		*gradŭ*		*gradu*
dat.	*gradu*		*gradomŭ*		*gradoma*
loc.	*gradě*		*graděchŭ*		*gradu*
inst.	*gradomĭ*		*grady*		*gradoma*

Adjectives follow comparable declensional schemes.

The verbal system of Indo-European has been drastically modified. There remain only three synthetic tenses of the indicative active, other tenses and the passive being formed periphrastically with *byti* 'to be' and various participles. Paradigms of *bĭrati* 'bear, take':

	Present	Imperfect	Aorist
Sg.1	*berǫ*	*bĭraachŭ*	*bĭrachŭ*
2	*bereši*	*bĭraaše*	*bĭra*
3	*beretŭ*	*bĭraaše*	*bĭra*
Pl.1	*beremŭ*	*bĭraachomŭ*	*bĭrachomŭ*
2	*berete*	*bĭraašete*	*bĭraste*
3	*berǫtŭ*	*bĭraachǫ*	*bĭrašę*
Du.1	*berevě*	*bĭraachově*	*bĭrachově*
2	*bereta*	*bĭraašeta*	*bĭrasta*
3	*berete*	*bĭraašete*	*bĭraste*

Imperf.sg. 2,3 *beri*, pl.1 *berimŭ*, 2 *berite*, du.1 *berivě*, 2 *berita*
Participles: (active) pres. *bery*, past (1) *bĭravŭ*, (2) *bĭralŭ*; (passive)
pres. *beromŭ*, past *bĭranŭ*. Supine *bĭratŭ*
   Numbers: 1 *jedinŭ*, 2 *dŭva*, 3 *trĭje*, 4 *četyre*, 5 *pętĭ*, 6 *šestĭ*, 7 *sedmĭ*,
8 *osmĭ*, 9 *devętĭ*, 10 *desętĭ*, 100 *sŭto*

Vocabulary
Typical elements include:

   OCS *gostĭ* 'stranger, guest': Eng. *guest* (OEng. *giest* 'stranger,
guest'), Lat. *hostis* 'stranger, enemy'
   OCS *sestra* 'sister': Lith. *sesuõ*, gen, *seseřs*, Goth. *swistar*, Lat.
soror, Ir. *siúr* ('sister in religion')
   OCS *bratrŭ* 'brother': Lith. *broterělis* (diminutive), Skt. *bhrǻtār-*,
Gk. *phrǻtēr* ('clansman'), Lat. *frāter*, Eng. *brother*, Ir. *bráthair*
('brother in religion')
   OCS *mĭgla* 'mist': Lith. *miglà*, Gk. *omíkhlē*
   OCS *noštĭ* 'night': Lith. *naktìs*, Skt. *nák*, pl. *naktîs*, Gk. *núx*, gen.
nuktós, Lat. *nox*, gen. *noctis*, Eng. *night*, Alban. *natë*, Welsh *nos*, cf.
Ir. *anocht* 'tonight'
   OCS *lěvŭ* 'left' (as opposed to 'right'): Gk. *laiós*, Lat. *laevus*
   OCS *sěditĭ* 'sits': Lith. *sědi*, Lat. *sedet*, Eng. *sits*

Text

Matthew vi.9–13

Otĭče našĭ iže   jesi na nebesĭchŭ: da   svętitŭ sę   imę   tvoje.
father our who art on heavens   may hallow itself name thy

Da   priidetŭ cěsarĭstvije tvoje. Da   bǫdetŭ volja tvoja, jako na
may come   kingdom   thy   may be   will thy   as   on

nebesi i   na zemlji. Chlěbŭ našĭ nastoję̆štajego dĭne
heaven and on earth   bread   our present   today ('daily')

daždĭ namŭ dĭnĭ sĭ.   I   otŭpusti namŭ dlŭgy našę, jako i   my
give us   day this and forgive us   debts our   as and we

otŭpuštajemŭ dlŭžĭnikomŭ našimŭ. I   ne vŭvedi   nasŭ vŭ
forgive   debtors   our   and not into-lead us   into

napastĭ   nŭ izbavi ny otŭ neprijazni (. . .)
temptation but deliver us from evil

RUSSIAN

Modern Slavonic languages are, by and large, rather conservative and Russian is no exception.

Phonetics

The acute accent (not ordinarily printed) marks the stress; *ë* is pronounced as though *jó*, ' denotes palatalisation of preceding consonant, other symbols as for Church Slavonic.

Accidence

The inflexions of noun and adjective are generally well preserved; the three genders remain. Apart from the vocative, the ancient cases survive, but the dual number has disappeared. Paradigm:

Sg.nom.acc. *górod* 'town', gen. *góroda*, dat. *górodu*, loc. *górode*, inst. *górodom*, pl.nom.acc. *gorodá*, gen. *gorodóv*, dat. *gorodám*, loc. *gorodách*, inst. *gorodámi*

The inflexions of the verb, too, are well preserved, though again the dual number has gone. However, the structure of the verb has been greatly modified, for the imperfect and aorist have been replaced by a periphrasis based on the verb 'to be' and a participle. As the auxiliary itself has disappeared in Russian, the past tense behaves like an adjective—it has no personal endings, but inflects for gender and number. OCS *bĭrati* appears as *brat'* 'take', the inflected forms being:

Pres.sg.1 *berú*, 2 *berës'*, 3 *berët*, pl.1 *berëm*, 2 *berëte*, 3 *berút*
Imperf.sg. *berí*, pl. *beríte*
Past tense: sg.m. *bral*, f. *bralá*, n. *brálo*, pl. *bráli*
Participles: passive pres. *berúščij*, past *brávšij;* active forms only adverbial: pres. *berjá*, past *bráv(ši)*
Numbers: 1 *odín*, 2 *dva*, 3 *tri*, 4 *četýre*, 5 *pjat'*, 6 *šest'*, 7 *sem'*, 8 *vósem'*, 9 *dévjat'*, 10 *désjat'*, 100 *sto*

Vocabulary

A large amount of Common Slavonic vocabulary has been preserved. Thus the examples of OCS on p. 165 are in Russian: *gost'* 'guest', *sestrá* 'sister', *brat* 'brother', *mgla* 'mist', *noč* 'night', *lev* 'left', *sidít* 'sits'. Doublets sometimes occur through borrowing from Church Slavonic, as *-grad* <OCS *gradŭ* beside native *górod*.

Texts

From the short story *Čem Ljúdi žívy* ('What men live by')
by L. N. Tolstoi

Eščë púšče vzjálo zlo Matrënu.
still   more took   evil Matryona ('still greater rage filled M.')

"Ne dárom ne chotéla   za tebjá, p'jánicu, zámuž   idtí.
not in-vain not (I) wished for you   drunkard for-husband to-go
('I had good grounds for not wanting to marry you, you drunkard')

Mátuška mne cholstý otdalá— ty   própil;   pošël   šúbu
mother me linen gave   you drank (it) (you) went fur-coat

kupít'— própil."   *Chóčet Semën rastolkovát' žené,   čto*
to buy   (you) drank (it) wishes Simon to-explain to-wife that

própil on tól'ko dvádcat' kopéek.   Ne daët emú Matrëna
drank he only   twenty   copecks (worth) not gives him M.

slóva   vstávit'. Govoríla, govoríla Matrëna, podskočíla k Semënu
of-word to-get-in talked   talked   M.   rushed   at S.

schvatíla egó na rukáv. "Daváj   poddëvku-to mojú.   A
seized   him on sleeve give (me) jacket-this   my ('of mine') for

tó odná ostálas'. Daváj sjudá,   konopátyj   pës,
this alone remained give   here (you) pock-marked mongrel,

postrél   tebyá rasšibí."
apoplexy you   strike ('strike you')

MODERN SLAVONIC LANGUAGES
(The Paternoster)

EAST SLAVONIC

Russian

Ótče naš, súščij na nebesách: da svjatítsja ímja tvojë. Da prijdjët
father our being on heavens   be-hallowed name thy   may-come

cárstvie tvojë. Da búdet vólja tvojá i   na zemlé, kak na nébe.
kingdom thy   may-be will thy and on earth as on heaven

Chleb naš nasúščnyj daj nam sej den'. I prostí nam dolgí náši,
bread our daily   give us this day and forgive us   debts our

kak i   my proščáem dolžnikám nášim. I   ne vvedí   nas v
as and we forgive debtors   our   and not into-lead us into

iskušénie, no izbáv' nas ot   lukávogo. Íbo tvojë jest' cárstvo
temptation but deliver us from evil   for thine is   kingdom

i síla i sláva vo véki.
and power and glory into ages

Ukrainian

9 *Otče naš, ščo na nebi: nechaj svjatyt' sja imja tvoje.*
10 *Nechaj pryjde carstvo tvoje. Nechaj bude volja tvoja, jak na nebi tak i na zemlji.*
11 *Chlib naš ščodennyj daj nam s'ɵhodnji.*
12 *I prosty nam dovhy naši, ja i my prošajemo dovžnykam našym.*
13 *I ne vvedy nas u spokusu, a izbavy nas ot lukavoho. Bo tvoje jest' carstvo j syla j slava po viky.*

Belorussian

9 *Ojča naš, katory jëść u nebe: śvjacisja imja tvajë.*
10 *Pryjdzi valadarstva tvajë. Budź volja tvaja, jak na nebe tak i na zjamli.*
11 *Chleba našaga štodzjënnaga daj nam cjënnja.*
12 *I adpuści nam grachi našy, jak i my adpuščaem vinavatym našym.*
13 *I nja ŭvodź nas u spakusu, ale zbaŭ nas ad zloga. Tvajë bo jëść valadarstva i sila i slava na veki večnyja.*

WEST SLAVONIC

Czech

9 *Otče náš, kterýž jsi v nebesích: posvěť se jméno tvé.*
10 *Přiď království tvé. Buď vůle tvá jako v nebi tak i na zemi.*
11 *Chléb náš vezdejší dej nám dnes.*
12 *A odpusť nám viny naše, jakož i my odpouštíme vinníkům našim.*
13 *I neuvoď nás v pokušení, ale zbav nás od zlého. Nebo tvé jest království i moc i sláva na věky.*

Slovak

9 *Otče náš, ktorý si v nebesiach: posväť sa meno tvoje.*
10 *Príď kráľovstvo tvoje. Buď vôľa tvoja ako v nebi tak i na zemi.*
11 *Chlieb náš vezdejší daj nám dnes.*
12 *A odpusť nám viny naše, ako aj my odpúšťame vinnikom svojim.*
13 *I neuvoď nás v pokušenie, ale zbav nás od zleho. Lebo tvoje je kráľovstvo i moc i sláva na veky.*

Upper Sorbian

9 *Naš wótče, kiž sy ty w njebjesach: swjećene budź twoje mjeno.*
10 *Přindź k nam twoje kralestwo. Twoja wola so stań, kaž na njebju tak též na zemi.*
11 *Naš wšědny chlěb daj nam džensa.*
12 *A wodaj nam naše winy, jako my wodawamy našim winikam.*
13 *A njewjedź nas do spytowanja, ale wumož nas wot teho złeho. Přetož twoje je to kralestwo a ta móc a ta česć haš do wěčnosće.*

Lower Sorbian

9 *Wošc naš, kenž sy na njebju: huswěšone buži twojo mě.*
10 *Twojo kralejstwo pšiži. Twoja wola se stani, ako na njebju tak též na zemi.*
11 *Naš wšedny klěb daj nam žěnsa.*
12 *A wodaj nam naše winy, ako my wodawamy našym winikam.*
13 *A njewjeź nas do spytowanja, ale humož nas wot togo złego. Pšeto twojo jo to kralejstwo a ta moc a ta cesć do nimjernosći.*

Polish

9 *Ojcze nasz, któryś jest w niebiesiech: święć się imię twoje.*
10 *Przyjdź królestwo twoje. Bądź wola twoja, jako w niebie tak i na ziemi.*
11 *Chleba naszego powszedniego daj nam dzisiaj.*
12 *I odpuść nam nasze winy, jako i my odpuszczamy naszym winowajcom.*
13 *I nie wódź nas w pokuszenie, ale nas zbaw ode złego. Albowiem twoje jest królestwo i moc i chwała na wieki.*

Kashubian

9 *Wójcze nasz, chteri jes v njebjesech: svjęce sę jimję twóje.*
10 *Przindze krolestwo twóje. Będze wólo twója, jak v njebje tak na zemji.*

11   *Chleba naszeho povszedneho daj nom dzis.*
12   *A wódpusce nom nasze vjine, jak e me wódpuszczome naszim*
     vjinovajcom.
13   *A njewódze nas na pokuszenje, ale nas zbavji wóde złeho (. . .)*

Polabian

9   *Nos fader, tå tåi jis vå něbiśai, sjǫtă vårdă tüji jaimă.*
10   *Tüjă rik komă. Tüjă viłă šinót, kok vå něbiśai, tok kăk no zimě.*
11   *Nosěj věsědanesnă st'aibě doj-năm dans.*
12   *Un vitědoj-năm nos grex, kăk moi vitědojimě nosěm gresnărüm.*
13   *Un ni brind'oj nos kå farsükoňě, tåi lözoj nos vit věsokăg ẋaudăg*
     (. . .)

SOUTH SLAVONIC

Slovene

9   *Oče naš, ki si na nebesih: posveti se ime tvoje.*
10   *Pridi kraljestvo tvoje. Zgodi se volja tvoja, kakor na nebu tudi na*
     zemlji.
11   *Kruh naš vsakdanji daj nam danes.*
12   *In odpusti nam dolge naše, kakor tudi mi odpuščamo dolžnikom*
     svojim.
13   *In ne vpelji nas v izkušnjavo, nego reši nas zlega. Ker tvoje je*
     kraljestwo in moč in slava na vekomaj.

Serbo-Croat

9   *Oče naš koji si na nebesima: da se sveti ime tvoje.*
10   *Da dodje carstvo tvoje. Da bude volja tvoja, i na zemlja kao na*
     nebu.
11   *Hljeb naš potrebni daj nam danas.*
12   *I oprosti nam dugove naše, kao i mi što opraštamo dužnicima*
     svojijem.
13   *I ne navedi nas u napast, no izbavi nas oda zla. Jer je tvoje carstvo*
     i sila i slava u vijek.

Macedonian

9   *Oče naš, što si na neboto: da se sveti tvoeto ime.*
10   *Da dojde tvoeto carstvo. Da bide tvojata volja, kako na neboto*
     taka i na zemjata.
11   *Lebot naš nasušen daj ni go deneska.*

12 *I prosti ni gi dolgovite, kako i nie što im gi proštavame na našite dolžnici.*

13 *I ne vovedubaj ne vo iskušenie, tyky izbavi ne od zloto (. . .)*

Bulgarian

9 *Otče naš, kojto si na nebesata: da se sveti tvoeto ime.*

10 *Da dojde tvoeto carstvo. Da băde tvojata volja kakto na nebeto tăj i na zemjata.*

11 *Nasăštnija ni chljab daj ni dnes.*

12 *I prosti nam dălgovete ni, kakto i nie proštavame na dlăžnicite si.*

13 *I ne văvedi nas v izkušenie, no izbavi ni ot lukavia. Zaštoto tvoe e carstvo i silata i slavata vo veki.*

THRACO-PHRYGIAN

Thraco-Phrygian is the term used to denote a group of languages whose earliest known homeland was South-East Europe. Three languages are distinguished: Thracian, Phrygian and Armenian. The first two have long been extinct and left but meagre traces of their former glory, but Armenian is still a flourishing language. The Ancient Greeks described the Armenian tongue as being similar to Phrygian, and the Phrygians, they said, were originally a Thracian tribe. Modern comparative philology has tended to accept these statements as a working hypothesis, though the character of the Armenian language as we know it and the exiguous nature of the Thracian and particularly of the Phrygian records are such that the postulated relationship cannot, strictly speaking, be demonstrated scientifically.

Thracian

At the time of its greatest known extent, in antiquity, Thracian was spoken throughout the eastern half of the Balkan Peninsula and stretched northwards into the Central European Plain. From the evidence of proper names it is possible to delimit approximately the area in which the language was used. Its frontiers ran from the Bosphorus to the mouth of the Dniestr, thence northwards as far as the Carpathians between the upper reaches of the Sereth and Theiss, turning south to cross the Danube about thirty miles east of Belgrade, passing through Nish and Skopje and down the valley of the Vardar to the Gulf of Salonica. The islands of Samos and Samothrace were Thracian, and so were Mysia and Bithynia across the Hellespont in Asia Minor. There were also several enclaves of Thracian speech far inside Greece, for instance in Boeotia, the Thracians here being colonists. Thracian was thus in contact with Greek in Europe and with Greek and other (unknown) languages in Asia Minor. Its neighbour to the west was Illyrian, to the north possibly Slavonic, to the east Iranian.

The surviving records of the Thracian language, which cover a period from Homer to the early Middle Ages, consist of a large number of proper names, a few glosses, a list of plant names and two inscriptions in Greek letters, of the fourth or fifth centuries B.C., giving twenty five words altogether. The character of the material precludes much discussion on the dialects of Thracian. Occasionally such terms as Bithynian, Mysian, or Samothracian are used in reference to names or glosses, but these are to be understood as dialects of Thracian. As for the Thracian spoken in Europe, modern research has identified one or two features which seem to distinguish the dialect of Dacia (the area north of the Danube) from the dialect of Thrace proper (south of the Danube), so that it has become usual to speak of Dacian as opposed to Thracian. The two may be referred to jointly as Daco-Thracian. Recently, a number of appellatives in Rumanian have been interpreted as Dacian. It is unlikely that the Slavonic languages now spoken in the area will offer anything comparable, as they arrived too late to be affected, at least not appreciably, but it is not improbable that a considerable Thracian element went into the making of Albanian.

The Thracians appear to have been expansive in Asia Minor until the middle of the first millennium B.C. Shortly afterwards, they began to come strongly under Greek influence. When, in 400 B.C., Xenophon and his Greeks made common cause with the Thracian king Seuthes, we read that an interpreter was sent to open negotiations, but later on in the account Seuthes is described as able to understand most of what was being said in Greek. From about this time, a knowledge of Greek must have spread rapidly among the Thracians. On the evidence of archaeology, they must have adopted Greek as their literary language, for inscriptions found in Thracian parts from about this period on are in Greek. The seaports in the Thracian-speaking areas were often Greek foundations and served as focal points for hellenisation. The second enemy of Thracian was Latin. In the year A.D. 9, Rome created the province of Moesia, in 46 the province of Thracia, each with a Roman administration. The country was thus wide open to romanisation also. Dacia was conquered in 107 and Roman colonists settled there in such numbers that the native language must soon have been hard pressed (see 'Rumanian').

How long the Thracian language continued in use we cannot say. Chrysostom in the fourth century speaks of the Thracians as possessing Christian literature in their own language, but the passage smacks of rhetorical exaggeration. However, a monk Theodosios (died 539) reports that he built a chapel in which certain of the Bessoi recited their prayers in their own language; the home of the Bessoi was the Rhodope Mountains in Thrace. In Asia Minor, Mysian is said to have been a living language in the sixth century.

The IE character of Thracian is clear from items of vocabulary, e.g. *pinon* '(barley) drink', cf. Alban. *pinë*, OCS *pivo* 'drink', further Gk. *pínō* '(I) drink', *pōma*, *pósis* 'drink'. Geographical names may point to IE affinities, e.g. *Strumṓn* (now *Struma*), cf. Eng. *stream*, Latv. *straume*, 'river', Ir. *sruaim* 'stream', Gk. *rheûma* 'a flowing'. Thus *Strumṓn* may be plausibly explained as meaning simply 'river', exactly as English (originally Celtic) *Avon*, cf. Welsh *afon* 'river'. Personal names are frequently evidence of IE connections. Even though the etymology of these names is usually quite elusive, the mode of composition is at once seen to be typically IE. One of the commonest Thracian names, *Bithys* (with several variants) is recorded more than 300 times in Greek and Latin sources. It readily formed compounds, e.g., the names *Asa-bithys*, *Di-beithys*, *Bithi-centus*, *Beithy-tralis*.

Phrygian

The Phrygians were the first people in the western half of Asia Minor to build a state of respectable proportions after the collapse of the Hittite Empire. They occupied the highland zone with Gordion as their centre. The older form of the language, Early or Old Phrygian, survives in nearly 25 short inscriptions of doubtful date (perhaps eighth to sixth centuries B.C.) written in an alphabet of an archaic Greek type. A more recent form of the language, Late or New Phrygian, is found in about a hundred inscriptions in the Greek alphabet dating from the first three centuries A.D. The texts, however, are monotonous, consisting principally of maledictory formulae which accompany the otherwise Greek inscriptions found in burial chambers. The following is an average example: *ios ni semoun knoumanei kakoun addaket etittetikmenos eiton*, which on the strength of a Greek parallel (*tìs dè taútēi thalámein kakòn pospoiěsei katēraménos ětó*) has been interpreted 'who, however, causes damage to this grave shall be cursed'. Among the Phrygian words, *knoumenai* is seen from other sources to be the dative of *knouma* 'grave' and *kakoun* 'damage', lit. 'evil, bad', may be regarded as the equivalent of Gk. *kakón* (perhaps a loan word from this language). Having got so far, it can be argued that *ios* must be the Phrygian reflex of the IE relative pronoun **yos*, otherwise seen e.g., in Skt. *yáh*, Gk. *hós*. Judging by the general use of Greek in their inscriptions at this period, the Phrygians were becoming bilingual, which would be the prelude to hellenisation.

In addition to the inscriptions, numerous Phrygian names and several glosses have come down to us. Philologically speaking, nearly all this material is highly problematic. Its interpretation is not made easier by the fact that the Greeks (who report the names and glosses) sometimes used the term Phrygian to include peoples ethnically distinct from the Phrygians proper.

ARMENIAN

The Pre-Armenians have been identified with the eastern group of a people, known to cuneiform records as *Muski*, who reached the Upper Euphrates at the beginning of the twelfth century. These are thought to have formed part of a wave of Thraco-Phrygian invasion across the Hellespont and through Asia Minor. As Thraco-Phrygians are never mentioned in the Hittite records it seems likely that they were the barbarians responsible for the destruction of the Hittite capital Hattusa about 1200 B.C. It is supposed that the Armenians existed as a separate ethnic group before the sixth century when the name *arminiya-* first occurs in inscriptions.

The present-day Armenians are, however, not the descendants of the *Muski* only. The IE immigrants imposed their language on both Hurrians and Urartians and doubtless these non-IE peoples are ulti-mately responsible for many of the peculiar and unexplained features of Armenian. Furthermore, at the time of the glottogonic process which resulted in the emergence of Armenian, Anatolian was still being spoken in adjacent territories to the west; perhaps Armenian owes something to Anatolian, too. The Armenian calls himself *Hay* (pl. *Hayk'*); it has been suggested that this name may continue *hatti-* 'Hittite'. In Georgian, however, the name for the Armenians is *Samekhi* (where *Sa-* is a prefix), which can hardly be separated from *Muski* of the cuneiform tablets. It seems possible to account for *Muski* (pl.) as a formation based on the geographical name which occurs in the Balkans as Moesia and in Asia Minor as Mysia. Remarkably enough, *Muski* appears to contain, as the sign of the plural, the suffix *-ki*, making it the prototype of the Armenian plural ending *-k'*, the provenance of which has always been such a mystery.

Armenian was, from an early date, subject to Iranian influence. The country was annexed by the Medes and by their successors the Persians until the destruction of the Persian Empire by Alexander in 330 B.C. From A.D. 66 until 387, Armenia was ruled by a Parthian dynasty (the Arsacids), when the country was divided between Persia and Byzantium. The last Arsacid was dethroned in 428 and the Persian part of Armenia was under Persian margraves until the end of the Sasanid Empire in 642. Especially during these last six cen-turies, Armenian adopted an immense number of words of Iranian provenance. It lost much of its older vocabulary in the process, reducing the original Thraco-Phrygian element to some nine hundred root words, say 10 per cent of the basic word stock. In fact, this foreign influence is so pervasive that early scholars (since Petermann 1837) were misled into classifying Armenian as an aberrant Iranian language until Hübschmann, in 1877, showed that the Iranian features were due to borrowing and that Armenian belonged to another branch of IE.

Old and Middle Armenian

Old Armenian is the language of a large number of texts produced, according to tradition, in the Armenian Golden Age, the first six decades of the fifth century A.D. They are written in an alphabet which has ever since remained the national alphabet of the Armenians. It is said to have been invented by St Mesrob, presumably at the beginning of the Golden Age. The works bear a mainly religious character and are principally translations: first and foremost the classical version of the Bible, then translations from Greek and Syriac (a West Semitic language) at that time the cultural languages of Eastern Christianity.

Old Armenian is an exceptionally uniform language; it is believed to have been based on the dialect of the Tarawn district by Lake Van. Although the spoken language subsequently underwent considerable changes, works continued to be composed in a language modelled on the classical style; such works could, however, only be understood by an élite. As early as the tenth century, the living language must have become considerably differentiated from this written style as solecisms in contemporary texts indicate. From this time onwards until the fifteenth century, we speak of Middle Armenian. This stage is attested chiefly in the rich profane literature of the immigrant Armenians in Cilicia who set up a kingdom which lasted from 1198 to 1375, where Armenian was the language of court and chancery. This colonial Armenian did not differ greatly from the language of Armenia proper, but as a western dialect it had taken part in the second Armenian sound shift by which *b, d, g* became *p, t, k* and vice versa. Thus the native form of the name of the Armenian king transcribed *Tigran* is so pronounced in Eastern Armenian (east of Erzurum), but becomes [dikran] in Western Armenian (Erzurum and westwards).

Modern Armenian

With the collapse of the Kingdom of Cilicia, written Middle Armenian came to an abrupt end and was soon forgotten. The Armenians were now everywhere under harsh foreign rule. Only in the seventeenth and eighteenth centuries did something like a cultural revival set in.

But this renaissance found its literary medium not in any dialect of contemporary Armenian but, following the old tradition, in a form which stood above all the spoken dialects, namely the strict classical tongue, even though this was no longer comprehensible without considerable study and application. Then, at the beginning of the nineteenth century, a movement developed which propagated the use of Modern Armenian as the ordinary literary medium. There ensued a struggle between the *grabareanner*, the supporters of the *grabar* or 'written form', and the *ašxarhabareanner*, the partisans of the *ašxarhabar* or 'secular form'. By the middle of the century, the latter had clearly won the day. But which dialect of Armenian was to be the basis of the new literary form?

Political events turned out to be decisive. In 1801, Russia had annexed Transcaucasia with the result that a very large number of Eastern Armenians became subjects of the Czar; most of the others were still to be found within the Ottoman-controlled lands. Mounting tension between Turkey and Russia inevitably tended to emphasise the differences between Western and Eastern Armenian. In the west, the dialect of the influential Armenian colony in Constantinople, in the east the dialect of the Ararat region gave rise to two distinct literary languages, sometimes spoken of as Turkish and Russian Armenian. Linguistically speaking, the former is somewhat more archaic than the latter, but nevertheless both literary languages are close enough to enable readers of one to follow the other easily. The differences between them are of the same order as, say, between Irish and Scottish Gaelic.

Emigration from the barren highlands of their original home has been a feature of Armenian life since the twelfth century at least. So it came about that Armenians are found scattered throughout Byzantine lands and even beyond, for instance in Polish Galicia. Others emigrated eastwards as far as India. The majority of Armenians eventually lived under Turkish rule. But they remained staunch Christians. Those in the diaspora, usually the more prosperous, maintained a strong, introvert communal life which enabled them, Jew-like, to preserve their national identity among the Muslim majority. At the same time, their separateness made them an obvious target for attack. Towards the end of the last century, they had the misfortune to become involved in big-power rivalries, the upshot of which was the massacre or dispersal of the greater part of the Armenians in Turkey. Hitherto, Western Armenian had been the more influential literary dialect, but now the balance was radically altered. Furthermore, in 1920, Eastern Armenian became the official language of the newly-formed Armenian Republic, which in 1922 became part of the Soviet Union.

Eastern Armenian is the native language of 85 per cent of the population of the Armenian SSR. Armenians also live in adjacent areas, especially in Georgia with a large colony in the capital Tbilisi (Tiflis). Smaller groups are found in North-West Iran, mainly in the province of Azerbaidjan. A few thousand live in India. Western Armenian dialects are spoken in Erzurum, Sivas, Van, Diyar Bekir and in other localities in Turkey, especially Istanbul; further in Syria and Lebanon, as well as by Armenian emigrants throughout the world. It is estimated that Armenian is known to more than three million people, of whom 1,100,000 live in the Armenian SSR. It is to be expected that the total number of Armenian speakers will, for some time to come, continue to decline. Whereas the language is so far secure in the Armenian SSR, the outlook for Armenian elsewhere, especially for Western Armenian, is not auspicious. Its speakers are scattered far and wide, the great majority are bilingual; in modern conditions they cannot hope to resist linguistic assimilation for long. Meanwhile the language is strongest in the Lebanon, where the influential Armenian community numbers 200,000.

THE STRUCTURE OF ARMENIAN

OLD ARMENIAN

Phonetics

The sounds of Old Armenian are inferred from the pronunciation of the modern language and from such information as can be deduced from the texts themselves, e.g., from the form of loan words. The following values of the transliteration current in philological works should be noted:

$p^{'}$, $t^{'}$, $k^{'}$ are aspirated p, i.e. $p + h$, etc.

c is pronounced [ts] and $\check{c}$ [tʃ]; ς and $\check{\varsigma}$ are the corresponding aspirates, i.e. $c + h$, etc.

$\check{s}$ [ʃ], $\check{z}$ [ʒ], j [dz], $\check{j}$ [dʒ], x [χ], l an undetermined form of l, r as in 'run' distinct from $\dot{r}$ which is strongly rolled.

Difference in vowel quantity has apparently disappeared: $\bar{e}$ represents closed e and $\bar{o}$ closed o. When initial, e and o are pronounced as ye and wo.

The stress falls uniformly on the final syllable.

Accidence

There is no grammatical gender. Nouns and adjectives have two numbers and seven cases, but in all declensions originally different

endings have to a considerable extent fallen together. Several termina-
tions are philologically problematic. Sample paradigm:

Sg.nom.	cer 'old (man)'	Pl.	cerk'
acc.loc.	cer		cers
gen.dat.abl.	ceroy		ceroç
inst.	cerov		cerovk'

The direct object may be denoted by the prefix z (really a preposition
'about, concerning'): haç 'bread', acc. zhaç.

There are no articles proper in Old Armenian.

There are three inflected tenses, both indicative and subjunctive:
present, imperfect and aorist. There is a passive voice, though the
forms are only partly distinct from those of the active. Original IE
endings have often been replaced by formations mostly of obscure
origin. Sample paradigm (indic. active):

Pres.sg.1	berem '(I) bear'	Imperf.	berei	Aor.	beri
2	beres		bereir		berer
3	berē		berēr		eber
pl.1	beremk'		bereak'		berak'
2	berēk'		bereik'		berēk'
3	beren		berein		berin

The aor.subj. very often functions as a fut.indic. and may be so
designated: sg.1 beriç, 2 berçes, 3 berçē, pl.1 berçuk', 2 berǰik', 3 berçen

Vocabulary

Armenian has lost by far the greater part of its IE lexicon. The oldest
language already contains loan words from Syriac, Greek and especially Persian (pp. 175f.). A considerable number of words are of unknown provenance, some of which are doubtless Urartian or Hurrian.
Nevertheless, some 900 root words have been provided with an IE
etymology. The outward appearance of these words has been significantly modified, the consonants, for instance, having been affected
by changes almost as extensive as in Germanic, known as the first
Armenian sound shift. The following give some idea of the nature
of the IE element:

kov 'cow': Eng. cow, Ir. bó, further with general sense of 'head of
cattle' Skt. gáús, Gk. boũs, Lat. bõs (all forms from an IE initial gw-)

hur 'fire': Gk. pũr, Umbrian pir, Hitt. pahhur, Eng. fire

li 'full': Gk. pléōs, cf. also Lat. plēnus, etc. (p. 80)

loys 'light': Lat. lūx, Ir. lóiche, Russ. luč ('ray of light'), Icel. logi
('flame')

mayr 'mother': Skt. mātár-, Gk. mḗtēr, Lat. māter, Ir. máthair, Eng.
mother, Toch. A mācar, B mācer, Russ. mat', gen. máteri

Numbers: 1 *mi*, 2 *erku*, 3 *erekʿ*, 4 *čorkʿ*, 5 *hing*, 6 *veç*, 7 *ewtʿn*, 8 *utʿ*, 9 *inn*, 10 *tasn*, 100 *hariwr*

Text

Matthew vi.9–13

Hayr mer or   erkins: surb eliçi   anun kʿo. Ekesçē
father our which in-heaven holy become name thy   come

arkʿayutʿiwn kʿo. Eliçin   kamkʿ kʿo orpēs erkins   ew erkri.
kingdom   thy become will   thy as   in-heaven and on-earth

Zhaç mer hanapazord tur mez aysōr. Ew tʿol   mez zpartis
bread our daily   give us this-day and forgive us   debts

mer, orpēs ew mekʿ tʿolumkʿ meroç partapanaç. Ew mi tanir zmez
our as   and we forgive our   debtors   and not lead us

i   pʿorjutʿiwn, ayl pʿrkea zmez i   čarēn. Zi kʿo ē arkʿayutʿiwn
into temptation but deliver us   from evil   for thy is kingdom

ew zōrutʿiwn ew pʿarkʿ yawiteans.
and power   and glory for-ever

MODERN ARMENIAN

The forms quoted in the following outline are those of the literary language of the Armenian SSR, i.e., Modern Eastern Armenian.

Phonetics

v and *w* have fallen together as *v*, but (the ligature) *ew* [jev] is still written. *e* and *ē* and *o* and *ō* have fallen together giving a compromise quality, half-open, half-closed: *e, o*. The spellings *ē* and *ō* are retained in initial position (and in composition) where the pronunciation is [e] and [o], since *e* and *o*, when initial, are pronounced [je] and [vo]. *l* is the voiced velar fricative [ɣ].

Accidence

The declension of nouns continues, though the endings have greatly changed; in particular a new locative has established itself.

Sg.nom.acc.	*cer* 'old man'	Pl.	*cerer*
gen.dat.	*ceri*		*cereri*
abl.	*ceriç*		*cereriç*
inst.	*cerov*		*cererov*
loc.	*cerum*		*cererum*

The adjectives are now uninflected: *cer* 'old'.

Modern Armenian has evolved articles. The definite article takes the form of an unstressed suffix, usually *-ə: cerə*, sometimes *n*. The indefinite article is *mə* which follows its noun: *cer mə*.

Numbers: 1 *mek*, 2 *erku*, 3 *erekʿ*, 4 *čors*, 5 *hing*, 6 *veç*, 7 *yotʿ*, 8 *utʿ*, 9 *inn*, 10 *tasə*, 100 *hariwr*

While retaining several features of the old language such as the subjunctive mood and the passive voice, Modern Armenian has largely remodelled the classical verbal system. In Eastern Armenian, for instance, the present and imperfect are now formed periphrastically: *berum em* '(I) bring' lit. 'at-bringing am', *berum ēi* '(I) brought' lit. 'at-bringing was', where *-um* is the locative inflection. On the other hand, the aorist and a future tense are still formed synthetically, the latter also taking a prefix *k-*. Paradigms:

Pres.sg.1	*berum em*	Imperf.sg.1	*berum ēi*
2	*berum es*	2	*berum ēir*
3	*berum ē*	3	*berum ēr*
pl.1	*berum enkʿ*	pl.1	*berum ēinkʿ*
2	*berum ekʿ*	2	*berum ēikʿ*
3	*berum en*	3	*berum ēin*

Aor.sg.1	*bereçi*	Fut.sg.1	*kberem*
2	*bereçir*	2	*kberes*
3	*bereç*	3	*kberi*
pl.1	*bereçinkʿ*	pl.1	*kberenkʿ*
2	*bereçikʿ*	2	*kberekʿ*
3	*bereçin*	3	*kberen*

Vocabulary

Although modern literary Armenian has drawn freely upon the copious word stock of the older language, it has been naturally influenced by neighbouring languages. In the case of Soviet Armenian, calques on Russian are exceptionally common and, in the nature of the case, inevitable, e.g., *xosum ē Erevanə* 'Erevan calling' lit. 'speaks E.', cf. Russ. *govorít Moskvá* 'Moscow calling' (*govorít* 'speaks').

7

Texts

Matthew vi.9–13

Modern Eastern Armenian

Mer hayr   or   erknkʻumn   es: surb lini kʻo anunə.   Ga   kʻo
our father which in-heaven-the art holy be thy name-the come thy

tʻagavorutʻyunə. Lini kʻo kamkʻə inčpes erknkʻum aynpes ew
kingdom-the   be   thy will-the as   in-heaven so   and

erkrum. Mer amenōrya haçə   aysōr   ēl   mez tur. Ew mer
in-earth our daily   bread-the this-day still us   give and our

partkʻerə nerir, inčpes or   menkʻ enkʻ nerum   mer
debts-the forgive as   which we   are at-forgiving our

partapannerin. Ew mez pʻorjankʻi meǰ mi tanir, ayl čariç
debtors-the   and us temptation in not lead but from-evil

azatir. Orovhetew kʻonnē tʻagavorutʻyunə ew zorutʻyunə ew
deliver for   thine is kingdom-the   and power-the and

havitenakan pʻaṙkʻ.
eternal   glory

Modern Western Armenian

Note. The consonants here transliterated *b*, *d*, *g* have the phonetic
values [p, t, k]; conversely, *p*, *t*, *k* have the values [b, d, g]. These
changes are known as the second Armenian sound shift.

9   *Ov hayr mer or erkinkʻn es: kʻu anund surb əllay.*
10 *Kʻu tʻagaworutʻiwnd gay. Kʻu kamkʻd əllay, inčpēs or erkinkʻə
     anank al erkris vray.*
11 *Mer amēn awur haçə aysōr mezi tur.*
12 *Ew mezi nerē mer partkʻerə, inčpēs or menkʻ al kə nerenkʻ mer
     partakannerun.*
13 *Ew mez pʻorjutʻean mi tanir, hapa čarēn mez azatē. Inču or kʻukd
     ē tʻagaworutʻiwnə ew zōrutʻiwnə u pʻaṙkʻə yawiteans.*

I I

ILLYRIAN

In antiquity, the Central European Plain and the Balkan Peninsula (except Greece) were divided between two IE languages, Thracian and Illyrian, the former occupying the eastern, the latter the western portion. The boundary between the two has been defined on pp. 171f. The Illyrian-Greek frontier ran across Epirus and through the mountains of Macedonia. In the north, Pannonia was Illyrian, i.e. present-day Hungary (in so far as it was not Thracian), Slovenia and Croatia, except Istria and adjoining districts which were Venetic. The linguistic position north of Illyria is obscure. In the north-west, the Rhaetians had been in possession of the Alpine area. Celts were also certainly in the area in the fifth century B.C., to be replaced apparently at the beginning of the Christian era first by Germanic, later by Slavonic tribes. Judging by tribal and place names, Illyrians were also established locally in Greece at an early date.

On the evidence of onomastics (chiefly river names), it is argued that Illyrians once populated a wide territory to the north of their known historical extension, including the southern part of Germany. From this area, however, they are supposed to have been withdrawing since the middle of the first millennium in the company of their neighbours to the west and north, the Venetians. Whereas a southward drift of tribes appears to be attested in the prehistoric period, definite linguistic labels cannot be given with certainty to peoples whose movements are only traceable archaeologically unless there is adequate supporting evidence from elsewhere. In the present case, as far as Illyrian goes at least, the validity of the supporting (onomastic) evidence is being more and more disputed.

The term Illyrian first occurs about 500 B.C. in a Greek description of the Adriatic coast, but it is likely that Illyrian-speaking tribes were established in the area before the first millennium. This is inferred from tribal names mentioned in Homer and from the fact that Illyrians appear to have played an important part in the Doric invasion of Greece. Naturally, little can be said with certainty about the linguistic configuration of the Balkans at this very early date, but it is known that, from about 400 B.C., Celtic invaders introduced a new linguistic element into the Illyrian area; the autochthonous language, however, succeeded in absorbing the intrusive Celtic. But then the Roman conquest of Illyria, which began in 230 B.C., led to the romanisation of the coastal area. The campaigns of Augustus in the interior greatly strengthened the Roman hold on the country and paved the way for the victory of Latin over Illyrian. Only in the remoter parts did the latter continue; it is possible that it still lives on in a much altered form in Albanian. Otherwise, such pockets of Illyrian as survived the Roman period succumbed to Slavonic which poured into the province at the beginning of the Middle Ages. There is, very occasionally, evidence from place names which seems to show that, here and there, Illyrian was still being spoken when the Slavs came. The form of the name Paraun in Bosnia, for instance, is held to demonstrate that the Illyrian language maintained itself there until at least the seventh century.

Illyrian linguistic studies are rendered exceptionally difficult owing to the scanty amount of material which has survived. Not a single inscription has yet been found in this backward province. Apart from a few glosses, the language is attested only in rather more than one thousand personal and geographical names, but the interpretation of most of these is far from certain. All the same, a few features are clear. Some elements of phonology have been worked out, but it is not certain whether the language belonged to the centum or satem type. A little can be gathered about word formation. It is noticeable, for instance, that derivation was preferred to composition—in convenient contradistinction to Thracian. Lastly, a few dozen words have been extracted from the onomastic material. The following are among the more certain identifications: *pantas 'fifth', *sastas 'sixth', *teutā 'people' (Ir. *tuath*, Old High Ger. *diot*), *apā 'water' (Skt. *ǎp-*), *mal- 'mountain' (Dacian *mal-* 'bank', Rumanian *mal* 'rising ground, bank', Alban. *mal* 'mountain, bank'), *mento-* 'mountain' (Lat. *mons, mont-*, Welsh *mynydd*), *vidu-* 'tree, wood' (OIr. *fid*, OEng. *widu* beside *wudu*).

Messapian

Archaeological evidence suggests that about 1,000 B.C. peoples living in Epirus crossed the Adriatic and colonised the coastal lands on the opposite side from Garganus to the south. These areas, Apulia and (ancient) Calabria, retained their individual character until Roman times. One of the tribes settled in Calabria took on the name of

Metapii (*met-* 'between', *ap-* 'water'), later hellenised to Messapii. Some 260 inscriptions, including two long ones, have been found in Apulia and Calabria, especially in the territory of the Messapii. The inscriptions are written in a form of the Greek alphabet and date from the fifth to the first century B.C. Not long after this, the Messapian language must have passed out of use. It was replaced by Latin. Previously it had yielded some ground to Greek established in Tarentum and environs since 708 B.C.

The IE character of the language is quite clear. Fragmentary paradigms have been recognised, e.g., four case endings of the IE *ā*-stems: sg.nom. *-a*, acc. *-an*, gen. *-as*, dat. *-ai*. A score of words have been identified with certainty, including *apa* 'from' (Skt. *ápa*, Gk. *apó*), *ma* 'not' (Skt. *mā́*, Gk. *mḗ*, Alban. *mos*), *bilia* 'daughter' (Lat. *fīlia*, Alban. *bijë*, archaic dial. *bilë*).

The Ancients held that the Messapians were immigrants from over the sea. Illyrian affinities were conjectured in 1876 by Helbig, who found significant correspondences in the toponymy on both sides of the Adriatic. As a working hypothesis Messapian may be considered to be a form of Illyrian, but the paucity of both the Messapian and the Illyrian records has so far precluded positive proof.

ALBANIAN

Albanian is the mother tongue of rather more than three million people, of whom a good half live outside the state frontiers of Albania, mainly in Yugoslavia. Approximate figures are: for Albania 1,800,000, for Yugoslavia 1 m., of whom 800,000 live in the Autonomous Region of Kosovo-Metahija and nearly all the rest in Macedonia. The present political boundaries of Albania are substantially those of 1913 when the state of Albania came into being out of the deliberations of the London Conference and the debris of the Turkish Empire. It goes without saying that the presence of a large Albanian minority on Yugoslav territory is a perennial bone of contention between Tirana and Belgrade. Albanian is, of course, the official state language of Albania. The language is also official in Yugoslavia within the defined Albanian-speaking areas, i.e., from the shores of lakes Prespa and Ohrid, northwards to Dibra, across to Priština in the Kosovo Plain and from there to the southern border of Montenegro. Here, however, a knowledge of the state language, Serbo-Croat, is widespread and increasing. In Macedonia, an exceptional number of Albanians are polyglot. The present state frontier between Albania and Greece bisects a zone of mixed population, Albanians being particularly numerous around Kastoria. The minorities on both sides are by now largely bilingual and are diminishing.

Albanian in the diaspora

At the behest of Greek landowners and, later, of Turkish potentates, Albanians emigrated to Greece in very large numbers. The movement began in the fourteenth century and continued until the third quarter of the eighteenth. The Albanians came in either as peasants to be settled on empty lands or as mercenaries to help keep the Greeks in order. Large parts of the country became Albanian-speaking, e.g., Epirus and about half the Peloponnese, and these parts maintained their exotic character for centuries. But after the War of Independence (1821–9), the Greek element vigorously asserted itself and the assimilation of the Albanians began. Many of the erstwhile Albanian colonies have today ceased to exist, all the others are much reduced in size. Speakers of Greco-Albanian nowadays know Greek as well and, given modern conditions, it is unlikely that the language will survive for long. Still, that day has not yet arrived, and it would surprise many a tourist to Greece to learn that in a score of villages between Athens and (including) Marathon, Albanian and not Greek is, or was until very recently, the home language of most of the villagers. P. A. Phurikis in his account of the Albanians of Attica, 1932–3, calculated that there were then about 70,000 speakers in that province alone. It is not possible to say what the present figure is either for Attica or for the whole of Greece. There has undoubtedly been a very sharp decline in the last few decades and a large number of Albanians were expelled after World War II. We suggest a total of not more than 60,000 Albanian speakers now living on Greek territory.

Albanian settlements in South Italy and Sicily date from the middle of the fifteenth century. The first settlers were refugees from Turkish oppression. Others followed, mostly from Greece, the last settlement being made in 1746. In spite of their isolation, many of these Italo-Albanian colonies still survive, conditions here, as in the Balkans, being static enough to enable many small communities to maintain their exclusiveness. Albanologists estimate that about 80,000 speak Italo-Albanian dialects.

Gheg and Tosk

How long Albanian has been in use in the main Albanian-speaking area is not known. The coastal plain was certainly Romance-speaking until late medieval times, while the more accessible parts of the interior were overrun by Slavs as is shown by the place names. But the Albanians, who held the mountainous areas, managed to assimilate the non-Albanian population and to make encroachments on the Greeks to the south in Epirus.

The dialects of Albanian are rather diverse. In the main Albanian area mutual comprehension is, however, always possible, though not always easy. The dialects of the diaspora, having little or no contact with the homeland, are naturally more divergent. The dialects fall into two distinct groups: Gheg to the north of the river Shkumbi, Tosk to the south, the capital, Tirana, being conveniently situated in the transition zone. With the exception of the Gheg-speaking village of Arbanasi on the Yugoslav coast, the dialect of all Albanian colonies is Tosk.

The dialect differences between Gheg and Tosk were accentuated by the cultural differences between the isolated tribal north and the more accessible feudal south. Under these circumstances, two literary languages arose, though neither could achieve uniformity within itself. Under Zog (1925–39) and during the Italian occupation (1939–44) a compromise style based on the usage of the Tirana district was employed for official purposes. Shortly after coming to power, the Albanian partisans, who were chiefly South Albanians, sponsored the use of the East Tosk dialect, which already had a respected literary tradition. By 1950 agreement on normative forms had been reached in Albania and these were then followed in official publications, the daily press, school books, etc. The chiefly Gheg-speaking Albanians in Yugoslavia, however, continue to write literary Gheg. There is, apparently, some feeling on both sides that the literary forms should be brought nearer together whenever possible, but as matters stand at present there are two distinct forms of literary Albanian, both official, and differing as much as, say, Czech and Slovak.

Albanian has been written in a variety of alphabets: Latin, Greek, occasionally Cyrillic and, under Turkish influence, Arabic. In addition, two national scripts were in manuscript use in the last century. One of these, called Büthakukje after its inventor, arose about 1840, apparently a development of contemporary Greek handwriting. The other was found in use in Elbasan about 1850; the origin of this, the Elbasani script, is unknown, but it is much older than the Büthakukje. The modern Latin alphabet is, in essentials, that decided upon at Monastir in 1908.

Origins

Although Albanoi are mentioned by Ptolemy about A.D. 150, the earliest documents in their language are not older than the fifteenth century, the first text being a baptismal formula (1462). There is not much more until 1555, when Albanian literature proper begins with a long devotional work. Scholars are thus very much in the dark about the earlier stages of the language. Albanian, as we know it, has suffered greatly from attrition. It has, moreover, adopted a host of words from the Latin once spoken in the Balkans. It has borrowed a large number of words from the surrounding languages, Serbian, Macedonian and Greek, and also, as a result of Ottoman suzerainty from 1479 to 1913, from Turkish. Consequently, Albanian has lost a great part of its earliest vocabulary. The amount of material in the language which can be safely interpreted as original is small, but more than enough to make it quite certain that Albanian is of IE origin.

Albanian has been established longer in the Balkans than the other languages (Rumanian, Slavonic) now spoken in this area. The question therefore arises: Does Albanian continue the ancient Illyrian or is it a descendant of Thracian? The nature of Albanian and the exiguous character of the records of the ancient languages concerned combine to make a definite answer impossible. For some scholars the scanty evidence points to Illyrian origin, but others have argued that the closest connections are with Thracian, while a third group would have the best of two worlds and see in Albanian a tongue incorporating elements of both. The theory of Illyrian descent appears to be fashionable in Albania itself. Nevertheless, it does look as though a Thracian component is present. It is noteworthy that Albanian has a number of traits in common with Rumanian. Some of these are held to stem from a period of contact between the two languages, but other features have been interpreted as belonging to the substratum common to both. In antiquity, Illyrian and Thracian met in the area in question. There is no information on the character of the linguistic boundary, though there is evidence that Illyrian power had been expansive here. One cannot ascertain how this affected the linguistic situation, but from what may be inferred from the unsettled mode of life among the mountaineers of those days, it seems clear that the linguistic boundary will have been anything but static. The languages in contact must have contaminated each other, so that some basically Illyrian dialects most likely contained a marked Thracian element, and vice versa. The development of Albanian lexicography and etymology can be expected to yield a certain amount of fresh information, while further investigation of the Illyrian and Thracian substratum in the other Balkan languages will doubtless bring new facts to light. Perhaps it will then be possible to make more definite statements about the ancestry of Albanian. Meanwhile one thinks in terms of an ancient migration southward, noting in this connection that the names of two important Central European mountain ranges, Carpathians and Beskids, are only explicable from Albanian where *karpë* and *bjeshkë* mean 'rock' and 'high mountain, upland pasture' respectively.

THE STRUCTURE OF ALBANIAN

The following material refers solely to the present official literary language of Albania.

Phonetics

The stress is fixed either on the last syllable but one (paroxytone) or, less usually, on the last syllable (oxytone) of the uninflected form. The following spelling conventions may be noted: *th* is voiceless as in 'think', *dh* is the corresponding voiced spirant as in 'this'; *j* is like Eng. 'y', *ll* is like 'll' in 'hill'; *gj* may be pronounced 'g + y', *q* is the corresponding voiceless 'k + y'; *ë* denotes the indistinct sound of 'er' in 'father'; *y* is like 'u' in French 'lune'.

Accidence

There are three grammatical genders: masc., femin. and neuter, though the last is much restricted and nearly obsolete. Many nouns are ambigene, i.e., the plural has a gender different from the singular. The noun has six cases, though the number of distinct case endings is considerably fewer. The original IE endings have been largely lost through phonetic attrition or have been altered analogically. As a sample paradigm we take *mal* 'mountain'; it is masc. in the sg., femin. in the pl.:

Sg.nom.voc.acc.	*mal*	Pl.nom.voc.acc.	*male*
gen.dat.abl.	*mali*	gen.dat.	*maleve*
		abl.	*malesh* or *maleve*

The definite article inflects for number, gender and case. When used with nouns, it appears as a suffix: *mali* 'the mountain' declined as follows:

Sg.nom.voc.	*mali*	Pl.nom.voc.	*malet*
acc.	*malin*	acc.	*malet*
gen.dat.abl.	*malit*	gen.dat.abl.	*malevet*

Adjectives usually come after the noun; they do not decline, but agree with the noun in number and gender. Nearly all adjectives are preceded by the article, as follows: *mal i naltë* 'a high mountain' lit. 'mountain the-high', *mali i naltë* 'the high mountain', *majë e malit të naltë* 'the top of the high mountain', *mali është i naltë* 'the mountain is high'.

The Albanian verb is rich in inflexions, both active and passive. The endings themselves, however, are largely the product of secondary developments. In addition, Albanian possesses a series of periphrastic tenses, using an invariable *do të* 'will' and an inflecting *kam* 'I have'. Eight tenses are distinguished. There is a subjunctive and an optative mood. The following commonly used tenses of the indicative give some idea of the system:

Pres.sg.1 *punoj* 'I work'	Imperf.sg.1 *punoja*	Aor.sg.1 *punova*
2 *punon*	2 *punoje*	2 *punove*
3 *punon*	3 *punonte*	3 *punoi*
pl.1 *punojmë*	pl.1 *punonim*	pl.1 *punuam*
2 *punoni*	2 *punonit*	2 *punuat*
3 *punojnë*	3 *punonin*	3 *punuan*

Fut.sg.1	*do të punoj*	Perf.sg.1	*kam punar*
2	*do të punosh*	2	*ke punar*
3	*do të punojë*	3	*ka punar*
pl.1	*do të punojmë*	pl.1	*kemi punar*
2	*do të punoni*	2	*keni punar*
3	*do të punojnë*	3	*kanë punar*

Vocabulary

From the lexical point of view, Albanian may be described as a semi-romanised language, but the fundamental IE affinities of the language are seen from the following words of native stock:

Alb. *njeri* 'man': Skt. *nár-*, Osco-Umbrian *ner*, with prothetic vowel Gk. *anér*

Alb. *ti* 'thou': Lat. *tū*, Gk. *sú*, dial. *tú*, Armen. *du*, OCS *ty*, Ir. *tú*, Welsh *ti*, Eng. *thou*

Alb. *pi* 'I drink': Gk. *pínō*, Lat. *bibō* (from **pibō*, cf. Faliscan *pipafō* 'I shall drink')

Alb. *njoh* 'I know': Lat. *(g)nōscō*, Gk. (dial.) *gnōskō*, Eng. *know*

Alb. *bie* 'I carry': Skt. *bhárāmi*, Armen. *berem*, Ir. *beirim*, Eng. *bear*, Gk. *phérō*, Lat. *ferō*

As a curiosity we mention a unique Albanian-Celtic isolgloss: Alb. *gju* (archaic dial. *glu*) 'knee': Ir. *glúin*, Welsh *glin*.

Numbers: 1 *një*, 2 *dy*, 3 *tri*, 4 *katër*, 5 *pesë*, 6 *gjashtë*, 7 *shtatë*, 8 *tetë*, 9 *nëntë*, 10 *dhjetë*, 100 *qind*.

Texts

Matthew vi.9–13

Ati   ynë që   je në qiell: u shënjtëroftë emri   yt.
father-the our who art in heaven be-hallowed name-the thy

Arthtë mbretëria   jote. U bëftë dëshira jote, si në qiell,   edhe mbi
come kingdom-the thy be-done will-the thy as in heaven and on

dhe. Bukën   tonë të   përditëshme jepna   neve sot.   Edhe
earth bread-the our the daily   give-us us   today And

falna   fajet   tona, sikundër edhe ne ua   falim
forgive-us debts-the our   as   and we them-it forgive

fajtorëvet   tanë. Edhe mos na shtjerë në   ngasje,   po
debtors-the our   and not us lead   into temptation but

shpëtona nga i   ligu.   Sepse jotja është mbretëria   e
deliver-us from the evil-the for   thine is   kingdom-the and

fuqia   e   lavdia   në jetët   të jetëvet.
power-the and glory-the in age-the the ages-the

We conclude with a version of the above in Gheg, the other form
of literary Albanian in use today, and which is the standard in
Yugoslavia.

9 *At' ynë që je në qiell: shêjtnue qoftë emni i yt.*
10 *Ardhtë rregjinija e jote. U bâftë vullnesa e jote, si në qiell, ashtu
   mbi dhe.*
11 *Bukën tonë të përditshmen epna ne sod.*
12 *E ndienaj ne fajet tona, si ndiejm na fajtorët tonë.*
13 *E mos na lem me ra në të keq, por largona prej gjith së keq. Sepse
   joteja âsht rregjinija e fuqia e lafti në jetët të jetëvet.*

I 2

ARYAN or INDO-IRANIAN

The name Indo-Iranian indicates in essentials the distribution of the languages comprising this branch of Indo-European with its two main divisions, Indian and Iranian. The designation Indian, however, leads to terminological difficulties, not primarily due to Partition (India 'Bharat' and Pakistan), but owing to the fact that many pre-Indo-European languages are also spoken on the territory of the Indian sub-continent. These have at least an equal right to be called Indian. On the other hand, expressions such as Old Indian, in reference to the old period of Indo-European in India, are part and parcel of acceptable usage.

Not infrequently, the term Aryan is used as a synonym for Indo-Iranian. This essentially ethnic term, free from geographical connotations, is all the more appropriate as traces of this branch of Indo-European have been found in the Near East. Furthermore, it now appears that there is evidence of a more fundamental threefold division, the Dardic languages or at least the Kafiri group of these languages properly constituting an intermediary division between Indian and Iranian. It is often convenient to characterise the Indian division as Indo-Aryan.

Prehistory

Though details of the movements of the Aryans into their historical seats in the Near East, Iran and India are lost, it is known that they were emigrants from an earlier home in Eastern Europe north of the Caucasus. Their neighbours at that remote epoch were Finno-Ugrians, whose languages preserve certain Aryan loan words of great antiquity. There can be little doubt that Aryan existed as a distinct branch of Indo-European before the second millennium B.C.

Aryans in the Near East

As told elsewhere (pp. 159–61), excavations at Tell el Amarna and Boğazköy brought to light great quantities of archival material which threw unexpected light on the early history of the Near East. One revealing fact was the discovery of positive evidence for the presence of Aryans in this area, as follows. Firstly, the Aryan divinities Mitra, Varuna, Indra and the (two) Nasatyau are named as treaty gods in a text in Hurrian, the language of the Mitanni kingdom, a powerful state embracing a wide tract of Mesopotamia, North Syria and Cappadocia. Secondly, a number of Aryan words occur in a Hittite text compiled by Kikkuli of Mitanni. The material is dated to between 1450 and 1350 B.C. and shows that at some time previously the Hurrians had assimilated a group of Aryans significant enough to make a tangible contribution to Hurrian tradition.

1. INDIAN

Indian scripts

Two alphabetic scripts were in use in ancient India. One of these, the Kharosthi, was confined to North-West India and is found only from the middle of the third century B.C. to the third century A.D. It occurs in coin legends and Ashoka inscriptions. The writing runs from right to left and is derived from the Aramaic alphabet which, at the time of the Seleucid Empire, was in use from Syria to the frontiers of India. Perhaps it was adopted in India about 300 B.C. or a little later.

The other ancient alphabet, the Brahmi, is first plentifully attested in Ashoka inscriptions, i.e. in the third century B.C. It occurs throughout the sub-continent and is the parent type of all the multifarious alphabets, some two hundred in number, subsequently developed in and around India. The ductus is from left to right. It seems certain that the Brahmi script, like Kharosthi, also goes back to a Semitic model, though this time the exact source is not identifiable. The Brahmi type is shadowly attested in a few inscriptions before the Ashoka period, when the letters may run from right to left, as is common Semitic practice. The Brahmi known to us, however, must have passed through a protracted period of special development in India itself, so that one imagines the borrowing could hardly have been later than, say, the middle of the first millennium B.C. Presumably Indian merchants visiting Mesopotamia became acquainted with alphabetic writing there and introduced the new art to their countrymen. There is no evidence that the pre-alphabetic Indian script of the third millennium, brought to light at Mohenjo-daro, survived the disappearance of the civilisation associated with it.

The alphabet most widespread in India today is the Devanagari, or simply Nagari. This has for long been the case, and the bulk of Sanskrit literature is written in this character. Hindi, the national language of Bharat, appropriately follows suit, as do a number of other languages. Nagari is of northern origin, first encountered in the fourth century.

Though alphabetic, all forms of Indian script are cumbrous when compared with Latin, some of them particularly so. Sometimes letters are written together to give a virtually new compound symbol, and in Sanskrit especially these ligatures, as they are called, run into the hundreds and can be tantalisingly complicated. Furthermore, in the writing of Sanskrit and some later languages the words are sometimes separated, but at other times joined together according to set rules, though in the modern languages words are separated as in European scripts. A peculiarity of Nagari and most scripts associated with it is the use of a bar (*mātrā*) over each letter; it may, however, be omitted in handwriting.

The following modern Indian languages, official in the constitutional sense (pp. 200–1), use scripts distinct from Nagari: Panjabi, Gujarati, Oriya, Bengali and Assamese, further the non-Indo-European Telugu, Kannada, Malayalam, Tamil. Many other languages may also appear in a local script of their own. Further, in Ceylon, Sinhalese is written in a related (Southern) Indian script.

The Muslim invasions brought Arabic script to India. Its characters are simpler than the Indian; on the other hand, they are not well fitted to represent the sounds of Indian languages. Muslims, however, may use their script for any language, and always do so in the case of Urdu, an official language in Bharat and the state language of Pakistan.

After the coming of Europeans to India, the Latin script obtained some currency, but mainly for minor languages, several of which were committed to writing for the first time by missionaries who often preferred Latin to an indigenous script.

In view of the many disparate scripts in use today, it is not surprising that proposals for the acceptance of a single script are sometimes made. The obvious choice is Nagari, but regional and communal feelings are so strong there that seems no possibility of such a move succeeding in the foreseeable future. An even more idealistic suggestion would be the adoption of an All-India Latin alphabet, i.e. Latin suitably enlarged by new letters to represent the sounds of Indian languages. Such an alphabet has been devised and used to some extent in the teaching of Indian languages to foreigners. It is the scientific answer to the problem. It is clearly superior to Nagari or any other Indian alphabet. It is also a marked advance on the traditional Latin transcription of Indian languages (used in our texts) which employs a disfiguring system of diacritics, often awkward to read, instead of creating additional, fully legible symbols.

OLD INDIAN

The Aryans are usually thought to have reached India about the beginning of the first millennium B.C., entering the country from the north-west. Reminiscences of their arrival and also of their pastoral life before this occur in passages of the Rig-Veda, a collection of hymns and the oldest Aryan text. Within the next few centuries, Aryan kingdoms had been set up in the Panjab and Doab as well as throughout North India generally. By the middle of the first millennium B.C. their language was in use at least as far as Bihar. Indian was at this time still very close to Iranian (p. 234).

Sanskrit

The language of the oldest texts is called Vedic Sanskrit, the most archaic parts being composed about the time the Aryans appeared in India. Vedic is followed by Classical Sanskrit, still a highly synthetic language, though morphologically somewhat simpler than Vedic. Its forms were regulated in the grammatical treatise attributed to Panini in the fourth century B.C., about which time Sanskrit will already have acquired something of the nature of a dead language. This so-codified language remained, however, as a most serviceable literary medium down to recent times.

After Hittite, Vedic is the oldest surviving Indo-European language. But the abundance of its records and the archaic character of the language, meticulously preserved by a priestly tradition, give to Vedic an unsurpassed importance. It shows but few traces of indigenous Indian influence, though lexical items of non-Aryan origin were freely absorbed by later Sanskrit. Vedic clearly reflects the usage of the early Aryans of North-West India, and the classical language follows suit in most respects. In addition, however, an artificial literary element is certainly present, a fact implied by the very name Sanskrit, i.e., 'perfected, refined'.

As the result of such a lengthy period of cultivation, Sanskrit is the vehicle of a most copious literature, nearly all of it composed long after it had ceased to bear any close resemblance to living speech. Indeed, the golden age of Sanskrit was the period of the Gupta or Brahmin renaissance of the fourth to the sixth centuries A.D. Every literary genre, both poetry and prose, is richly represented. The wisdom of India is stored up in compendious Sanskrit works on philosophy, religion, law, medicine and many other sciences. Sanskrit has been to India what Latin was to Europe. It has provided much of the literary vocabulary for nearly all subsequent Aryan, and from an early date likewise influenced the Dravidian languages of the south. Sanskrit has been a considerable unifying force in India, and although it now plays hardly any part as a means of communication, its prestige remains so great that it has been declared one of the official languages of the Indian Union.

A dead language is notoriously difficult to write correctly, for there is no native feeling to guide one. Just as Latin documents produced, say, in Italy may show corruptions due to the Italian mother tongue of the composer, so do many Sanskrit monuments bear witness to the perverting influence of the Indian vernaculars. In one class of literature such distortions are so pervasive that the case calls for mention as follows. The earliest known Buddhist literature is written in the Middle Indian language Pali (see below), but later on the North-Indian Buddhists are seen to employ a curiously artificial type of Sanskrit, which consists essentially of Pali sentences mechanically transposed into the older language. The idiom is thus Middle Indian, while the outward appearance of the words is—more or less—that of Classical Sanskrit. This style has often been referred to as the Gatha dialect, but is more appropriately termed Buddhist Hybrid Sanskrit. Exact datings are not possible; one may think in terms of the first to the sixth centuries A.D.

Sanskrit is normally written in Nagari script.

MIDDLE INDIAN

A number of Middle Indian languages have been recorded. The oldest makes its appearance in the third century B.C., others become known at different times down to the tenth century A.D., after which the New Indian period may be said to begin. The attested Middle Indian languages arose in various geographical areas and reflect the naturally evolving differentiation of Aryan speech over the vast terrain of North India. Middle Indian is commonly known as Prakrit, a word understood as meaning 'unrefined' in contrast to the refined Sanskrit (see above). It is noteworthy, however, that several Prakrits themselves became the basis for petrified literary languages, to this extent being actually comparable to Sanskrit. Middle Indian languages, even the earliest, have a relatively advanced phonology, but the grammatical structure, especially of the older Prakrits, is still largely faithful to the inherited Indo-European type. There is, however, a growing amount of exotic vocabulary taken up from the substratum as Aryan consolidated its positions in the north and spread farther to the east and into the centre of the sub-continent.

Old Prakrit, Pali

Old Prakrit is the term applied to the earliest monuments of Middle Indian. The milieu is Buddhist and the use of Prakrit in these circles to be interpreted as a demonstration against the Sanskrit cultivated by the Hindu brahmins. Old Prakrit is present in variant forms in the Ashoka inscriptions from around the middle of the third century B.C. It is also represented in fragments of the work of the dramatist Ash-vaghosa, *c.* 100 B.C.

But the chief witness to Old Prakrit is Pali. This, the sacred tongue of the Buddhists, is moreover the most significant of all Middle Indian languages. Its texts go back to the third century B.C. The basis for the language was probably the spoken Aryan of the present-day province of Bihar, but the Pali known to us is doubtless a somewhat mixed language, already the product of a measure of literary cultivation. In this it resembles Sanskrit and, again Sanskrit-like, was destined to live on as an ossified bookish medium. In India itself the use of Pali decreased with the decline of Buddhism there. Outside India, however, particularly in Ceylon, but also in Burma, Siam and elsewhere, Pali has been used throughout the centuries as a literary language.

The word *pāli* means 'rule, canon (of the Buddhist faith)'; as the name of the language it is an abbreviation of *pālibhāṣā* (*bhāṣā* 'language'). Pali is usually written in the appropriate local alphabet, as Sinhalese, Burmese, etc. European scholars use a Latin transcription.

Middle and Late Prakrit

A number of Middle Prakrits are found in literary texts from the second century A.D. onwards. Maharashtri, the language of Maharashtra, enjoyed a great vogue as the medium of lyric and to a less extent of epic poetry. Ardha-Magadhi 'Half-Magadhi'—Magadha being a district of Bihar—is the language of the older Jainist works, often therefore called Jaina-Prakrit. It is not far removed from Pali. Some Prakrits are particularly associated with the Sanskrit drama, where noble men converse in that tongue, but their consorts and children are usually represented as speaking Shauraseni, the dialect of Shaurasena and its capital Mathura. Other conventions of the drama include the use of Magadhi, the speech of Magadha (see above), and Paishachi, the dialect of the North-West; these two Prakrits are put into the mouths of low-caste personages. Finally, several late Prakrits, collectively known as Apabhramsha, lit. 'degenerate', are similarly attested in the Sanskrit drama. With Apabhramsha we are approaching the New Indian stage represented by modern languages.

It may be stated that the Prakrit languages are, by and large, much of a muchness. Though naturally varying in place and time, their

common origin in Old Indian remains transparent. The great re-
structuring of Indo-Aryan which characterises the modern languages
appears, for the most part, as a post-Prakritic development.

NEW INDIAN

Problems of classification

At the level of the spoken language, conditions in India today are
reminiscent of those in parts of Europe during the Middle Ages. There
is a predominantly rural population, largely illiterate, whose speech
is entirely dialectal. There is a saying in India that every twelve *kos*
(a *kos* is about two miles) the language changes as the branches differ
on trees. But though the spoken tongue does vary from place to place,
there appear to be no hard and fast geographical boundaries between
the dialects and languages. From Sindh in the west eastwards to
distant Assam, from the Himalayas in the north to the southernmost
tip of Aryan in the Konkan, the languages in question form a continuum, interrupted only by colonies of immigrants or by enclaves of
exotic, pre-Aryan speech. This was the exact situation, for example,
in the Romance or Slavonic world in medieval Europe. But in later
times, modern states came into being and out of the various regional
varieties of Romance and Slavonic arose the standard national
languages, as French and Spanish, Russian or Polish, which have by
now, in greater or lesser measure, replaced traditional dialect speech.
But in the retarded historical evolution of India such a development
did not take place, though it doubtless will. In these circumstances,
classification by dialect or even by language becomes highly problematic. Indeed, the question of what is dialect and what is language
must be raised afresh and appropriate definitions sought. In our
classification ('The Modern Languages' below) we have followed the
Census of India which in turn is indebted to Grierson's Linguistic
Survey. Of necessity much is tentative, including statistics.

The two following examples illustrate the situation. Grierson
recognised a Rajasthani language, and in contemporary India there
exists the state of Rajasthan. The language Rajasthani, however, is
essentially a linguist's term to denote a theoretical concept. The vast
majority of the speakers of those dialects classed as Rajasthani do not
think of themselves as using a form of such a language. For them, the
name of the language they speak is the name of the local dialect, as
Marwari, Malwi, Mewari, Dhundhari, Lamani, to mention only the
largest. According to the 1961 census, forms of Rajasthani were given
to the enumerators under seventy-two different names. Not more than
one in ten used the term Rajasthani; we surmise that the overwhelming

majority of the others had never heard of it in the linguist's sense. Although there has be.n a small amount of literary activity in some of these dialects, there is no literary Rajasthani as such. Nor is it likely that there ever will be, as the not too dissimilar Hindi/Urdu is bidding fair to become the literary medium for Rajasthan. At any rate, Hindi is now the official language of administration and education in that state.

Panjabi is a much more solid proposition than Rajasthani and we take it as our second example. There exists a flourishing Panjabi literature based on the usage of the central area. But how far does the Panjabi-speaking area extend, and how many persons speak this language? For the sake of argument, we look in a south-easterly direction and see at the end of the Indus Valley the province of Sindh, where Sindhi, also with a standard literary language, is an entity quite as tangible as Panjabi. The two literary languages differ considerably, as much as Italian and Spanish, But if we follow a line from the heartlands of the Panjab to the centre of Sindh, we cannot find a point where the spoken dialects change more than at any other point, so that at this level Sindhi and Panjabi merge imperceptibly. Where there are no clear boundaries, there can be no exact statistics. Moreover, in the present case, many linguists, among them Grierson, regard what we would imply as being western Panjabi dialects as comprising a separate language, termed Lahnda. As a linguist's construction, Lahnda is the analogue of Rajasthani. In terms of this latter classification, therefore, we should say that Sindhi merges into Lahnda, which in turn merges into Panjabi.

The New Indian languages have sometimes been first divided into groups, e.g., a western group, a central group, etc. This procedure admittedly raises as yet unanswerable questions and we have preferred a simple geographical classification.

In conclusion, we notice that most Indian languages have not only regional dialects, but also communal dialects, cf. 'Islamic influence' below. Furthermore, caste dialects are an equally significant feature of Indian speech.

Islamic influence

Muslim invaders entered India over the passes of the North-West as early as 712. Subsequent inroads led to permanent settlement, at first in the North-West, later (around the turn of the twelfth and thirteenth centuries) in Nothern India generally. The Sultanate of Delhi was founded in 1206 and that city remained the effective centre of government until Aurangzeb's death in 1707, while the office of Moghul emperor formally survived until 1804. As a result of these developments, Islam became an established religion especially in the north of India, where its adherents now total upwards of a hundred million.

At Delhi and later in a number of other Muslim states, Persian became the official language, and a rich literature in that tongue, both in prose and verse, was created on Indian soil. Many Persian loan-words—themselves frequently Arabic in origin—passed into Indian languages, particularly as spoken by Muslims. The very existence of Urdu is the direct result of Islamic influence (p. 213). The use of Arabic script by Indian Muslims has already been referred to (p. 194).

Linguistic states

During the period of British rule, it was axiomatic that English should be the chief official medium. But an independent India could hardly uphold that attitude. The practical requirements of the new situation meant that Indian languages would henceforth play the main role. The obvious candidate for the honour of state language in a united India would be Hindustani. But India was in fact partitioned: the Hindu variety of Hindustani, Hindi, became the state language of the Indian Union, while the Muslim variety, Urdu, assumed the same function in Pakistan.

Although Hindustani with some 170 million native speakers is the major language of India, it is far from being a majority language in that vast, multilingual sub-continent, which has a total population of 603 millions. There are quite a dozen significant regional languages, each playing a dominant role in its own area. The importance of the regional language was well shown by the success in 1956 of the moves to secure full official rights for the Bengali language in East Pakistan, while in India the strength of the regional languages led to the creation of the present linguistic states. In the British era, the country was organised in units which were historical, but not essentially linguistic. The Bombay Presidency, for example, incorporated the territories of two major languages, Gujarati and Marathi. The reorganisation on linguistic lines, which had long been mooted, began in 1952 when Andhra Pradesh was constituted as a Telugu-speaking state with that language as its official medium. Root-and-branch changes—and proposals for such changes—almost inevitably lead to tension in some situations, and there has been violence and loss of life in the present connection. In 1964, there were sixteen major states largely formed on the basis of linguistic homogeneity, though it will be un-derstood that, in the conditions actually obtaining, each such state includes minor languages and also some speakers of other major lan-guages. It may also be noted that Hindi is used not only in its own main areas, i.e. in Uttar and Madhya Pradesh and the eastern part of Panjab, but also in Bihar and Rajasthan. The following languages in addition to Hindi/Urdu are official in the above sense: Assamese, Bengali, Gujarati, Kashmiri, Marathi, Oriya, Panjabi and the non-Indo-European Kannada, Malayalam, Tamil, Telugu. Further, the dead language Sanskrit has also official status, while English, still of immense practical value, has the standing of an associate official language.

THE MODERN LANGUAGES

Sindhi

This is the language of the historical district of Sindh, now a province of West Pakistan, on the Lower Indus. It is in touch with Balochi and Pashto to the west and north-west respectively, with Lahnda to the north-east, and with Rajasthani and Gujarati to the east and south-east. Sindhi is spoken by considerably more than five million persons.

After Partition, about one-quarter of the population left for Bharat, where about half a million Sindhis now live in Gujarat, the remainder spread mainly over Rajasthan, Madhya Pradesh and Maharashtra. The founding of Pakistan had a further consequence: the creation of an influential Urdu enclave in the heart of traditional Sindhi territory. Karachi was chosen as the capital of the new state, and immediately the population increased explosively as Muslims from all parts of the sub-continent congregated there. For the new-comers, Urdu was the native language or at least the lingua franca, and Urdu is the official language of West Pakistan.

Sindhi may be printed in a local alphabet close to Nagari, but since Muslims constitute the majority of Sindhi users, the language most frequently appears in Arabic script. Although Sindhi was hardly written at all until the middle of the last century, it has since developed a considerable literature. It is not easy to predict the future for the language in Bharat. Some assimilation seems inevitable, but the language is officially recognised and is thriving. In its homeland, too, Sindhi remains a vigorous idiom in spite of competition from Urdu; it is, in fact, the only regional language in West Pakistan to support a modern press. Sindhi is said to be gaining ground at the expense of Balochi.

Lahnda

Lahnda ('West') denotes those dialects spoken north-east of the Sindhi-speaking area and west of Panjabi and Rajasthani. They are bounded to the west and north-west by Pashto, to the north they form a confused border with Dardic. These dialects, which are often classified as Western Panjabi, are normally oral media only, their speakers, some ten millions in number, having Urdu as their official language.

Panjabi

Panjabi is spoken by, say, twenty-five million persons, of whom half live in the Indian state of Panjab and half in an area of comparable size across the frontier in Pakistan. Panjabi also spreads into neighbouring Indian states: there are some 200,000 speakers in Rajasthan and about as many in Uttar Pradesh, while in Jammu over a million use Dogri, a form containing Kashmiri elements. To the west and south-west of Panjabi territory as defined above lies the Lahnda-speaking area, to the south Rajasthani, to the east Western Hindi, to the north-east Western Pahari, to the north Dardic.

As a vehicle of culture, Panjabi is particularly associated with the Sikh religion founded towards the end of the fifteenth century. Much early Sikh literature is in Hindi, some of the Sikh rulers used Persian as their official medium, but there was always some literary cultivation of the vernacular, for which an alphabet, the Gurmukhi, based on Nagari, was devised. With the heightening of communal consciousness in the last century, Sikhs began to look on Panjabi as the distinctive medium of their community. Much less significant has been the written use of Panjabi by the Muslims, though they have produced a modest literature in a language borrowing from the usual Islamic sources. Literary Panjabi follows the usage of the central area with the influential cities of Amritsar and Lahore. In India, Panjabi is the official language of the state of Panjab, where the Sikh element, now accounting for about half the total population, has been strengthened by refugees from the west. In Pakistan, on the other hand, Panjabi remains chiefly an oral medium, and little used as a literary form. For Muslim Panjabis, Urdu is the usual literary language, a development begun under the British who encouraged Urdu as an administrative medium after the annexation of the Panjab in 1848. With its Western Hindi base, Urdu is of course particularly close to Panjabi.

Gujarati

Gujarati is the state language of Gujarat and the native tongue of twenty-two and a half million persons, of whom close on two millions live outside the state, chiefly in neighbouring Maharashtra (approaching one and a quarter million, of whom 900,000 live in Bombay), but also in Rajasthan (50,000). Considerable emigrant populations are found in Madhya Pradesh (150,000) and especially in Madras (200,000), where the principal settlements may be a thousand years old; their dialect is called Saurashtra. In its homeland, Gujarati is in touch with Katchi to the north-west, Rajasthani to the north, Bhili to the east, and has Khandeshi and Marathi along its southern border. In addition to the usual differences between Hindu and Muslim usage, a third form of Gujarati is used by the exclusive Parsi ('Persian') community, over 100,000 strong, now mainly resident in Bombay. Their idiom admits Persian loans not found in the other varieties.

The written records of Gujarati go back to the fourteenth century. In common with Bengali, Hindi/Urdu and Marathi, Gujarati developed a modern literature in the second half of the last century. The presence of an influential Gujarati component in the population of Bombay, the leading commercial centre, has not been without significance in these matters, a Gujarati-language newspaper appearing in that city as early as 1822. The standard language is based on the major dialect spoken in the central area from Baroda to Ahmedabad. The alphabet is a cursive form of Nagari, omitting the *mātrā*.

Katchi

Some 400,000 persons, natives of the Cutch (Katch), speak non-literary dialects intermediate between Gujarati and Sindhi, as their geographic location implies. These dialects are sometimes considered as forming a separate language. The Cutch belongs administratively to Gujarat State, and Gujarati is the literary language for speakers of Katchi.

Rajasthani

Rajasthani is essentially a linguist's term to denote collectively the dialects proper to Rajasthan, both those actually in use there and those now spoken elsewhere, but known to have originated in, or have close connections with Rajasthan. There is no Rajasthani literary language, much less any recognised norm. Rajasthanis normally practice literacy through Hindi/Urdu, and Hindi is the official language of the Rajasthan State.

Statistics must be used with especial caution, as many of the speakers of these dialects return Hindi/Urdu as their native tongue. We reckon with a figure approaching twenty millions, of whom at least one-third uses the Marwari dialect. Other large groups with approximate number of adherents are Malwi (3 m. mostly over the border in Madhya Pradesh), Mewari (2 m.), Dhundhari (1½ m.), Lamani (¾ m.), also Banjari, Harauti and (in Madhya Pradesh) Nimadi, each with well over half a million. Rajasthani dialects are further spoken by large emigrant groups, chiefly about 600,000 in Andhra Pradesh and half as many in Mysore. In Jammu, 200,000 persons use Gojri, a dialect of Rajasthani provenance.

Rajasthani's neighbours are, to the west Sindhi, to the north-west Lahnda, to the north Panjabi, to the east Western Hindi, to the south Marathi and Bhili, to the south-west Gujarati.

Bhili and Khandeshi

These two non-literary languages are situated south of the Rajasthani-speaking area, the former being in contact with it. Bhili is spoken by rather more than two and half million tribesmen, as follows: in Madhya Pradesh (950,000), Maharashtra (500,000), Rajasthan, where nearly all speak the Wagdi dialect (900,000), and Gujarat (300,000). Their homelands are the mountainous tracts where these states converge. Khandeshi is used by 450,000 persons, 85 per cent of whom live in Maharashtra, the remainder across the state border in Gujarat. In the former the dialect is called Ahirani, in the latter Dangi.

The dialects of the Bhils contain a residuum of Munda words and it is likely that these tribes were aryanised in quite recent times.

Marathi

Marathi is the native tongue of at least thirty-six million persons, of whom thirty three millions live in Maharashtra, where it is the state language. Marathas also inhabit adjoining areas, particularly in Mysore and Madhya Pradesh with over a million each, further in Andhra Pradesh (300,000) and Gujarat (200,000). In the district of Bastar, some 300,000 persons describe themselves as Halbi-speaking. These we have counted in with the Marathas, but according to some classifications their speech is closer to Bhatri, an aberrant dialect of Oriya. On the other hand, we have excluded the Konkani-speakers from the Marathi total (see below). Neighbours of Marathi to the north are Gujarati, Rajasthani and Western Hindi, to the east Eastern Hindi, to the south Telugu and Kannada. There is contact with Gondi in the north-east, east, and south-east, sometimes in enclaves surrounded by Marathi. To the north, further, there are areas of Bhili and Khandeshi; Marathi is also in touch with Korku.

Bombay, the capital of Maharashtra, has a cosmopolitan character. Of its four and a half millions, only about two speak the state language as their mother tongue. There are no less than 900,000 Gujaratis, residents of long standing, and about as many Hindustani speakers, often recent arrivals. The remainder come from all over India, but especially from the Dravidian south.

In common with Bengali, Hindi/Urdu and Gujarati, Marathi came to be extensively used as a literary medium in the second half of the last century, the standard language being based on the usage of Poona and district. The earliest literary compositions in the language

date from the thirteenth century, but inscriptions go back to about
A.D. 1000. The script is Nagari. It will be remembered that Maharashtra is an ancient province, whose kings were a force in the land. Their
influence reached its height in the eighteenth century, when they
successfully challenged the Moghuls, but British intervention brought
about their downfall in 1804. Marathi is well attested at the Middle
Indian stage in Maharashtri Prakrit.

Konkani

This language, akin to Marathi, takes its name from the Konkan, a
coastal district beginning in the southern part of Maharashtra and
continuing through Goa into Mysore. Konkani forms the southernmost tip of the Aryan continuum. The chief centre of the language is
Goa and the name Goanese is often applied to it. Speakers number
nearly one and a half million: about a quarter of a million in Maharashtra, upwards of 600,000 in Goa, 550,000 in Mysore, with a further
75,000 or so emigrants in Kerala.

   Konkani is frequently classified as a dialect of Marathi. It has,
however, been going its own way for some time now, partly due to
the administrative separateness of the Goa territory, a Portuguese
colony until 1961, and the language is much used in local affairs. It is
generally written in Nagari, but through Portuguese influence, the
Latin alphabet may also be used. As a frontier language, Konkani has
acquired a sizeable Dravidian (Kannada) element.

Hindi

The Hindi dialects are spoken over an extensive area in North-Central
India. One distinguishes Western and Eastern Hindi, an approximate
dividing line passing north–south through Lucknow. Western Hindi
is the language of the eastern half of Panjab State, including the
Delhi Enclave, and of the western and central areas of Uttar Pradesh
and Madhya Pradesh up to the dialectologist's demarcation line
referred to. Eastern Hindi dominates over the remainder of the two
last-mentioned provinces. It thus extends much farther south than
Western Hindi, its broad Chattisgarhi wedge reaching as far as
Bastar in a linguistically confused area. The western division of
Hindi is bounded essentially by Pahari, Panjabi, Rajasthani and
Marathi, its eastern division by the following major languages:
Nepali, Bihari, Oriya, Telugu, Marathi, while in the southern and
south-eastern regions of Madhya Pradesh various minor Dravidian
and Munda languages adjoin Hindi or form enclaves within it.
Eastern Hindi also extends into Nepal, where there are about a
million speakers. There are furthermore close on three million Hindi
speakers in border districts in Maharashtra. In the whole contiguous

area under discussion, some 160 millions speak Hindi, two-thirds using dialects characterised as Western.

Forms of Hindi are spoken outside its native area (see section 'Hindustani: Hindi/Urdu' below).

Bihari

Bihari is the collective name for those dialects spoken mainly in Bihar State, transitional between Eastern Hindi on the one hand and Bengali and Oriya on the other. To the north there is contact with Nepali, to the south also with Dravidian and Munda languages. Three dialect groupings are distinguished: Bhojpuri, in the western half of the state, spoken by perhaps twenty-five millions, contrasts with the eastern dialects Maithili in the north-east and Magahi or Magadhi in the south-east with, say, fifteen and ten million speakers respectively. None of these are contemporary literary languages in the full sense, though poetic compositions in Maithili go back to the fourteenth century. For official, educational and ordinary literary purposes, Hindi is the recognised medium in Bihar.

Oriya

Oriya is the state language of Orissa, where it is the native medium of sixteen and a half millions, or 70 per cent of the population. It is also spoken in adjacent areas, particularly in Andhra Pradesh (200,000), West Bengal (200,000) and Bihar (300,000), as well as by emigrants, chiefly in Assam (150,000). The divergent Bhatri dialect is used by some 100,000 persons across the state border in Madhya Pradesh. Altogether, Oriya is the native language of some seventeen and a half millions. To the south it is bounded by Telugu, to the west by the Chattisgarhi dialect of Hindi, to the north by Bihari and Bengali, here also by Munda languages, notably Santali.

The Oriyas reached their present seats after advancing from the west, apparently in the tenth century, since which time they have absorbed many autochthonous groups. Their language can be traced back to the fourteenth century, but no literature proper is older than the sixteenth, and consists mainly of poetry. But with its present status, Oriya is developing the resources of a modern standard language. It employs its own very distinctive script which, judging by the circular forms of its letters, will be of southern origin.

Western Pahari

The Aryan languages of the Himalayan zone are classified as Pahari. The eastern division is represented by one language only, Nepali, at the same time the most important member of the whole group. In the central division are Kumaoni and Garhwali, in the western a medley of minor non-literary languages.

Western Pahari languages are spoken in the Dehra Dun District of Uttar Pradesh, in Himachal Pradesh, in the Kangra and Simla Districts of Panjab, in the Chamba Exclave of Himachal Pradesh, whence into the bordering areas of Jammu. Western Pahari is thus in touch with Tibetan languages, notably Kanauri, to the north and north-east, with Garhwali to the south-east, Western Hindi to the south, Panjabi to the west and Kashmiri to the north-west.

Towards two million mountain dwellers today speak forms of Western Pahari, but details for the individual languages or dialects are obscure, since more than half the census returns simply give 'Pahari' without further, or with insufficient qualification, distributed as follows: over half a million in Himachal Pradesh and nearly a quarter of a million each for Panjab and Jammu. We recall, too, that much field work remains to be done on Indian languages, especially those in the remote mountain areas, before all details necessary for an exact classification are available. Below, we indicate the numerically significant vernaculars listed as languages, as opposed to dialects, in the Census of India (1961), and supply figures based on this source. The languages are, from east to west, in Uttar Pradesh: Jaunsari (54,000), in Himachal Pradesh: Sirmauri (111,000), Churahi (44,000), Mandeali (227,000), in Panjab: Kului (50,000), in the Chamba Exclave: Bharmauri (56,000), Chamelai (46,000), in Jammu: Bhadrawali (33,000). In considering these figures, we again remind the reader that more than half of the Pahari languages were returned to the census as 'Pahari Unspecified'.

The literary language of Western Pahari speakers is Hindi.

Kumaoni and Garhwali

These are the languages of the historical districts of Kumaon and Garhwal in the far north of Uttar Pradesh. Together they form the central division of the Pahari group. To the north we find Tibetan languages, to the south Western Hindi. East of Kumaon lies Nepal, west of Garhwal the territory occupied by Western Pahari. Kumaoni is spoken by over a million persons, Garhwali by somewhat less than that figure. The official language and normal literary language of Kumaoni and Garhwali speakers is Hindi.

Nepali

Nepali forms the eastern division of Pahari and was introduced into the region of present-day Nepal from the west not later than the twelfth century. By the fourteenth century, advanced groups had entered the Valley of Kathmandu, and in the seventeenth century

their form of Pahari, later to be called Nepali, was in official use side
by side with the indigenous Newari, a language of the Tibeto-Burman
group. Then the conquest of the Valley by the Gurkhas in 1769
destroyed the political power of the local Newari kings and established
a single kingdom of Nepal with Kathmandu as its capital and Nepali
as its state language. Nepali has since spread vigorously at the expense
of the many Tibetan and similar languages spoken in the country.
According to the 1952–4 census, rather more than four million
Nepalese subjects out of a total of some eight and a quarter millions
spoke Nepali as their mother tongue, while the majority of the
remainder could use it as a second language. Nepali has also spread
outside its homeland. In 1961 there were 75,000 Nepali speakers in
Sikkim making it the major language in that territory, 215,000 in
Assam, and 525,000 in West Bengal, in all over a million in India. We
estimate that native speakers of Nepali now number at least seven
millions.

It is noteworthy that Nepali is decidedly a minority language both
in Kathmandu and the Valley, constituting less than 30 per cent of the
inhabitants of the former and about 40 per cent of the latter, the rest
being chiefly Newari speakers. Spoken in 1952–4 by close on 400,000
persons in Nepal, Newari is the only Himalayan language of the
Tibeto-Burman group to have developed a considerable literature.
The Newars have evolved a high degree of material culture and a
distinctive social organisation, factors which have assisted them to
preserve their language so well in the face of competition from Nepali.

Bengali

Bengali is the most important modern Aryan language after Hindi/
Urdu. It is spoken by no less than 100 millions in Bengal and bordering
areas of neighbouring states, as follows: West Bengal (38 m.), East
Bengal (57 m.), Orissa (150,000), Bihar (over 1 m.), Assam (approx.
3 m., of whom 800,000 live in Tripura—two-thirds of its population).
Understandably, in Indian conditions, the spoken dialects of a
language spread so far and wide are not only numerous, but in
extreme cases not mutually intelligible. Bengali is bounded on the
south-west by Oriya, on the west by Munda languages, especially
Santali, and by Bihari, on the north by Nepali and Tibeto-Burman
languages (Lepcha, Bhutani, Boro). In the north-east, Bengali adjoins
Assamese, the Tibeto-Burman Garo and the isolated language Khasi,
then veering south faces in turn other Tibeto-Burman languages,
notably Meithei, Tripuri, Lushai.

Bengali initiated and led the movement for the literary cultivation
of modern Indian languages at the beginning of the eighteenth
century. There was a considerable tradition, at least in verse, upon

which to build; the oldest specimens go back to the twelfth century. The modern literary standard is based on the usage of Calcutta and district. Bengali is written in an alphabet of the Nagari type, commonly described as being aesthetically the most pleasing of Indian scripts. This script is also generally employed by the Muslims of East Bengal. Needless to say, Bengali is the state language of both West Bengal (Bharat) and East Bengal (Pakistan).

Bengal was for a long time very much a peripheral province, but took on a new importance with the weakening of the Moghuls and the establishment of British power in Calcutta in the eighteenth century. Calcutta remained the capital of British India until the central government was transferred to New Delhi in 1911. Such things were naturally not without effect on the growth of a Bengali national conscience and hence of a literature in the Bengali language.

Assamese

Assamese, the state language of Assam, is the native idiom of over seven million persons. It is proper to the middle and upper parts of the Assam Valley as far as Dibrugarh. It represents the most easterly conquest made by Aryan speech, which here advanced from northern Bihar and Bengal to push its way along the Brahmaputra into a geographical cul-de-sac. In so doing, it drove a wedge between the Tibeto-Burman languages already established in the area and which at the present time occupy the hill districts and encompass the intrusive Aryan on three sides (see 'A note on Tibeto-Burman languages' and 'A note on Khasi' below).

Spoken Assamese is close to Bengali. Literary Assamese, however, has developed almost exclusively on the basis of the spoken style and, unlike literary Bengali, has made very sparing use of Sanskritisms. Assamese is written in Bengali script. It has a considerable literature, including chronicles dating back to about 1300. Historical writing in an Indian vernacular is exceptional, and the Assamese chronicles were in fact initiated by the (originally Thai-speaking) Ahon invaders who made themselves masters of the country in 1228.

Sinhalese

Sinhalese, formally often Singhalese, is an Aryan language introduced into Ceylon from Northern India. Tradition ascribes its introduction to Prince Vijaya, dating the event to about 500 B.C. The linguistic contours of Ceylon at such a remote date are entirely unknown. One assumes the existence of a lost indigenous language spoken by an autochthonous population, perhaps represented today by the (now Sinhalese-speaking) Veddas. It is further assumed that Tamils had most likely already reached the island across the Palk Strait. The Aryans will have absorbed these Tamils, just as they absorbed those who are known to have filtered into the island subsequently. But after about A.D. 1000, large numbers of immigrant Tamils remained unassimilated. They began to constitute a majority in the north, where they founded a kingdom. Their descendants today are the so-called Ceylon Tamils. Much later, in the nineteenth and twentieth centuries, Tamils were brought in as estate labourers; these are termed Indian Tamils. At present, Ceylon and Indian Tamils number over three millions, the former being nearly twice as numerous as the latter. The Ceylon Tamils form more than three-quarters of the population of the Northern Province, reaching 97 per cent in Jaffna. They also account for close on half the population of the Eastern Province. Indian Tamils are concentrated in the Central and Uva Provinces, constituting a third of the inhabitants. The Tamil-speaking minority is thus widely dispersed among the Sinhalese-speaking majority, who number upwards of eight millions, and the conditions of modern life tend to mingle further the territorial basis of the two languages. Over a million persons are described as bilingual in Sinhalese and Tamil.

The beginnings of literacy in Ceylon are associated with the coming of Buddhism, an event traditionally placed in the third century B.C. The earliest literary works composed in Ceylon are in Pali or Sanskrit, the first known composition in Sinhalese belonging to the mid-tenth century. On the other hand, inscriptions in the vernacular go back to the centuries before our era, the language being termed Old Sinhalese or Elu. Sinhalese, especially in its literary form, has borrowed extensively from Pali and Sanskrit. It is written in an alphabet of Southern Indian provenance (p. 194).

Owing to isolation and long-standing exposure to an exotic environment, the basically Aryan character of the language is only faintly apparent. The speech of the Veddas (above), now numbering less than one thousand, is particularly aberrant, due possibly to exceptional substratum influence. But from which part of North India the Sinhalese language originated has not yet been agreed.

As in other places, the anti-colonial movement in Ceylon took up the language question and especially after Independence in 1948, *Svabasa* 'Native Language' became a leading political issue. The Sinhalese majority interpreted this as 'Sinhalese only', which in 1956 was declared the sole official language of Ceylon, thus replacing English. After ensuing communal violence, amendments (1958, 1966) protected Tamil-medium education and provided for the use of the minority language in administration and local government, though Sinhalese remains the exclusive language of the state. English is known to about one-tenth of the population and still plays an important part in intellectual life. It remains the usual medium of university instruction.

Maldivian

Maldivian or Divehi is the official language of the Republic of the Maldives. It is also the vernacular of the 3,000 natives of the Indian island of Minicoy, 70 miles to the north, and is spoken by about 100,000 persons in all.

The islands in question were occupied by colonists from Ceylon perhaps about the year A.D. 1000, but Maldivian has been appreciably distinct from Sinhalese for at least 500 years, if not longer, and the languages are not mutually intelligible. Until about 250 years ago, Maldivian was written in a local alphabet akin to Sinhalese and a small amount of traditional literature has been preserved. In more recent times, however, a peculiar script with South Asian connections but modified by Arabic and similarly written from right to left has become universal. The Maldivians became Muslims about 1200, an event which tended to increase their isolation from the Buddhist Sinhalese. Maldivian has borrowed considerably from literary Arabic.

Romany

The Romany or Gipsy languages are basically Indo-Aryan, though a more precise classification has not so far been possible. It is known that the people themselves migrated from North-West India, but whether they were of local origin or had reached that area from elsewhere is undecided. Nor can their emigration from the Indian homeland be dated with any certainty, though the eleventh century is considered likely. During their westward movement through Persia, the wanderers split into a southern and a northern group. The former reached Syria, the latter Armenia, in which countries some of their descendants continue to speak Romany. Parties from the northern group then moved through Asia Minor and by the fourteenth century had crossed into the Balkans. From the beginning of the fifteenth century, these nomads spread rapidly throughout Europe; they are said to have first arrived in Britain in 1430.

In Europe, some thirteen Romany dialects have been classified. The basic structure of the language is everywhere substantially the same, but the large numbers of loan words adopted from the languages of their various hosts has meant that the dialects are often mutually unintelligible. Thus two-fifths of the basic vocabulary of British Romany is non-Indian, approximately as follows: English one-fifth,

Iranian, Greek, Balkan Slavonic, and miscellaneous, 5 per cent each.
How many speakers exist today is a moot point. Many perished under
Hitler when Gipsies shared the fate of Jews. In modern conditions,
assimilation is almost everywhere the trend, made all the easier since
the Gipsies have been essentially bilingual since the time of their
emigration from India. Perhaps something like a quarter of a million
persons still use a Romany dialect as their communal or domestic
idiom.

By the nineteenth century, most British gipsies had abandoned
their native idiom as the primary medium, though some remembered
enough to use as a corrupt jargon. Only in Wales did some members of
a local clan preserve the language with remarkable purity into the
present century, so that a few are still alive who heard grandparents
conversing among themselves in Romany. Incidentally, these speakers
were trilingual, having in addition fluent English and Welsh. The remnant of the travelling people in this country today retain at most a
few relics of Romany in the shape of single words or short phrases.

Romany has been used to a limited extent in writing. Publications
chiefly on religious subjects, mostly of pamphlet size, have appeared
in many countries. In Eastern Europe especially, literature designed
for Gipsies often contains material written in one or other of the forms
of Romany found in that area. The script is that of the host country.
The earliest record of Gipsy speech dates from 1542, when Andrew
Boorde published thirteen short sentences of English Romany in his
Fyrst Boke of the Introduction of Knowledge.

It was for long believed that the Gipsies spoke a secret jargon. Only
in 1777 when Rüdiger compared the language with Hindustani, did
its Indo-Aryan affinities become evident. In Britain, these strangers
were thought to be Egyptians, hence the term 'Gipsies'.

Something like a score of 'Gipsy' dialects have been reported from
India itself, but these appear to be no more than varieties of already
known Indo-Aryan languages, and there is no evidence of any
special relationship with Romany proper, i.e. emigrant Gipsy. (For a
possible exception, see Dumaki below).

Dumaki

Among the Burushaski of Hunza and Nagar (pp. 228f.) lives a caste of
blacksmiths and musicians, in all some three hundred persons,
speaking Dumaki 'Romany' as their domestic tongue. Dumaki is a
language of an Aryan type, but closer affinities are undetermined. It
has, however, been suggested that Dumaki may be an Indian survivor
of the otherwise emigrant Romany tribe. The language is much
affected by Burushaski, which the Dumaki-speakers naturally use as
their second tongue.

Hindustani: Hindi/Urdu

We have referred above to the Hindi dialects and their homeland in the central part of Northern India. On the basis of a western type of Hindi, a modern literary language has emerged in two communal styles: (High) Hindi, used by the Hindus and written in Nagari, and Urdu, used by the Muslims who employ Arabic script. At the simplest level, that of ordinary conversation or artless writing, the two styles are substantially the same. This common language has been termed Hindustani.

The history of Hindustani can be traced to the Hindi of the eleventh century. Eventually three dialects came into literary use: Awadhi (region of Awadh), Braj, properly Bhasha Braj 'Language of (the region of) Braj', i.e. Mathura and district, and Khariboli 'Pure Speech' native to an area south of Delhi. The last named became the most influential, at the same time spreading far and wide in the north as a lingua franca. At the Muslim courts, including Delhi, which employed Persian for official purposes, the Khariboli adopted large numbers of loan words from that language, and the resultant Islamic style was known by a Persian name *zabān-e-urdū* 'language of the camp', subsequently abbreviated to *urdū*, in origin incidentally the same word as Eng. *horde*. Urdu became a familiar literary style whereever the Muslim element predominated, not only in parts of the Hindi-dialect area proper, but beyond notably in the Panjab, in Kashmir, in Sindh, and even in Hyderabad in spite of its mainly non-Indo-European, Telugu-speaking population. The British administration encouraged the use of Urdu in local affairs in these areas, so that from 1837 onwards Urdu effectively replaced Persian in this respect.

The earlier literature had been poetry, but towards the middle of the last century, a prose literature came into being, the language being based on Khariboli. Now both Muslims and Hindus were using the same basic medium, but the latter strove to replace the Persian element, where possible, with words of native Indian origin—in the case of neologisms drawing freely on Sanskrit—and their style was called (High) Hindi. In 1947, Hindi and Urdu became the state languages of Bharat and Pakistan respectively; in the former Urdu is also an official language (p. 201). Since that time, the term Hindustani has tended to fall into disuse, speakers now usually expressing their communal or political allegiance by declaring themselves speakers of Hindi or Urdu, as the case may be. Statistics are of the order of 145 millions for Hindi, thirty millions for Urdu. It goes without saying that the influence of Hindi/Urdu has immensely increased since Independence in all fields of public life, as government,

8

education and the mass media, and also as a lingua franca, even though English remains, and remains almost supreme, at several levels (p. 113). Such an upsurge has naturally encouraged the further development of a modern, technical vocabulary, expressed in the one style largely by Sanskrit elements, in the other by Persian, hence a growing lexical divergence between the two styles which can seriously hinder mutual comprehension in certain contexts.

It will be noticed that Urdu is not historically native to any part of Pakistan. The eastern region is essentially Bengali-speaking, the western region heterogeneous. Here the most significant traditional language is Panjabi, in its wider sense including Lahnda and Dogri, followed by two important languages, Sindhi and the (Iranian) Pashto, and a medley of minor tongues. However, Partition brought a great influx of native Urdu speakers, making some three and a half millions in all, chiefly in West Pakistan. Karachi (p. 201) is now a predominantly Urdu-speaking city, forming a two-million strong enclave in Sindhi-speaking Sindh. It is quite possible that Urdu, now naturalised in West Pakistan, will prove expansive as a primary medium also. In spite of the relatively small number of its native speakers and their slender territorial basis, Urdu is nevertheless the language of prestige, as indeed it has been since British times, and is by far the most influential literary medium. This situation is, in general, accepted by the population. There has been no agitation in West Pakistan on behalf of local languages comparable to that in East Bengal, or in the Indian Union (p. 200).

Native Hindustani speakers are found elsewhere in India outside the Hindi-dialect area, most notably in Bombay. Here some 900,000 of them compete with the Gujaratis for the position of second largest linguistic group in that remarkably polyglot city.

Hindustani has also been carried beyond India. The successes of British arms against the Burmese, from 1824 onwards, led to a considerable Indian immigration, mainly after 1852, when the Irrawaddy Delta was annexed. Before World War II, quite half of the population of Rangoon was Indian, and Hindustani had become the lingua franca of the Burmese capital. But the Japanese invasion led to a precipitate exodus of at least half a million Indians. In 1955, there were still 600,000 remaining, but large-scale repatriation has since reduced the Indian minority to relative unimportance. Needless to say, Burmese is back in the saddle now (p. 114).

Since 1840, when the practice of drawing on India for indentured labour began, Hindustani has been carried even farther afield. In common with various other Indian languages, it has been established chiefly in Mauritius, South and East Africa, the West Indies, especially Guyana and Trinidad, and finally in Fiji. In many areas, assimilation has become the rule, chiefly to English (British West Indies, South Africa, and also to Swahili in East Africa). Elsewhere, Indian languages remain in communal use, a lingua franca being employed in dealing with outsiders, as in Mauritius (Creole French) or Dutch Guyana (Sranan). In Fiji, however, that 'Little India of the Pacific', the Indians number 235,000 as against 195,000 native Fijians. About 200,000 are native Hindustani speakers whose language is the lingua franca of the whole Indian community and to a large extent the medium of primary education. Hindustani in Fiji seems to represent a permanent colonising achievement; it dates from 1879.

THE STRUCTURE OF INDIAN

SANSKRIT

Phonetics

There are three short vowels: *a, i, u,* five long vowels: *ā, e, ī, o, ū,* and the diphthongs *ai, au.* The consonants include aspirated occlusives: *bh, ph,* i.e. *b + h, p + h,* etc., further cerebrals (occlusives with retroflex articulation): *ṭ, ṭh,* etc. Other consonants occurring in the examples below are the palatals *ñ* and *ś,* similarly *c* (approx. *t + y*), and secondary variants of *h* and *m* written *ḥ, ṃ.* The acute accent denotes a stressed syllable.

Accidence

There are three genders, three numbers, and eight cases, the fullest representation of the Indo-European system. IE **ekwos* appears in the oldest language as follows:

Sg.nom.	*áśvas*	Pl.	*áśvās*	Du.	*áśvau*
voc.	*áśva*		*áśvās*		*áśvau*
acc.	*áśvam*		*áśvāṃs*		*áśvau*
gen.	*áśvasya*		*áśvām*		*áśvayos*
dat.	*áśvāya*		*áśvebhyas*		*áśvābhyām*
abl.	*áśvād*		*áśvebhyas*		*áśvābhyām*
loc.	*áśve*		*áśveṣu*		*áśvayos*
inst.	*áśvā*		*áśvais*		*áśvābhyām*

The adjective follows comparable declensional schemes.

The verb is highly synthetic and morphologically complex. It has six tenses in the indicative (pres., fut., imperf., aor., perf., pluperf.). There is an optative and an imperative mood, further a large number of participles and verbal nouns, one of the latter becoming in Classical

Sanskrit a regular (active) infinitive. There are two basic voices: active and middle, with a passive developing out of the latter. Sample paradigms:

ACTIVE

Infin. *bhártum* 'to bear'

Present

	Indicative	Optative	Imperative
Sg.1	*bhárāmi*	*bháreyam*	*bhárāṇi*
2	*bhárasi*	*bháres*	*bhára*
3	*bhárati*	*bháret*	*bháratu*
Pl.1	*bhárāmas*	*bhárema*	*bhárāma*
2	*bháratha*	*bháreta*	*bhárata*
3	*bháranti*	*bháreyur*	*bhárantu*
Du.1	*bhárāvas*	*bháreva*	*bhárāva*
2	*bhárathas*	*bháretam*	*bháratam*
3	*bháratas*	*bháretām*	*bháratām*

Participle sg.nom. *bháran* n., *bháratī* f., *bhárat* n.

Imperf. (indic. only) sg.1 *ábharam*, 2 *ábharas*, 3 *ábharat*, pl.1 *ábharāma*, 2 *ábharata*, 3 *ábharan*, du.1 *ábharāva*, 2 *ábharatam*, 3 *ábharatām*

MIDDLE/PASSIVE

Present

	Indicative	Optative	Imperative
Sg.1	*bháre*	*bháreya*	*bhárai*
2	*bhárase*	*bhárethās*	*bhárasva*
3	*bhárate*	*bháreta*	*bháratām*
Pl.1	*bhárāmahe*	*bháremahi*	*bhárāmahai*
2	*bháradhve*	*bháredhvam*	*bháradhvam*
3	*bhárante*	*bháreran*	*bhárantām*
Du.1	*bhárāvahe*	*bhárevahi*	*bhárāvahai*
2	*bhárethe*	*bháreyāthām*	*bhárethām*
3	*bhárete*	*bháreyātām*	*bháretām*

Participle: sg.nom. *bháramāṇas* m., *bháramāṇā* f., *bháramāṇam* n.

Imperf. (indic. only) sg.1 *ábhare*, 2 *ábharathās*, 3 *ábharata*, pl.1 *ábharāmahi*, 2 *ábharadhvam*, 3 *ábharanta*, du.1 *ábharāvahi*, 2 *ábharethām*, 3 *ábharetām*

Numbers: 1 *ékas*, 2 *dvaú*, 3 *tráyas*, 4 *catvåras*, 5 *páñca*, 6 *ṣáṭ*, 7 *saptá*, 8 *aṣṭaú*, 9 *náva*, 10 *dáśa*, 100 *śatám*

Vocabulary

dámas 'house': Gk. *dómos* ('hut'), Lat. *domus*, Russ. *dom*, Armen. *tun*

mū́s 'mouse': Gk. *mūs*, Lat. *mūs*, Eng. *mouse*, Russ. *myš*, Alban. *mi* *vidhávā* 'widow': Lat. *vidua*, Eng. *widow*, Russ. *vdová*, Welsh *gweddw*, older Irish *feadhbh*

ávis 'sheep': Lat. *ovis*, Gk. *oĩs*, with restriction of sense Eng. *ewe*, Lith. *avìs* 'do.'

sāmí- 'half': Gk. *hēmi-*, Lat. *sēmi-*, Old High Ger. *sāmi-* *svādús* 'sweet': Gk. *hēdús*, Lat. *suāvis*, Eng. *sweet* *vártate* 'turns, becomes': Lat. *vertit*, Russ. *vértit*, Lith. *veřčia*, all meaning 'turns', Goth, *wairþiþ* 'becomes'

Text

(In writing Sanskrit many words are joined together when phonetic changes may take place. In the following, the component parts of such orthographic compounds have been given in brackets)

Matthew vi.9–13

Bho asmākaṃ svargastha pitaḥ: tava nāma pavitraṃ   pūjyatāṃ.
o   our   heavenly father thy   name holy   be-hallowed

Tava rājyamāyātu (rājyam   ā-yātu). Yathā svarge
thy   kingdom come   as   in-heaven

tathā medinyāmapi (medinyām api) tavecchā (tava icchā) sidhyatu.
so   earth   on   thy   will   be-done

Śvastanaṃ bhakṣyamadyāsmabhyaṃ (bhakṣyam adya asmabhyaṃ)
daily   food   today us

dehi. Vayañca (vayam ca) yathāsmadaparādhināṃ (yathā
give   we   and   as

asmat   aparādhinaṃ) kṣamāmahe, tathā tvamasmākamaparādhān
against-us trespassers   we-forgive so

(tvam asmākam aparādhān) kṣamasva. Asmāṃśca (asmāms ca)
thou our   trespasses forgive   us   and

parīkṣāṃ   *mā naya, api-tu durātmata uddhara. Yato rājyaṃ*
into-temptation not lead   but   from-evil deliver   for   kingdom

parākramaḥ pratāpaśca (pratāpas ca) yuge-yuge tavaiva (tava
power   glory   and for-ever   thine

eva).
indeed

PALI

We print next a Paternoster in Pali to give an idea of the relationship between this earliest Middle Indian language and the Old Indian stage as seen in the foregoing Sanskrit.

(Writing conventions approximately as for Sanskrit; *ṁ* denotes nasalisation of preceding vowel)

Saggaṭha no pitā: tava nāmo pavitto hotu. Tava rajjamāgacchatu
heavenly our father thy   name holy   be   thy

(rajjam ā-gacchatu). Yathā sagge   *tathā paṭhaviyaṁ tavecchā*
kingdom come   as   in-heaven so   on-earth

(tava icchā) kariyyatu. No denikāhāram (denikam āhāram) ajja
  thy will   be-done   our   daily   food   today

no dehi. Iṇāyikānaṁ no yathā khamāna, tathā no iṇaṁ
us give trespassers our as   we-forgive so   our trespasses

khama. Amhe parikkhaṁ   *mā nehi, amhe ādīnavā mocehi.*
forgive us   into-temptation not lead us   from-evil deliver

Kiṁ rajjañ   *ca parakkhmañ ca mahimañ ca sadā*
for   kingdom and power   and glory   and for-ever

tav'eva.
thine-indeed

HINDUSTANI: HINDI/URDU

New Indian languages have moved very far away from the Indo-European type still well represented in Middle Indian. In general they are predominantly analytic, the reduction of old synthetic forms being most advanced in the central languages, of which Hindustani is a characteristic example. Phonetic changes have often been far-reaching, e.g., Skt. *ghṛtám* 'clarified butter', MInd. *ghidaṃ, ghiaṃ*, Hind. *ghī* (Anglo-Indian 'ghee').

Details of the transitional developments between Middle and New Indian are often obscure, particularly as there is a considerable gap between the later Prakrits and the earliest attestations of the modern tongues.

Phonetics

$a = $ [ə], *ṇ* nasalises the preceding vowel or diphthong, *v* is more like *w*, *q* (only in loan words from Persian) is formally uvular, but *k* may be substituted. The macron essentially denotes quality rather than quantity. Other conventions comparable to those for Sanskrit.

Accidence

The three-gender pattern of Old Indian is reduced to masculine and feminine only. The old dual has disappeared. The case system distinguishes nominative and oblique, though these are not always morphologically distinct. There are some half-dozen declensional classes, e.g., sg.nom. *laṛkā* 'boy', obl. *laṛke*, pl.nom. *laṛke*, obl. *laṛkon*; sg.nom.obl. *laṛkī* 'girl', pl.nom. *laṛkīāṇ*, obl. *laṛkīoṇ*. Postpositions governing the oblique correspond to the prepositions of English, e.g., *laṛke ko* 'to (the) boy'. Adjectives are indeclinable, except for most of those ending in -*ā* which go as follows: masc.sg.nom. *burā* 'bad', obl. and pl. *bure*, fem. (both cases and numbers) *burī*.

The verbal system has been drastically reshaped and so simplified that most verbs have become regular. Tenses are typically periphrastic. Example: *bolnā* 'to speak':

Present habitual: sg.1 *maiṇ boltā huṇ* lit. 'I speaking am', 2 *tū boltā hai*, 3 *voh* 'he' *boltā hai*, pl.1 *ham bolte haiṇ*, 2 *tum bolte ho*, 3 *voh bolte haiṇ*. Except for pl.1, the participle varies for gender, e.g., sg.1 *maiṇ boltī huṇ*, 3 *voh* 'she' *boltī hai*, pl.3 *voh boltī haiṇ*. Similarly present continuous: *maiṇ bol rahā (rahī) huṇ*, etc. Other tenses: *maiṇ boltā thā (boltī thī)* 'I used to speak', *maiṇ bol rahā thā (rahī thī)* 'I was speaking', *maiṇ bolungā (bolungī)* 'I shall speak', *maiṇ bolā (bolī)* 'I spoke', *maiṇ bolā (bolī) huṇ* 'I have spoken', *maiṇ bolā hungā (bolī hungī)* 'I shall have spoken', *maiṇ bolā thā (bolī thī)* 'I had spoken'. There is an inflected subjunctive: pres.sg. *maiṇ boluṇ, tu, voh bole*, pl. *ham boleṇ, tum bolo, voh boleṇ*. Imper.sg. *bol*, pl. *bolo*

Numbers: 1 *ek*, 2 *do*, 3 *tīn*, 4 *cār*, 5 *pañc*, 6 *chai*, 7 *sāt*, 8 *āṭh*, 9 *nau*, 10 *das*, 100 *sau*

Texts

(Etymological *ṣ* commonly pronounced as *ś*)

Matthew vi.9–13

Hindi

He hamāre svargbāsī pitā: *terā nām*   *pavitra kiyā*   *jāe. Terā*
o our   heavenly father thy name holy   made be thy

rājya   *āe.*   *Terī icchā jaise svarg*   *meṇ vaise pṛithvī par pūrī ho.*
kingdom come thy will   as   heaven in   so   earth on full be

Hamārī dinbhar kī roṭī   *āj*   *hamen de.* *Aur jaise ham apne*
our   daily   bread today us   give and as   we our-own

ṛiṇiyon ko kṣamā   *karte*   *hain taise hamārī ṛiṇon ko kṣamā*
debtors forgiven making are   thus   our   debts   forgiven

kar.   *Aur hamen parīkṣā*   *men mat*   *ḍāl,*   *parantu duṣṭ se*
make and us   temptation in   do-not thrust but   evil from

bacā.   *Kyonki rājya*   *aur parākram aur mahimā sadā tere*   *hain.*
deliver for   kingdom and power   and glory   ever thine are

Urdu

Ai hamāre bāp,   *tū*   *jo*   *āsmān* *par hai*: *terā nām*   *pāk mānā jāe.*
o our   father thou who heaven on art thy name holy made be

Terī bādśāhat āe.   *Terī marzī jaise āsmān* *par pūrī hotī*   *hai,*
thy kingdom come thy will   as   heaven on full being is

zamīn par bhī *ho. Hamārī roz kī roṭī*   *āj*   *hamen de. Aur jis*
earth on also be our   daily bread today us   give and what

tarah *ham apne*   *qarzdāron ko muāf*   *kiyā hai, tū*   *bhī*
manner we our-own debtors   forgiven made is   thou also

hamāre qarz *hamen muāf*   *kar. Aur hamen āzmāiś*   *men na*
our   debts us   forgiven make and us   temptation in not

lā,   balki burāī se   bacā.   Kyonki bādśāhat aur qudrat aur jalāl
bring but   evil   from deliver for   kingdom and power and glory

hameśa terā   hain.
ever   thine are

OTHER MODERN INDO-ARYAN LANGUAGES
(The Paternoster)

(Final *-a* in some transliterations may not be realised in speech, thus
Gujarati, Marathi *nāma* 'name' pronounced *nām*, as in Hindi)

Sindhi

9   *E asān-jā piu, jo āsmāna men āhe: tunhin-jo nālo pāku kare
    j'anije.*
10 *Tunhin-jī bādśāhī ace. Tunhin-jī marzī jian āsmāna men āhe tian
    zamīna te thie.*
11 *Asān-jī toni asān khe aj'u ḍ'e.*
12 *Ain asān-jani ḍ'ohani khe māf kar jian asīn panhin-jani ḍ'uhāriani
    khe māf thā kariūn.*
13 *Ain asān khe āzmāiśa men na nen, uṭlo asān khe buchiṛāia khān
    chaḍ'āi. Jo bādśāhī ain qudrata ain vaḍ'āī tunhin-jī hameśa āhe.*

Panjabi

9   *He sāḍe pitā, jihṛā surg vic hai: terā nān pavittar mannyā jāve.*
10 *Terā rāj āve. Terī marjī jihī surg vic tihī dhartī utte bī pūrī kītī
    jāve.*
11 *Sāḍī gujar jogī roṭī aj sānūn dih.*
12 *Ate sāḍe karj sānūn māph kar, jiven asān bī āpne karjāīān nūn
    māph kītā hai.*
13 *Ate sānūn partāve vic nā lyā, sagon duṣṭ ton bacā. Kyonki rāj ate bal
    ate partāp terā sadā hai.*

Gujarati

9   *O ākāśamānnā amārā bāpa: tārun nāma pavitra nanāo.*
10 *Tārun rājya avo. Jema ākāśamān tema prithvi para tāri icchā puri
    thāo.*
11 *Divasani amāri roṭali āja amane āpa.*
12 *Ane jema ame amārā riṇione māpha karyā che tema tun amārān
    riṇo amane māpha kara.*
13 *Ane amane parikṣanamān na lāva, pana bhunḍāthi amāro chuṭako
    kara. Kemake rājya tathā parākrama tathā mahimā sarvakāla
    sudhi tārān che.*

Marathi

9 *He āmacya svargātila pityā: tuzhen̄ nāma pavitra mānilen̄ zāvo.*
10 *Tuzhen̄ rājya prakaṭa hovo. Svargātlyāpramāṇen̄ pṛithvivarahi tuzhā manoratha purṇa hovo.*
11 *Āmaci rojaci bhākara āza āmhān̄sa de.*
12 *Aṇi zaśi āmhin̄ āpalyā aparādhyān̄nā kṣamā keli āhe taśi tun̄ āmacyā aparādhān̄ci āmhān̄sa kṣamā kara.*
13 *Aṇi āmhān̄sa kasoṭisa lāvun̄ nako, tara āmhān̄sa tyā duṣṭācyā hātātuna mukta kara. Kāraṇa kin̄, rājādhikāra, sāmarthya va gaurava hin̄ anantakāḷa tujhin̄ca āheta.*

(mark of nasalisation etymological)

Konkani (Original Goanese Latin orthography)

9 *Amchea bapa, tum sorgar assai: tujem naum vodd zaum.*
10 *Tujem raj amcam eum. Tuji khoxi, zoxi sorgar zata, toxem sounsarant zaum.*
11 *Amcho dispotto giraz aiz amcam di.*
12 *Anim amchim patcam bogos, zocem amim amcher chucleleanc bogsitaum.*
13 *Anim amcam tainent poddunc dium naca punn amcher sorvoi vaitt vign eta itleim niver. (. . .)*

Oriya

9 *He āmbhamānañka svargasha pitā: tumbha nāma pabitra bali manyā heu.*
10 *Tumbhara rājya āsu. Yepari svargare separi pṛithibīre tumbhara icchā saphala heu*
11 *Āji āmbhamānañku prayojanīya āhāra dia.*
12 *Āmbhemāne yepari āpanā āpanā aparādhīmānañku kṣamā kariyacchnu separi āmbhamānañkara aparādha sabu kṣamā kara.*
13 *Parīkṣāre āmbhamānañku āna nāhi, mātra mandaru rakṣā kara. Yeṇu rājya, parākrama o gaurava yuge yuge tumbhara.*

Nepali

9 *He hāmrā svargavāsī pitā: timro nāū pavitra bhaniera sammānya hos.*
10 *Timro rājya āos. Svargamā bhaejhāī yas pṛithivīmā timro icchā siddha hos.*
11 *Ājakā din hāmro dāinik āhār hāmīlāi deū.*
12 *Tathā hāmrā sārā aparādh kṣamā gara, jasarī hāmīle pani āphnā aparādhīharulāi kṣamā garekā chāū.*

13 *Hāmro parikṣā maleū, tara kubhalodekhi hāmro uddhār gara.
Kinabhane rājya timro ho, parākram timro äu mahimā timro ho
sadākā nimti.*

Bengali

9 *He āmāder svargastha pitā: tomār nām pabitra baliyā mānya hauk.*
10 *Tomār rājya āisuk. Tomār icchā siddha hauk, yeman svarge temni
pṛithivīte.*
11 *Āmāder dainik āhār ei dine āmādigake dāo.*
12 *Evan āmāder aparādh sakal kṣamā kara, yeman āmrāo nij
aparādhīdigake kṣamā kariyāchi.*
13 *Ār āmādigake parīkṣāy ānio nā, kintu manda haite rakṣā kara.
Kāran rājya, parākram, o mahimā yuge yuge tomāri.*

Assamese

9 *He āmār svargat thakā pitri: tomār nām pujânīya haok.*
10 *Tomār rājya haok. Ŷenêkâi svargat, tenêkâi pṛithibīto tomār
icchā pūr haok.*
11 *Āmār prayojânīya āhār āji āmāk diyā.*
12 *Āmār dhâruvahatak āmi ŷenêkâi kṣamā kârilõ, tenêkâi āmāro
dhār kṣamā karā.*
13 *Āmāk pârīkṣālâi ninibā, kintu pāp-ātmār parā āmāk dhâri
rākhā. (. . .)*

Sinhalese

9 *Svargayehi väḍasiṭina apagē piyāṇeni: obagē nāmayaṭa gaurava
vēvā.*
10 *Obagē rājyaya ēvā. Svargayehi men pṛithiviyehida obagē kämätta
karanu läbēvā.*
11 *Apagē davaspatā bhōjanaya apaṭa ada duna mänava.*
12 *Apaṭa väradi karannavunṭa apa visin kamā vennāk men apē
väradivalaṭat kamā vuva mänava.*
13 *Apa parīkṣāvaṭa nopamuṇuvā napuren apa gaḷavā gata mänava.
Maknisāda, rājyayat balayat mahimayat sadākalma obava-
hansēgēya.*

Romany (Bulgarian)

9 *Dáde amaré, kaj isién k'o devlé: te evél svete to anáv.*
10 *Te avél teṛé tagaripé. Te evél teṛí velja sar k'o devlé, kidijá ci k'i
phuv.*

11   *Dí amén avzí kata sisotnó maṛé.*
12   *Ci bašla amengé amară bórdži, sar amé-da bašlădăk amară*
      borčlúnge.
13   *Ci ma ingál amén andé xoxaibé, ami kurtár amén bengestár.* (. . .)

APPENDIX

NOTES ON NON-INDO-EUROPEAN LANGUAGES IN INDIA

Dravidian languages

When the Aryans reached North-West India they are generally believed to have come into contact with Dravidian peoples. Though today found mainly in Central and especially in South India, the considerable influence exercised by Dravidian on Sanskrit and later Aryan strongly suggests the one-time presence of a large Dravidian population in the north also. The Dravidian languages constitute a separate family. The problem of origins is quite unsolved, but it is usually assumed that, like Aryan, Dravidian entered India from the north-west. It is not impossible that the bearers of the pre-Aryan Indus civilisation, best known from excavations at Mohenjo-daro, were of Dravidian stock. The total number of those speaking Dravidian languages is of the order of 125 millions.

The Dravidian languages fall into three groups: northern, central and southern. The northern group is represented by three languages: Brahui (say 250,000 speakers), isolated in the central highlands of Balochistan and much influenced both by Indo-Aryan and Iranian (p. 241), and very different from the other two, Kurukh and Malto. The former, also termed Oraon, is used by 150,000 persons in the western ranges of the Chota Nagpur Hills, in the districts of Raigarh and Sambalpur. It is in touch with Hindi and Bihari, and to the east with Munda languages. Malto, the vernacular of 100,000 tribesmen, is found in the Rajmahal Hills. It is surrounded by Munda. Kurukh and Malto are closely related, and both have been much influenced by Munda.

Of the central languages the most important is Gondi, scattered in numerous enclaves over a wide area of mountainous country in Central India, essentially as follows: a large part of the area between Bhopal and Jubbulpore north of the Narbada and a parallel strip centred on Pachmarhi a little to the south of the river. The south-western end of the latter adjoins an enclave of Korku, a Munda language. To the east, in the Maikal Range, is another small area of Gondi. Apart from the contact with Korku, the above-mentioned enclaves are surrounded by Hindi. To the south-east of the Korku enclave lies yet another area of Gondi with Nagpur at its centre, and a further one in Balaghat, both within Marathi-speaking country. Gondi is also spoken in pockets inside the northern part of the territory occupied by the major Dravidian language, Telugu, as well as in districts of mixed Aryan and Dravidian speech, particularly in Andhra Pradesh. Little is known about the origin of the Gondi enclaves, as indeed of most others. Local migrations during historical times have often been attested in India, but in the present case it is probable that Gondi was once the language of a large central area so that the enclaves seen today are those parts of the original territory which have not succumbed to the advance of Aryan (Hindi, Marathi) or Telugu. Other numerically significant central languages are: Kolami (60,000 speakers), chiefly in the Wardha district of Madhya Pradesh with Marathi as the influential Aryan neighbour, and Parji (30,000) to the south of Bastar in a mixed Aryan-Dravidian milieu. Lastly, the two closely related, but now mutually unintelligible languages of the Khonds, the one spoken in Orissa by 400,000 persons, the other in the Vizagapatam region of Andhra Pradesh by nearly 200,000. The former language is termed Kui, the latter Kuwi, variant pronunciations of a name by which the people call themselves. They are in touch with Oriya, Telugu, and Munda languages.

There has not been any great amount of literary activity in these northern and central Dravidian tongues. Where some literacy is practised, it is usually in the scripts of influential neighbours. Thus Gondi and Kurukh use Nagari. Some owe the little literature they possess to European missionaries who generally employed the Latin alphabet. Brahui may be written in Arabic characters.

The south of India is exclusively Dravidian. It is the home of four traditional literary languages, all official state languages in the con-temporary Indian sense (pp. 200–1): Telugu, Kannada (Canarese), Tamil, Malayalam. Telugu is the language of Andhra Pradesh with forty-three million speakers and a literature commencing in the tenth century. Kannada, spoken by twenty millions, dominates in Mysore. Its earliest literature dates from the ninth century, but the language is first known from fifth-century inscriptions. Both these languages have frontiers with Aryan: Telugu with Oriya and Hindi, Kannada with Marathi and Konkani. The best documented Dravidian language is Tamil, the records of its profuse literature going back nearly two thousand years. It claims thirty-eight million adherents, thirty-five millions of them in India, mainly in Madras, and a further three millions in Ceylon (p. 210). Malayalam, the language of a more than nineteen-million strong population, chiefly in Kerala, is in origin simply a variety of Tamil, which however developed aberrant features and has been used as a written medium in its own right since the ninth century. Literary styles in Dravidian, as in Aryan, may differ considerably from vernacular forms. The literary languages in particular are heavily indebted to Sanskrit, from the ample vocabulary of which they have extensively borrowed. Each of these major Dravidian languages employs its own alphabet. Telugu and Kannada are closely akin, the others very different, both from these and each other. A characteristic feature of these South Indian scripts is the expansion of the Brahmi prototype (p. 194) into complexes of round and curling forms.

There are also a small number of minor Dravidian languages in the south. The principal one is Tulu, spoken by a million persons in and around Mangalore, between speakers of Kannada to the north and Malayalam to the south. In recent years it has been used on a modest scale as a written medium; it has adopted the Canarese script.

Munda languages

Munda or Kolarian are names given to a group of languages spoken today in the central part of India. It is believed that speakers of Munda lived in India before the coming of the Dravidians. According to one school of thought, Munda is related, though very remotely, to the Mon-Khmer group further east (see 'Khasi' below). But since the comparative philology of the groups concerned has not yet been adequately worked out—a difficult task in the absence of historical records of these languages—statements about ultimate affiliations are safest regarded as tentative.

The Munda languages are nowadays found only in less accessible districts. This has not always been so, since it appears that Munda people were once present in the Ganges Valley where they developed a society advanced enough to offer stubborn, though unsuccessful, resistance to the invading Aryans. It is likely, too, that Munda has yielded ground to Dravidian. More information on such subjects can be expected when these languages have been more thoroughly studied. Much remains to be done, for several of the languages involved have not yet been sufficiently recorded, let alone properly analysed.

Although, by Indian standards, all the members of the Munda group are seen to be minor languages, they appear in general to be flourishing with the total number of speakers substantially rising and now above the six-million mark. The chief stronghold of Munda is the Chota Nagpur Plateau, where the languages of the numerically most significant, northern group are located. They occupy a contiguous area and go under the collective name of Kherwari. They have been considerably influenced by the surrounding Aryan (Hindi, Bihari, Oriya, Bengali), some of them also by the Dravidian (Malto, Kurukh, Kui) used in adjacent areas. The languages in question are chiefly

Santali ($3\frac{1}{2}$ millions), Mundari (800,000), Ho (700,000), Bhumij (175,000), Koda (35,000) and Korwa (25,000). A much smaller, central group, situated in a similar milieu also in Chota Nagpur, comprises two languages: Kharia (200,000) and Juang (over 15,000). Separated from the foregoing groups by Aryan (Oriya) and Dravidian (Telugu, Kui) lies the southern group in the Orissa-Andhra Pradesh borderland. There are two languages: Savara (300,000) and Gadaba (50,000), of which the former has been, relatively speaking, only slightly modified by its non-Munda neighbours. Finally, far away in the Mahadeo and Satpura Hills, Korku or Kurku (200,000) is the sole representative of West Munda, in contact with Aryan (Marathi) and Dravidian (Gondi). The more significant languages are often used in writing, the script being usually that of the most influential Aryan neighbour. Thus Santali commonly appears in Bengali script, Mundari and Ho generally used Nagari. Some of them, under European missionary influence, use the Latin alphabet.

Tibeto-Burman languages

The Aryan languages of India are bounded on the north and east by a host of mainly minor languages belonging to the Tibeto-Burman group of the Sino-Tibetan family. The languages in question are to a large extent used by hill-dwelling, often primitive, tribes, and hence the remarkable linguistic heterogeneity of the areas concerned. The group is named after the two major languages belonging to it: Tibetan and Burmese. These are, of course, the official languages of two of India's neighbours, but neither is, properly speaking, native to the borderlands adjoining India.

The more significant languages on Indian territory are, in Kashmir: Balti (over 40,000) and Ladakhi (60,000); in Himachal Pradesh: Kanauri (30,000)—we add here in Nepal: Newari (400,000)—in Sikkim: Lepcha (30,000); along the northern frontier of Assam: Aka, Dafla, Abor-Miri, Mishmi (over 150,000 on the Indian side), in the Lower Assam Valley: Boro (400,000), in the Garo Hills: Garo (400,000), in the Mikir Hills: Mikir (approaching 200,000), the last two being separated geographically by an apparently isolated language, Khasi (p. 228). Nagaland contains a bewildering assemblage of tongues, of which the numerically preponderant are Ao (65,000), Angami (45,000), Kabui (30,000), Konyak (65,000), Lotha (30,000), Mao (30,000), Sema (50,000), Tangkhul (50,000). Manipuri or Meithei, the chief indigenous language of Manipur, is spoken by some 700,000, and Tripuri, the language of Tripur, by 350,000, while to the south of these places, in the southern tip of Assam, the local language is Lushai with 250,000 speakers.

Several of these languages have been cultivated in writing within the last hundred years or so, thanks to the efforts of European missionaries who usually employed Latin script. Others, in particular Newari (see also p. 208) and Manipuri, have an older, native tradition using Indian script. Languages in Assam now often employ Bengali script.

Khasi

Khasi is spoken by 400,000 persons inhabiting the Khasi and Jaintia Hills in Assam. Missionaries in the last century provided the language with a Roman alphabet and initiated a modest literature. The language may also be written in Bengali script. The oldest neighbours of Khasi are the Tibeto-Burman languages, Mikir and Garo, spoken to the east and west respectively, while its Aryan neighbours, Assamese to the north and Bengali to the south, are relative newcomers. The genetic affinities of Khasi are not evident. According to one view, however, Khasi is to be regarded as a divergent member of the Mon-Khmer group, at one time widely spoken in South-East Asia. The greater part of the original territory of this linguistic group has since been occupied by languages of the Tibeto-Burman and Thai branches of the Sino-Tibetan family, hence the Mon-Khmer languages now appear in dispersed enclaves. The group takes its name from two of its members: Mon, the vernacular of the coastal districts round the Gulf of Martaban between Rangoon and Moulmein, and Khmer or Cambodian, the state language of Cambodia. Mon-Khmer is sometimes described as being ultimately connected with Munda (p. 226).

Nahali

In view of the meagre amount of information at present available for some of the minor languages of India, it is likely that details of classification, at least here and there, will require modification. It is, indeed, not impossible that relics of hitherto unrecognised linguistic families may have survived, and one case is at present under discussion. It concerns Nahali, spoken by about 1,000 tribesmen near the village of Tembi, 25 miles east of Burhanpur, Nimar District, Madhya Pradesh, which has been regarded as an outlandish dialect of the West Munda language, Korku. It now transpires, however, that Nahali contains elements, grammatical as well as lexical, which show no apparent affiliation with any other Indian language. If these elements prove to be basic, then Nahali will appear as a genetically isolated language though heavily overlaid with Munda.

Burushaski

In the western part of the Karakorum an isolated language, Burushaski, survives in two enclaves: an eastern form found in Hunza and

Nagar, a western form in Yasin, where it is termed Werchikwar. To the north there is contact with Wakhi, in Yasin also with Khowar, otherwise with Shina, a language which has advanced in the Gilgit area at the expense of Burushaski, and in so doing has broken the former geographical continuity between the western and eastern forms of the language. It is also possible that Burushaski at one time extended further eastwards, where before a deterioration in climate there was access to Baltistan, now the territory of the Tibetan-like Balti. Dumaki forms a diminutive Indo-European enclave within the Burushaski of Hunza and Nagar. To all intents and purposes, Burushaski is a purely oral medium. It is probably used by about 20,000 persons.

Andamanese

The autochthonous inhabitants of the Andaman Islands are a Negrito race, and consequently of great anthropological interest. They numbered several thousands when they first made permanent contact with outsiders in 1858, at which time a penal settlement was established at Port Blair to receive deportees after the Mutiny of the previous year. Today, the Negritos are numbered only in hundreds. They speak the divergent dialects of the isolated Andamanese language, as yet far from adequately recorded. Meanwhile continuing immigration has raised the population to some 40,000. As in the Nicobars (below), the newcomers are linguistically heterogeneous, half of them Bengali and Hindi speakers, but with a large Dravidian minority and not a few Mundas. There is also some Burmese.

Nicobarese

This language, indigenous to the Nicobars, is spoken by 15,000 islanders. It is said to have genetic affinities with the Mon-Khmer group (see 'Khasi' above). The population of the Nicobars has been swollen in the last two decades by settlers from all parts of India, forming a polyglot element comparable to that in the Andamans, and about as numerous as the native Nicobarese.

2. DARDIC

Certain phonological peculiarities, thought to be ancient, distinguish the Dardic languages from other Aryan, and for this reason the languages concerned may be classified as members of an independent sub-branch. Research into origins is, however, grievously hampered by the nature of the material. Apart from Kashmiri, the languages in question are known solely from the most recent period, the great majority recorded only during the last hundred years, and documentation is far from complete in most cases. More information is needed before the mutual relationship of the various languages can be precisely defined—the question of what is here language and what is simply dialect is often acute. The problem of affinities is further bedevilled by the fact that all the languages involved have been much affected by Iranian or Indian, often by both. Understandably, the evidence is sometimes ambiguous and differences of opinion are found. In this connection we must also state that, according to a more recent view, only those languages native to Kafiristan (see below) are to be ascribed to an independent sub-branch of Aryan, the others—these then the Dardic languages proper—representing a particular development of Primitive Indo-Aryan. In other words, Dardic is a group genetically close to Indian. the two groups resulting from an early division of Primitive Indo-Aryan.

Dardic languages are spoken in some of the least accessible mountain tracts in the world, and the proliferation of language and dialect found in these regions is a classical example of the linguistic heterogeneity commonly associated with an environment of this type. But how many speak the various forms of Dardic is, in the majority of cases, not exactly known. Most of the territory concerned lies outside the area covered by the census enumerations carried out by the Government of India. Elsewhere figures tend to be less precise, some indeed are no more than estimates made by researchers in the field. It seems, however, that the total number of persons using the minor Dardic languages, i.e. all except Kashmiri, will hardly exceed 400,000.

Both suggested classifications (above) recognise three divisions of Dardic: western, central and eastern. Where the Kafiri languages are regarded as Dardic, they are held to form part of the western division; It will be convenient to follow this arrangement here.

WEST DARDIC

Kafiri languages

These languages are proper to that district in the Hindukush nowadays called Nuristan ('Land of Light'), but known until the subjugation and conversion of the local tribesmen to Islam by the Afghans in 1896 as Kafiristan ('Land of the Unbelievers'), hence the term Kafiri languages or dialects. They are: Kati, Prasun, Waigali and Ashkun, possibly also Dameli. Kati, also named Bashgali from its centre along the Bashgal Valley, is spoken on both sides of the Afghan-Pakistan frontier. Prasun, closely allied to the foregoing, is confined to three villages in Chitral. Waigali or Veron is the language used in districts immediately to the west of the Kati-speaking area, while Ashkun is indigenous to the Afghan district of the same name lying due south of that area. On Dameli, see below.

Kalasha

This language is current in a few villages along the Kumar, south-east of Drosh, in Pakistan.

Gawarbati

South of the Kalasha-speaking villages, the next language is Gawarbati or Narsati, spoken on both sides of the frontier.

Bashkarik

This language is used in several villages in Dir Kohistan, hence the alternative name Diri.

Phalura and Dameli

Phalura is used by some thousand persons living in remote villages on the east side of the Lower Chitral Valley. It is said to have affinities with Dameli, another very minor speech used by a few hundreds in an isolated village in the Gid Valley in South Chitral. Dameli has been described as being basically a language of the Kafiri type.

Pashai

Pashai was formerly in use over a wide area centring on the Upper Kabul Valley. But the expansion of Pashto has confined Pashai to various side valleys, namely the Nijran and Tagau, the Alishang and Alingar, and finally the lower part of the Kumar Valley and its right confluent, the Darrai Nur. There is great dialectal diversity and mutual comprehension may not always be possible, not surprising in view of the extent and nature of the terrain occupied.

Tirahi

This most southerly of the West Dardic languages is now isolated from its congeners by Pashto. It takes its name from Tirah, the frontier district south of Kabul. Tirahi is now found only on the Afghan side, where it survives in a few villages south-east of Jalalabad. It was doubtless at one time more widespread and shows some affinities with the East Dardic of Kohistan.

CENTRAL DARDIC

This division of Dardic is apparently represented by a single language only, Khowar, whose main centre is the Valley of Chitral as far south as Drosh. It takes its name from Kho, the indigenous name for the district. Khowar is in touch with both West and East Dardic, forming a bridge between the two. It is spoken by rather more than 100,000 persons.

EAST DARDIC

Shina

Shina is the language of the Gilgit Valley and of the Upper Indus
Valley from Baltistan to the Tangir Valley and further south-east. It
is spoken in a great variety of dialects by perhaps as many as 150,000
persons. To the north it is in contact with Khowar and the non-Indo-
European Burushaski (p. 228). To the east it is flanked by the
Tibetan languages Balti and Ladakhi, to the south by Kashmiri.
Elsewhere it is in touch with various minor Dardic languages.

Kashmiri

Kashmiri is the chief language of the Kashmir District of the Province
of Jammu and Kashmir, its centre being the Vale of Kashmir with the
capital Srinagar. To the north and west are Dardic languages (Shina,
Kohistani group), to the south Indo-Aryan (Panjabi, Western
Pahari), to the east the Tibetan Ladakhi. Kashmiri is the only Dardic
tongue regularly used as a written medium; it is one of the fourteen
official state languages of the Indian Union. It was formally written
in a script of its own, akin to Nagari, now superseded by Nagari
itself, but in fact the language most usually appears in an Arabic
character, some four-fifths of its speakers being Muslims. Kashmiri
is spoken by about two and a quarter millions, of whom over two
millions live in Bharat, the remainder across the demarcation line in
Pakistan. Kashmiri literature goes back to the fourteenth century,
though the language is actually attested somewhat earlier in quotations
in Sanskrit works.

Kohistani group

The rugged region of Kohistan (*koh* 'mountain') is the territory of a
group of three languages, Maiya, Garwi and Torwali, often collectively known as Kohistani, spoken by some 70,000 persons altogether.
Maiya is the idiom of Indus Kohistan, while Garwi and Torwali are
used in the northern and southern parts of Swat Kohistan respectively.
The Kohistan languages are in contact with other Dardic, except to
the south where the language is Pashto.

Text

Matthew vi.9–13 in Kashmiri

Ai sāni māli   yus asmānas p'aṭh chu: cōn nāv   sapạnin pākh. Cə̄n'
o our father who heaven in   is   thy name become holy thy

pātśāhath yiyin. Cōn' marzī yithạpọ̄ṭh' asmānas p'aṭh chi zamīnas
kingdom come thy will as   heaven in   is earth

p'aṭh' ti   sapạnin. Sōn' dọhạc tsọṭ   bakhś az   asi. Tạ sōn'
in   also become our daily bread grant today us and our

karz kar asi muāf   yuth əs' ti   panạn'an karzdāran chi muāf
debts do   us forgiven as   we also our-own debtors   are forgiven

karān. Tạ asi ma an   āzmāiśi   andar, balki badas niśạ rach.
doing and us not bring temptation into   but evil   from deliver

Tik'āzi pātśāhath tạ   kudrath tạ   jalāl chu hamēśạ cōn.
for   kingdom and power and glory is   ever   thine

3. IRANIAN

Languages of the Iranian group have been known since the first half
of the first millennium B.C., when they were already distributed over a
vast territory including the Iranian Plateau, Central Asia and Southern
Russia. One distinguishes East and West Iranian.

OLD IRANIAN

The earliest Iranians in Southern Russia were the Scythians who were
certainly living there in the seventh century B.C. They were joined,
from the third century onwards, by other nomadic Iranian peoples
moving westward from Central Asia; they are often classed indis-
criminately as Sarmatians, among whom were the Alans. The immigrant Goths (p. 96) came into contact with the latter and made
common cause with them against the Huns in the fourth century A.D.
Large troops of Alans accompanied the Goths into Central Europe
and Spain, where they shared a common fate. But a section of the
Alanic-speaking tribes remained in the steppe country between the
Sea of Azov and the Caspian until medieval times and were well
known to Byzantine writers. Their East Iranian language survives
today in Ossetic (p. 246). The ancient Iranians of Southern Russia
left no written records, but we have the testimony of their personal
names. There is also some evidence from toponymy: for example, the
name of the Don is simply Iranian for 'river' as in Ossetic *don.*

Avestan

Undoubtedly the earliest Iranian texts are the Gathas ('Hymns') of the
Avesta, the ancient Iranian scriptures, though a precise dating is not
possible. The Gathas are traditionally ascribed to Zoroaster himself,
said to have lived in the sixth century B.C. This is perhaps a little late,

but at all events the language of the Gathas so closely resembles that of the Indian Vedas—the one can often be mechanically transposed into the other—that Iranists are inclined to place their composition considerably before the middle of the first millennium. The other parts of the Avesta are in somewhat less archaic language. Avestan belongs to the East Iranian type, most probably based on dialects once spoken in Central Asia. Tradition speaks of Bactria, but it has been suggested that a more likely centre will have been ancient Chorasmia (p. 236).

Avestan has often been called Zend or Zend Avestan, a misnomer which arose as follows. Zoroastrianism was flourishing by the end of the Achaemenid age. Subsequent political events pushed it into the background, until revived by the Sasanids under whom, in the third and fourth centuries A.D., the surviving Avesta was edited and provided with a *zand* (Zend) or 'commentary'. This, however, was drawn up in Pahlavi (p. 235), a very different language from that of the Avesta itself. Zoroastrianism has now all but disappeared from Persia, but survives vigorously in India, whither Zoroastrians began to repair in the seventh century. Their descendants, the Parsees (i.e. 'Persians'), over 100,000 strong, live mainly in Bombay and district. They pre-served a knowledge of Avestan and Pahlavi as the languages of their sacred literature, but their vernacular and ordinary literary medium is the Indian language Gujarati. It was from manuscripts in Parsee hands that the first knowledge of the Avesta reached Europe just after the middle of the eighteenth century.

The older Iranian alphabets are of Aramaic origin and usually suffer from the defect that, as in Aramaic, the vowels are in general unmarked. This is standard Semitic practice, the structure of these languages being such that they are tolerably legible even without letters for vowels, but it is a much less satisfactory method of writing an Indo-European language. It is possible that the Avesta was first written in such an alphabet. However, the texts available today have been handed down in a special development of Middle Persian script which contains carefully distinguished vowel signs. The intention was to fix as accurately as possible the forms of a language already then extinct. One may compare in principle the introduction of vowel pointing into the consonantal text of the Hebrew Bible between the fifth and seventh centuries A.D.

Old Persian

Iranians are first reported in the west in an Akkadian source of 836 B.C. The tribes concerned were Medes, who in 612 took Nineveh from the Assyrians. To the south of the Medes were the Persians, who eventu-ally assumed the leading role among the West Iranians and provided the Achaemenid kings who ruled the Persian Empire (546–330 B.C.).

The exiguous records of the Median language are of the same character as those of Scythian and Sarmatian, but the Persians left a number of inscriptions, chiefly monumental, from the Achaemenid period. Many of them are trilingual: Akkadian, Elamite and Persian. Akkadian was the Semitic language of Mesopotamia, while Elamite, of unknown affinities, was confined to the small country of Elam. At an undeterminable date, but most likely in antiquity, Elamite was replaced by Persian, the language of the area today. The inscriptions are engraved in a cuneiform alphabet, especially devised for writing in Persian. After the fall of the Empire, the art of cuneiform writing was lost. It was, however, from Persian materials that Grotefend in 1802 took the first decisive steps in the decipherment of this script. The language of the Achaemenid records is called Old Persian. In spite of the relatively small quantity available, an outline of the structure of the language can be obtained. It is closely comparable to Avestan— a fact which assisted the later stages of decipherment—but is less conservative.

Persia (*Pārsa*) properly denotes the homeland of the Achaemenids and lives on in the name of the present-day province of Fars. Likewise, Persian originally referred to the dialect of this district only, and its native name today is appropriately *Fārsī*.

MIDDLE IRANIAN

WESTERN

Middle Persian

Thanks no doubt to the political pre-eminence of the Achaemenids, Persian early began to spread at the expense of adjacent Iranian dialects, at the same time incorporating many elements proper to those dialects. The expanding Persian took on a progressively composite character. From the time of Alexander's conquest, however, until the end of the Arsacid dynasty in A.D. 226, Persian was not a state language and, save for occasional inscriptions, is not in evidence in the surviving records. Then, on the accession of the Sasanid line in 226, Persian again assumed official status and there rapidly came into existence a rich theological literature, mainly Zoroastrian and Manichean, but also Christian. Various adaptations of Aramaic script were in use to write Middle Persian or Pahlavi, as the language of this literature is also called. In reference to script, the term Pahlavi denotes a vowelless form which makes use of ideograms and is notoriously inconsequent. Sometimes Pahlavi texts are found transcribed into vocalised Avestan script (p. 234), such texts being called

Pazend. Lastly, the Manicheans borrowed the Estrangelo Syriac script and used it to write other Middle Iranian languages as well, i.e. Parthian and Sogdian. It is therefore customary to speak of Manichean Middle Persian, etc.

Middle Persian is grammatically very different from Old Persian. The inherited declensional pattern, still well preserved in the Achaemenid material, is seen to have broken down completely. The system of the verb has been reorganised as a consequence of the simplification of the traditional morphology. Literary Middle Persian was rudely pushed aside by the Arab conquest in 642 but the Zoroastrian communities continued to employ it until the tenth century. They sometimes used Arabic script; such texts are characterised as Parsi.

EASTERN

Chorasmian, Sogdian, Saka

These are the medieval representatives of the eastern division of Iranian. They have significant features in common which, moreover, they share with Pashto and Ossetic. This indicates a period of close continuity between the ancestral forms of all these languages in antiquity, when the tribes concerned lived on the plains of Central Asia.

Chorasmian (or Khwarazmian) was the language of ancient Chorasmia, a province along the Lower Oxus (Amu Darya), so called from its chief city Chorasm (Khwarazm), now Khiva. Excavations during the thirties of this century revealed for the first time the former magnificence of the province and a few inscriptions in Iranian writing came to light. A few hundred glosses in Chorasmian were, however, already known from their occurrence in Arabic sources. The Chorasmian state came to an end in 1231. Turkicisation had already begun, as is apparent from the presence of Turkic words in the glosses mentioned above. Chorasmian was probably extinct by the fourteenth century and today the area is shared by three Turkic languages: Turkmen, Karakalpak and Uzbek.

Sogdian (Soghdian) was the language of the ancient kingdom of Sogdiana and its capital Samarkand. As a lingua franca, it spread through Central Asia to China and Mongolia. A few letters in Sogdian, written in China, may be as old as the fourth century A.D. The latest documents belong to the tenth or eleventh centuries, but the bulk of the surviving literature dates from the seventh to ninth centuries. It is chiefly religious in content, Manichean, Christian and Buddhist, the material coming from archaeological sites in Chinese Turkestan explored in the first two decades of the present century. In the thirties, more modest archival finds were made among ruins in Sogdiana itself. In its homeland, Sogdian began to be displaced by Persian perhaps as early as the ninth century. Most likely it also yielded some territory to Turkic dialects introduced by nomads from the north. Today Sogdian has vanished except for the diminutive Yaghnobi enclave (pp. 246–7).

The Persians are said by Herodotus to have called the various Scythian tribes Saka. In the second century B.C., Saka Iranians invaded North-West India and the present province of Sinkiang (Chinese Turkestan). Traces of their language are faintly discernible in loan words occurring in Indian inscriptions of the first two centuries B.C. But rich manuscript remains of Saka came to light in Turkestan as the result of archaeological discoveries in the first two decades of this century. The chief finds are from Khotan, south of the Takla-Makan desert. Lesser finds were made at Maralbashi, an oasis north of the desert some 200 miles east of Kashgar, and at Tumshuq, a little to the east of Aksu. The texts are for the most part translations of Buddhist missionary materials, though medical and administrative documents are also present. They date from the beginning of the seventh to the second half of the tenth centuries. The language falls perceptibly into two periods: in the earlier one the inflexional endings of East Middle Iranian are well preserved, but in the later period are much decayed. The language of Khotan is called Khotanese Saka or simply Khotanese, the dialectally divergent records from the northern oases may be distinguished as Maralbashi or Tumshuq Saka. The monuments themselves are written in varieties of Indian Brahmi script and Indian loan words are commonplace, a clear reflection of the cultural influence of India upon ancient Sinkiang. Middle Iranian had as neighbours other Indo-European dialects belonging to the Tocharian branch. It is considered that the latter were already settled there when the Iranians arrived. Today, Uigur, a Turkic language, is the dominant speech of the region and was most likely responsible for the extinction there of Saka, as of Tocharian, an event which may conceivably be placed at the beginning of the second millennium. On the other hand, Saka appears to survive in the mountains to the west, see Pamir dialects (below).

NEW IRANIAN

WESTERN

New Persian

The Arab conquest of 642 brought to an end the official use of Persian and led to a catastrophic decline in its employment for literary purposes generally. It inaugurated the period of arabisation when

Persian and the other Iranian languages (except the isolated Ossetic) absorbed a notable Arabic element, in the case of Persian comparable in quantity and character to the Latinate component of modern English. It is this Arabic element which chiefly distinguishes New from Middle Persian. In the second half of the tenth century, Persian again became the dominant literary language, but it was now written in Arabic script. This is the formal beginning of New Persian.

Although Arab hegemony robbed Persian of its former status, the conquests of the Arabs laid the basis for the further territorial expansion of the language. Persian-speaking garrisons in the main centres of Afghanistan spread the use of the colloquial language at the expense of indigenous East Iranian languages. Persian was similarly introduced into Central Asia, Bukhara and Samarkand evidently giving up their native Sogdian by the ninth or tenth centuries. From the administrative centres, the language spread to the countryside.

Persian expansion in these areas was, however, soon afterwards checked by intruding Turkic languages and many gains were quickly turned into losses. Turkic-speaking nomads had been in evidence in Central Asia since the early centuries of the Christian era. But now they were becoming well-nigh irresistible and made powerful inroads deep into Iranian territory. In the eleventh century large bands passed south of the Caspian to settle in Azerbaijan or crossed over into Asia Minor. Others penetrated to the south where enclaves remain to this day. The northern area won from Parthian was lost and Merv, for a while a centre of Persian expansion, became a Turkmen-speaking city. Much of the old province of Sogdiana was similarly turkicised, especially the plains, where the Uzbeks began to infiltrate in the sixteenth century. Even the great cities succumbed, but the Jews of Bukhara and Samarkand have maintained the use of Persian—albeit much corrupted by Uzbek—as their community idiom. It has been termed Bukhari.

The present extent of the Persian-speaking area is as follows. Persian is spoken as the native language over the greater part of the modern state of Iran, of which it is the sole official language. It dominates from the Persian Gulf to the frontier with the Turkmen SSR, but the north-west in particular remains largely non-Persian. However, the state language is in many places simplifying the complicated linguistic map as it assimilates various minor speeches, and is everywhere making progress, at least as a second language. The number of native speakers is of the order of fourteen millions out of a total of twenty-six millions for the whole country. Of the other languages, the numerically most significant is the Turkic Azeri, spoken by five millions in Persian Azerbaijan. Well over a further million use other Turkic languages in various enclaves elsewhere in

Iran. The majority live in districts adjacent to the Turkmen SSR, but upwards of 300,000 lead their nomadic existence in the very heartland of Persia, the province of Fars. Otherwise the most important non-Persian languages are Kurdish (p. 240) and Balochi (p. 241).

About 100,000 Persian speakers live in enclaves in Iraq, about half that number at various points on the western shore of the Persian Gulf and in Oman.

Persian is further spoken over wide areas of Afghanistan, chiefly in the northern half of the country, and is the language of the capital, Kabul, the number of speakers approaching the two and a quarter million mark. Until 1936, it was the state language of Afghanistan, but was then replaced by Pashto. Persian continues in use as a second official language, but its former high standing has been adversely affected by the policy of afghanisation (p. 245).

The predominantly Persian-speaking area of Afghanistan continues across the state frontier into the Tajik SSR with one million Persian speakers. Another half million inhabit neighbouring areas of the Uzbek SSR. These territories have been under Russian suzerainty since the closing decades of the last century. In considering the prospects for Persian in the USSR, one should not forget the pressure from Uzbek and, more recently, from Russian. Particularly the presence of the latter seems ominous for the local Persian which is not strong enough to assimilate the growing number of Russians now settling in its territory. At the present time Tajiks—the Persian speakers—comprise rather less than one-third of the population of their own republic, the remainder being principally half a million Uzbeks and 300,000 Russians. Tajiks often speak Uzbek, latterly also Russian.

The Persian of Afghanistan and Central Asia may be called Tajiki, and this is the official name for Soviet Persian. Tajiki is traditionally written in the Arabic character, but in the USSR the Latin alphabet was introduced in 1928, changing to Cyrillic in 1939. Unlike their cousins in Iran and Afghanistan, the Soviet Tajiks are now highly literate. The form of their language differs from other Persian notably by reason of its Turkic (Uzbek) element, which effects both lexicon and syntax. It is the state language of the Tajik SSR, and also the literary language for speakers of the minor East Iranian dialects spoken in the republic.

Another form of Persian is worthy of note here. This is Judeo-Persian with an ample literature of considerable philological value, the earliest document being a letter dated 718. This variety is distinguished from standard literary Persian chiefly by the use of semitisms peculiar to the Jews. It is written in Hebrew characters.

Thanks to the vitality of its literature, the Persian language made a notable impress upon the Turkic languages with which it has been in intimate contact since the eleventh century. Persian has played a most significant role in India, where it became an official language and the medium of an extensive literature (p. 200).

Kurdish

The homeland of the Kurds is a mountainous area historically known as Kurdistan; it extends over the territories of four political states: Iran, Turkey, Syria and Iraq. Here the Kurds comprise 80 per cent of the population, a large proportion of whom are nomadic. The present linguistic boundary proceeds from a point just south-west of Hamadan to the southern tip of Lake Urmia, along its western shore and on to the junction of the Persian, Soviet and Turkish frontiers. It continues for 100 miles along the Turkish-Soviet border without appreciably extending into the USSR and then turns due west as far as the Euphrates, then south with it to the Syrian border which it crosses for a short distance. It then runs eastward through the Turkish borderland, making room for a large enclave of Arabic speech on the Turkish side. Entering Iraq, it passes north of Mosul and then veers south-east to the frontier with Iran near Khanekin, whence east a little below Kermanshah to the starting point near Hamadan. Kurdish is in contact with many and varied languages: the main ones are Persian, Azerbaijani and Osmanli Turkish, Arabic, while among the minor ones, mostly in Eastern Anatolia, are Armenian and Syrian, the latter a Semitic language. There are also isolated Kurdish centres, mainly in Iran and Turkey. There is a particularly strong enclave, with about a quarter of a million speakers, immigrants of long standing, in the northern part of the Persian province of Khorasan; a very small portion of this enclave extends into the Turkmen SSR as far as the environs of Ashkhabad. The most notable Kurdish enclave in Turkey lies immediately south-west of Ankara. This and other enclaves between here and Kurdistan are the result of transplantations carried out by the Turkish authorities during World War I and after the Kurdish risings in the twenties and thirties. It is not possible to calculate the number of Kurdish speakers exactly. One may, however, think in terms of between seven to eight millions at the most, of whom two and a half to three millions live in Turkey, up to two millions in Iran and nearly as many in Iraq, plus at least a quarter of a million in Syria. About 60,000 live on Soviet soil, mostly in the Armenian SSR. There are perhaps a further 200,000 in Afghanistan and Pakistan.

Kurdish falls into a number of dialects, often much differentiated. It is mainly an oral medium, its speakers being in any case very largely illiterate. Printing in Kurdish only began at the end of the last century— a news-sheet first appearing in 1898 and continuing at long intervals until 1902. There is no written standard for the whole Kurdish area, but regional varieties have in some places achieved literary status, the most significant being that of Sulaimaniye in Iraq. Here Kurdish nationalism is most effective and, since 1966 in the predominantly Kurdish parts of Iraq, the language may be used officially in local administration and elementary education. The Iraqi Kurds are also the most active culturally and publishing started here in 1920. Arabic characters are now employed, an experiment in the use of Latin letters having been given up. The large communities in Turkey are practically unable to publish in their native language. Between 1931 and 1956, Kurdish was permitted to be published in Syria, and here the Latin alphabet was in use. There is also some publishing in Kurdish in the USSR. The first productions, from 1921, used the Armenian alphabet; in 1929 this was changed to Latin, in 1946 to Cyrillic characters. The earliest texts in Kurdish are poems doubtfully ascribed to the twelfth century. The medieval literature is written in Arabic script. Kurdish is an essentially south-western Iranian language which reached its present stronghold by migration at an unknown date. The origin of the name Kurd is unexplained.

Balochi

Balochi (or Baluchi) is the spoken language of the greater part of the historic province of Balochistan, lying between Afghanistan and the sea, today divided between Iran and Pakistan. In this, its main territory, Balochi extends from Jask on the Gulf of Oman north-east to the Afghan border 100 miles north of Khormek. From here, its northern limit traverses the southern districts of Afghanistan, entering Pakistan a little south of Quetta and continuing due east to within 100 miles of the Indus. It then sweeps south, coming close to the Indus near Kashmor before turning south-west to the sea which it reaches 50 miles west of Karachi. Balochi thus faces Persian to the west, Pashto to the north, and the Indo-Aryan language, Sindhi, to the east. There is, however, a further neighbour, one actually situated inside the compact area of Balochi. This is Brahui, spoken by some quarter of a million persons inhabiting a large enclave which spreads out on either side of a line from Bela through Kelat to about 50 miles south of Quetta. Brahui is a Dravidian language (p. 224), profoundly influenced by Indo-Aryan with which it was in contact before being surrounded by the advancing Balochi.

Balochi is further spoken by emigrant groups in considerable enclaves in Western Afghanistan and North-Eastern Iran. Smaller communities are found in India (Bharat), in Muskat and Oman, and finally in the Mari Region of the Turkmen SSR. Balochi is the mother tongue of about two million souls. Half of these live in Pakistan, 600,000 in Iran, 200,000 in Afghanistan, 50,000 in India, 10,000 in the Arabian Peninsula, 8,000 in the USSR. Balochi is nowhere an official language and appears to be losing ground, especially to Sindhi. On the other hand, it is making some gains at the expense of Brahui.

Balochi is known only from the modern period, the first publication being in 1833. The Balochi-speakers are still, in the overwhelming majority, illiterate. Nevertheless, since the 1940s there has been a small amount of publishing in Pakistan, where Arabic letters are used. In the thirties, a Balochi-language newspaper and a few textbooks were issued in Latin characters in the USSR but the practice has been discontinued, education now being conducted in Turkmen.

The Baloch are first mentioned in the tenth century, when they were located in Fars, around Kerman and on the north-west border of present-day Balochistan, which was presumably entered during the Middle Ages. Dialectology shows that Balochi belongs to a north-west type of Iranian, so that its speakers were clearly on the move at the time of the first historical reference.

Tati

Tati is spoken in areas of mixed speech in Soviet Azerbaijan east of Baku on the Apsheron Peninsula and in districts stretching north-west of that city along the coast almost to the frontier of Daghestan and extending between 50 and 75 miles inland. The speakers here are chiefly Muslims. Tati is further spoken in various parts of Daghestan, particularly around Derbent, where it is in the main the language of the Mountain Jews. These were culturally more active than the Muslims and produced a literature in their language written in Hebrew letters. Their variety of Tati includes a lexical element of Hebrew-Aramaic origin. The Muslims remained without any literature in the mother tongue until the Soviet administration introduced the use of Tati in education. Today, however, the language is no longer so used in Azerbaijan, where the Tat population is bilingual, having the language of their neighbours, the Azerbaijani Turks, as the second medium. But in Daghestan the language continues to be used officially. In 1928 a Latin alphabet was devised for Tati, to be replaced ten years later by Cyrillic. In the south, Tati has been yielding to Azeri for at least a century. The position in Daghestan is less clear. Here there is no comparable indigenous major language, only a medley of local idioms spoken by relatively small populations. The number of speakers of Tati today will be of the order of 10,000 in Azerbaijan and 25,000 in Daghestan. Tati has south-western characteristics, its speakers being most likely descended from colonists planted during the Sasanid era (226 to 642).

Talishi

In addition to Tati, a second Iranian language is used in Soviet Azerbaijan. This is Talishi, which extends across the state frontier into Persian Azerbaijan where it is in contact with the main body of Iranian languages. In the north it occupies the Lenkoran Depression covering a strip of territory 20 miles wide which runs due south along the coast of the Caspian Sea. It then continues in the same fashion for an equal distance on the Persian side, though it now leaves the Caspian coast which here swings to the east. North of the state frontier Talishi is in contact with Azeri, south of the frontier with Azeri to the west, but with closely related Iranian dialects to the east. Talishi is the mother tongue of close on 200,000 persons, of whom half live in Soviet Azerbaijan. For at least a century, Talishi has been losing ground to Azeri. In Iran it is increasingly exposed to the levelling influence of Standard Persian.

Talishi has never been a literary language in any proper sense. Nevertheless at the beginning of the thirties it was decided to create a literature in Soviet Talishi. But this policy was soon abandoned, and the bilingual Soviet Talish now practise literacy through the medium of Azeri. Many of the Persian Talish also know this language, but in Iran Azeri may not be used for literary purposes. The Talish in Iran, therefore, in so far as they can read at all, use Persian as their literary medium.

Gilani and Mazandarani

The type of north-western dialect exemplified by Talishi is continued in the dialects spoken in the provinces of Gilan and Mazandaran along the southern shore of the Caspian. Collections of poetry in the language of the latter province go back to medieval times, but Mazandarani, like Gilani, is today a purely oral medium, in modern conditions more and more affected by Standard Persian.

Gorani and Zaza

The area of the north-western dialects of Iranian was largely overrun by Turkic, subsequently known as Azeri or Azerbaijani, introduced in the eleventh century. By the sixteenth century, this language had ousted the indigenous Iranian except from the peripheral area along the Caspian coast. Two of these north-western dialects, however, survive outside the area; they are Gorani and Zaza. The Gorans moved south, but their language, now much declined, survives only in the neighbourhood of Kermanshah. As the language of an obscure sect, Gorani became the vehicle of a considerable literature, but is no more than a patois today. The Zaza people, living in some small communities among the Kurds of Eastern Turkey, are descended from immigrants from Dailam on the southern shore of the Caspian and have in part retained the language of their ancestors, which they themselves call Dimli. It is an almost unwritten language.

Other West Iranian languages

The dialects of the Luri and Bakhtiyari tribes, chiefly inhabiting the Persian province of Luristan, comprise a division of south-west Iranian. These dialects, which are probably spoken by as many as a million souls, have produced no written literature, though as every-where in these parts, the people have a rich oral tradition. More to the south, in various districts of the province of Fars, smaller groups of other south-west Iranian dialects are found, also unwritten.

Finally, in West and Central Persia, there are a number of inde-pendent dialects, some of which are still imperfectly known. Differ-ences between them may be so great that mutual comprehension is excluded.

EASTERN

Pashto

By far the most important East Iranian language today is Pashto. Its main area is as follows. The western limits correspond partly to the state frontier between Afghanistan and Iran, except in the south-east where the indigenous language is Balochi. At certain points, however, Persian extends into Afghanistan; similarly Pashto extends into Iran, though only for short distances. Pashto occupies essentially the southern half of the State of Afghanistan, except for Balochi in its southern borderland and enclaves of Persian, mostly in the western part. The northern limit of the compact area of Pashto speech now runs in an arc from just below Herat down to Taivara, then up again to a point 100 miles north of Kabul—the capital itself is a Persian-speaking city though its hinterland uses Pashto. The linguistic frontier then turns due west to reach the Indus in Pakistan, whose course it follows to a little south of the confluence of the Kabul. It then moves away from the Indus slightly, but continuing parallel to it as far as Dera-Ghazi-Khan, where it bends sharply east, reaching the Afghan state frontier just south of Quetta. Pashto is thus in contact with Balochi to the south, Persian to the west and north, and with various Dardic and Indo-Aryan languages to the north-east and east. There are further a number of large enclaves of Pashto in the northern half of Afghanistan, several of them abutting on the territory of the USSR. The dominant language here is Persian (p. 239), but the most northerly districts, except for the extreme north-east, are largely Turkic-speaking, the main languages concerned being Turkmen in the westerly and Uzbek in the easterly parts.

It is thought that the ancestors of the Afghans originally inhabited the plains of Central Asia (p. 236), but already in antiquity migrating to the south-east where they assimilated other East Iranian and Indo-Aryan and some Dardic dialects. Afghans are first mentioned by name at the end of the tenth century, about which time they were settled in the area of the Sulaiman Mountains, largely in present-day Pakistan. Afterwards, they became expansive, but their colonisation of the low land by the Indus and the movement into the areas of Kandahar and Kabul did not begin until the thirteenth century. Afghans reached the outskirts of Herat in the sixteenth century. Subsequently the newcomers consolidated their position in all these areas with their language spreading at the expense largely of various East Iranian, Indo-Aryan and Dardic dialects. In the north and west, however, Persian was the loser. Meanwhile the language was also advancing in the north-east in the region of the Hindukush and more recently large enclaves of Pashto speech have been established in South Turkestan, a territory not finally conquered until the end of the nineteenth century. This is the area of mainly Turkmen and Uzbek speech, referred to above.

A language so widely dispersed over a mainly mountainous terrain naturally falls into numerous dialects. One distinguishes two main divisions, south-west and north-east, with Kandahar and Peshawar as their respective centres. The language is known in the former dialect as Pashto, in the latter as Pakhto. It is morphologically archaic, more so than, for example, Middle Persian. On the other hand, the traditional phonetic system has been subject to drastic changes and partly indianised. There are no texts older than the seventeenth century. The language is written in Arabic characters.

In 1936 Pashto, in older writings often called Pushtu, replaced Persian as the state language of Afghanistan, and since then the administration has pursued a policy of afghanisation in all parts of the country. Such official recognition has led to the rapid growth of a modern literature in Pashto in a wide variety of subjects. By contrast, the literature in Pakhto is very limited, for in Pakistan the official language is Urdu. About thirteen millions speak Pashto/Pakhto as their mother tongue, of whom seven live in Afghanistan, about half the population of that multilingual state, and six in Pakistan, where they are known as Pathans. Finally, about 50,000 Pashto speakers are found in the eastern frontier districts of Iran.

9

Ossetic

The only other East Iranian language spoken by a numerically significant population and in use as a literary medium is Ossetic, a language
long cut off from the rest of the Iranian world. It is employed by about
425,000 persons whose homeland lies in the Central Caucasus on both
sides of the main range which also divides their territory administratively into the North Ossetic Autonomous Republic and the South
Ossetic Autonomous Region of the Georgian SSR. The Ossetians are
descended from those Alans (p. 233) who remained in the Pontic-
Caspian steppes. In the twelfth and thirteenth centuries, they withdrew into the mountains to escape Turkic and Mongol invaders. The
settlements in Transcaucasia were affected by a secondary migration
of the fourteenth and fifteenth centuries.

The language falls into two main dialects: Iron spoken by fully
three-quarters of the population, and the more archaic Digor confined to the western and northern areas of North Ossetia. The Alans
have left but a single inscription; it is in Greek letters and dated 941.
But if they actually had a regular literary tradition, it was lost in subsequent centuries, for the modern language was only committed to
writing about the middle of the eighteenth century as the result of
orthodox missionary activity by the Georgian and Russian Churches.
Both dialects were cultivated and the language transcribed in two
types of script, Georgian and Russian. A modest literature arose,
chiefly in Iron. Since the twenties of this century literacy has developed
apace on the basis of the Iron dialect, for only Iron has any official
standing, Digor being no longer a normally written form. In 1923
Latin characters were introduced, but replaced in 1938 by Cyrillic in
North and Mkhedruli in South Ossetia. In 1954 the latter also went
over to Cyrillic. Ossetic has been profoundly influenced by the
Caucasian languages which surround it on every side and, like
Armenian, it shows this influence not only in vocabulary, but also in
phonetics. Ossetic is the only modern Iranian language without an
appreciable Arabic element (pp. 237–8). Through Alanic, its early
form, Ossetic is closely akin to the recorded languages of the eastern
division of Middle Iranian.

Yaghnobi

This is the speech of approximately 2,000 persons living along the
course of the Yaghnob, an affluent of the Zarafshan, and in other high
valleys in that neighbourhood. The area in question lies some 50 to
75 miles north and north-east of Dushanbe, the capital of the Tajik
SSR. Yaghnobi is the sole survivor of Sogdian. It is entirely surrounded by Tajiki which has greatly influenced it in matters of voca-

bulary, the more so since Yaghnobi speakers use this language as their second tongue.

Munjani and Yidgha

Between 1,000 and 1,500 persons inhabiting Munjan, a locality in the south-east of Afghan Badakhshan, speak this language. Closely related is the dialect known as Yidgha, spoken by 1,000 persons living in the upper valley of the Lutkuh about 60 miles south-east of Munjan near the frontier with Pakistan. Yidgha is a relatively recent colonial offshoot of Munjani. Whereas the latter is encompassed by Tajiki, to which it is losing ground, the former is in touch with the Dardic language Khowar.

Parachi

This language survives today in small enclaves within areas of Tajiki, Pashto and the Dardic language Pashai, situated on Afghan territory 60 to 100 miles north-east of Kabul. About 5,000 persons speak Parachi.

Ormuri

Today, Ormuri is confined to two small areas, one in Afghanistan in the valley of the Logar, 60 to 100 miles south-west of Kabul, the second 150 miles to the south-east in the district of Kaniguram, Pakistan. The latter is most likely a colonial settlement and its dialect is considerably more archaic. Ormuri is mentioned as early as the sixteenth century, when it was said to be in use in Kabul and environs. Reports from the nineteenth century show that it was even then much more widely used than it is today. It has lost ground to Tajiki in the extreme west, elsewhere to Pashto—the Ormuri in Pakistan likewise constitutes an enclave in Pashto-speaking territory. The number of speakers is not known exactly. One may think in terms of a few thousand for Afghanistan, and a much smaller figure for Pakistan.

Pamir dialects

The Pamir dialects are spoken by populations inhabiting the Western Pamirs. They form the native stock of the western part of the Gorno-Badakhshan Autonomous Region of the Tajik SSR and of adjacent districts of Afghanistan and the Chinese province of Sinkiang. The ancestors of these Iranians, presumably Saka, began moving into this most inaccessible territory at the time of the Muslim invasions in the eighth century. The dialects in question have only been studied within the last hundred years, some only in this century.

First, the Shughni group, which comprises Shughni proper, then

Roshani, Bartangi, Oroshori, Sarikoli. All these dialects are, in essentials, mutually comprehensible and, apart from Sarikoli, occupy contiguous areas. Shughni itself is the language of Shughnan, a historic region on both sides of the Pyanj (Upper Amu Darya) which here forms the border between Afghanistan and the USSR. Its centre is Khorog, at the confluence of the Pyanj and Gunt, now the administrative centre of Gorno-Badakhshan. Shughni is the native language of some 20,000 persons on the Soviet and of, roughly speaking, an equal number on the Afghan side of the frontier. North of Shughnan lies the district and town of Roshan. Roshani is spoken by about 15,000 persons, again approximately half on each side of the frontier. East of Roshan, the 4,000 inhabitants of the upper valley of the Bartang use the Bartangi dialect, while at the head of the same valley lies the kishlak of Oroshor, the distinct dialect of whose 2,000 inhabitants is accordingly known as Oroshori. Finally, the geographically isolated Sarikoli. Sarikol is a small region in Sinkiang and here, close to the frontier south of Tashkurgan, about 5,000 souls (at a very rough guess) use the Sarikoli dialect as their native vernacular. It is an offshoot of Shughni, brought in the not too distant past by emigrants from Shughnan.

Just north of Roshan lies the Yazghulam valley; its 2,000 inhabitants speak the Yazghulami dialect.

North of the Yazghulam and parallel to it runs the now Tajiki-speaking Wanch valley, where in the second half of the last century the Wanchi dialect could still be heard. Materials gathered in 1915 from informants who had used the dialect in their youth show that Wanchi belonged to the Pamir group.

Immediately south of the Shughni-speaking area, at the point where the Pyanj turns north, the dialects of the settlements at and around Ishkashim, Zebak and Sanglech form an entity of their own which we shall here call Ishkashimi. These dialects are spoken by 2,000 souls, of whom three-quarters live on the Afghan side. Ishkashimi is in contact with Shughni and Tajiki, except to the east where the neighbouring language is Wakhi.

Wakhi takes its name from the historic region of Wakhan situated in the area of the sources of the Pyanj, now divided between Afghanistan and the USSR. The majority of all Wakhi speakers live here, but smaller numbers are found along the Yarkhun in the Chitral district of Pakistan, in the Gilgit and Hunza districts of the Indian province of Jammu and Kashmir, and finally in the Sarikol district in Sinkiang near the junction of the frontier with Afghanistan and the USSR. Speakers of Wakhi may thus be in contact with many other languages, e.g., Tajiki, Ishkashimi, Sarikoli, the non-Indo-European Burushaski. Figures for the number of speakers in the different areas vary, but a round total of 15,000 will be about right, the largest group of six to seven thousand living on Soviet soil.

The Pamir dialects are essentially oral media, though there was a little publishing in Shughni in the thirties in Gorno-Badakhshan, a short-lived attempt to create a literature in this dialect. Today Tajiki is the literary medium for speakers of Pamir dialects in Gorno-Badakhshan. Elsewhere they also turn to more significant languages.

THE STRUCTURE OF IRANIAN

In view of the relative paucity of material, full paradigms for Old Iranian are sometimes unobtainable. This is invariably the case with Old Persian. However, in view of the close affinities between Old Iranian and Old Indian, the outline of the latter given on pp. 215–8 may serve by proxy as a rough guide to the oldest Iranian conditions.

Text

Beginning of an Old Persian inscription of Xerxes I (486–465 B.C.) at Persepolis

Baga vazarka Ahuramazdā, hya imām būmim adā, hya
god great A. (Lord of Wisdom) who this earth created who

avam asmānam adā, hya martiyam adā, hya šiyātim
yon heaven created who man created who well-being

adā martiyahyā, hya Xšayāršām xšāyaθiyam akunauš aivam
created for-man who Xerxes king ('shah') made a

parūnām xšāyaθiyam, aivam parūnām framātāram. Adam Xšayāršā
of-many king a of-many commander I Xerxes

xšāyaθiya vazarka, xšāyaθiya xšāyaθiyānām, xšāyaθiya dahyūnām
king great king of-kings king of-lands

paruvzanānām, xšāya θiya ahyāyā būmiya vazarkāyā, duraiyapiy,
of-many-peoples king on-this earth great far-and-wide

Dārayavahauš xšāyaθiyahyā puθra, Haxāmanišiya.
of-Darius (the) king son Achaemenid

MODERN PERSIAN

Phonetics

kh, gh are [χ, γ], *ch, sh, zh* [ʧ, ʃ, ʒ] respectively. ' (in words of Arabic origin) represents a glottal stop, ignored in informal speech. Doubled consonants are long. Vowel length is not phonemic, vowels being short or long according to position. The macron used in the transcription is not a mark of length, but of quality. Thus the phonemically distinct *a* and *ā* are (roughly speaking) front and back *a*-like vowels respectively, both occurring short and long. Stress falls on the last syllable.

Accidence

Modern Persian has been called the English of the East since it is so highly analytic. Grammatical gender has disappeared, nouns have no case inflexions, adjectives are invariable. A distinctive feature is the joining of adjectives to nouns and of nouns to other nouns by an (originally relative) particle *e*, after vowels *ye*, thus *Dōlat-e-Shāhan-shāhī-ye-Īrān* '(the) Imperial Government of Persia'.

The verb is built up from two stems, present and past, partly with the help of prefixes, as follows:

Infin. *bordan* 'bear away'

	Pres. indic.	Past indic.
Sg.1	*mibaram*	*bordam*
2	*mibarī*	*bordī*
3	*mibarad*	*bord*
Pl.1	*mibarīm*	*bordīm*
2	*mibarīd*	*bordīd*
3	*mibarand*	*bordand*

	Pres.subj.	Imperf. indic.
Sg.1	*bebaram*, etc.	*mibordam*, etc.

Imperf.sg. *bebar*, pl. *bebarīd*

Vocabulary

Although Modern Persian is phonetically far removed from the ancient language, a number of traditional words are easily recognisable, e.g., *pedar* 'father', *mādar* 'mother', *dokhtar* 'daughter'. Since the Islamic conquest an exceptionally large number of Arabic terms have passed into Persian, a close analogy being the influx of French and Latin words into English.

Numbers: 1 *yak*, 2 *do*, 3 *se*, 4 *chahār*, 5 *panj*, 6 *shesh*, 7 *haft*, 8 *hasht*, 9 *noh*, 10 *dah*, 100 *sad*

Text

Matthew vi.9–13

Ei pedar-e-mā, ke   dar āsmān ast: nām-e-to   moghaddas bād.
o father of-us that in   heaven is   name of-thee hallowed   be

Malakūt-e-to   beāyād. Erādat-e-to chonān dar āsmān ast bar
kingdom of-thee come   will of-thee as   in heaven is on

zamīn nāfez   bād. Nān-e-rūzīne-ye-mārā dar īn   rūz be-mā
earth effective be   bread daily of-us   in this day to-us

bebakhsh. Va ān chonān ke gharzdārān-e-khodrā mībakhshīm,
bestow   and that way   that debtors of-our-own we-forgive

gharzhā-ye-mārā bemā bebakhsh. Va mārā dar ma'raz-e-āzmāyesh
debts of-us   to-us forgive   and us   into arena of temptation

nayāvar, balke az   sharīr khalāsī   deh. Zīrā ke molk   va
not-bring but   from evil deliverance give for   kingdom and

ghodrat va jalāl tā abad az ān-e-to 'st.
power   and glory to eternity thine   is

OTHER IRANIAN LANGUAGES
(The Paternoster)

Balochi

9 *Phiṯẖ manī, ki bihishtā asti: thai nām pāk bī.*
10 *Thai rāj khāi. Thai marzī cho ki bihishtā phīlave, īrge jihānā phīlav bī.*
11 *Mai harro whard maroshe mārā de.*
12 *Cho ki mā waṯẖī wāmdārār bashkṯẖo dāṯẖa, īrge thau mai wām bashk de.*
13 *Mārā sai ma khanain, aẕẖ Shaitānā darbar.*

Kurdish (of Sulaimaniye)

9   *Yā bāwk-ī ēma, ka la āsmān-ā-y: nāw-it muqaddas bibē.*

10 *Pāšāyatī' tō bē. Ārazū-t, wakū la āsmān-ā, wā-š la sar dinyā ba jē bēnrē.*

11 *Nān-ī řōžāna-y amřō-š-mān pē bida.*

12 *Wa gunāhakān-mān bibaxša, harwakū ēma-š lawāna abūrīn ba gunāh-yān pē-mān-a.*

13 *Wa ma-mān-bar-a bar tāqī kirdinawa, baɫkū řizgār-mān bika la xirāpa. Čunka pāšāyatī w hēz ū fařaka hī tō-ya hatā hatāyē.*

Ossetic

9   *Max fyd, kæcy dæ ærvty midæg: syydæg ŭæd dæ nom.*

10 *Ærcæŭæd dæ patcaxad. Dæ bar ŭæd arvy kŭd u, zæxxyl dær aftæ.*

11 *Næ dzul nyn onynæn radt maxæn abon.*

12 *Aemæ nyn nyppar næ xæstæ, max næ xæsdžyntæn kŭd baræm, aftæ.*

13 *Æmæ næma bakæn fydævzaræny, fælæ næ fervæzynkæn fydbylyzæj. Cæmæjdæridtær dæŭ u patcaxed æmæ tyx æmæ kad mykkagmæ.*

Pashto

9   *Ay jmuǧ plāra, če pa āsmān kxe ye: stā num de pāk wi.*

10 *Stā bāčahī de rāši. Stā irāda, ləka če pa āsmān kxe pura keǧi, pa dunyā kxe de həm hase ši.*

11 *Nənanay rozi nən muǧ la rā kře.*

12 *Aw muǧ ta gunāwe wəbaxxe, ləka če muǧ haγuy baxxəli di če muǧ ta gunāgār wi.*

13 *Aw azmoyəxt ta mo ma byāye, magar la bado na mo wəsāte. Jəka če stā di bāčahi aw wāk aw jalāl təl tar təla.*

I 3

TOCHARIAN

By the nineties of the last century the comparative philology of the IE languages had been pretty thoroughly worked out. Research was still able to throw light on many points of detail, but the main outlines seemed clear and the general conclusions unassailable. In particular, the IE languages had all been securely identified and much attention was given to determining precisely the relationship of the various branches of the great IE family to each other. There was a generally held theory of a primary division into two groups, a *centum* or western group and a *satem* or eastern group, a theory based on the geographical distribution of the known IE languages. But an unexpected discovery, made in far-off Chinese Turkestan, was to ruffle the placid world of comparative philology and seriously call into question, if not invalidate entirely, a number of acknowledged views on the mutual relationship of the IE languages.

In the heart of Central Asia, between the Tienshan range, the eastern edge of the Pamir plateau and the mountain chains which mark the northern limit of Tibet, lies an arid depression, the Tarim basin, so-called from the Tarim river which flows along the northern side to the shifting Lobnor. Somewhat to the north of the Tarim, an ancient caravan route runs parallel to the river passing through the three oasis towns of Kucha, Karashahr and Turfan, respectively 400, 600 and 800 miles east of Kashgar. Travellers, among them Sven Hedin, had brought back to Europe accounts of ancient ruins buried in the desert sands of the Tarim basin, and archaeological expeditions in the closing decade of the last and the early years of the present century brought to light an astonishing number of documents in various languages. As we have already seen, some of these turned out to be Iranian (p. 236). In the neighbourhood of the above-mentioned three settlements, however, a great deal of material in an unknown language

10

was found. The records date from the seventh to the eighth centuries A.D. and are written in a North Indian alphabet of the Brahmi type. Not only could the language be read off more or less at once, it could also be fairly soon satisfactorily interpreted as it was seen that the bulk of the material consisted of translations from Sanskrit originals. Some of the texts are actually bilingual. The remaining material consists of monastery correspondence and accounts. An unusual curiosity are the caravan permits written on wooden tablets. The literary texts are mostly written on palm-leaf, occasionally on (Chinese) paper, the authors being apparently Buddhist missionaries. The new language was given the name Tocharian as it was believed that a name *twγry* occurring in a contemporary Uigur colophon referred to it. It was concluded that here was the language of a vanished Central Asian people known to Strabo as Tocharoi and considered to have been of Iranian stock.

In 1908 appeared the celebrated treatise *Tocharisch, die Sprache der Indoskythen* by E. Sieg and W. Siegling, scholars who had been work-ing on the materials removed to Berlin. This publication showed that Tocharian was indeed an IE language, sixteen years after S. von Oldenburg had first drawn attention to it when he published a photo-graph of a single page from the collection of the Russian consul at Kashgar, Petrovsky, who had acquired the material from local inhabitants. But though Tocharian was unmistakably IE, it showed no close relationship with any other known branch, least of all with Iranian. In other words, the newly discovered language constituted an independent branch of the IE family. It has apparently close links with the western languages, e.g. it formed a medio-passive with the characteristic ending -*r* which up to that time has been associated chiefly with Italic and Celtic. Most remarkable of all, it turned out that the Tocharian word for 'hundred' was *känt* or *kante*, according to dialect, that is to say the most easterly of all IE languages was found to be stamped with the supposed hallmark of western IE. It was, of course, arguable that the Tocharians were originally westerners who had worked their way or fought their way across Asia, but the old thesis of a major centum-satem division could never carry the same conviction again.

It was early realised that the Tocharian materials were written in two distinct dialects: one could indeed speak of two languages. They received the names Tocharian A and B, the former found at Karashahr and Turfan, the latter at Kucha as well. It was subsequently established that Tocharian B was the language proper to Kucha and may therefore be called Kuchean, while Tocharian A was spoken at Karashahr and Turfan; it is sometimes called Turfanian. The presence of Kuchean at these latter settlements is perhaps evidence of missionary activity emanating from Kucha. Some authorities refer to the dialects as Eastern and Western Tocharian. The terminological question has been further confused by the discovery that the name Tocharian itself is almost certainly a misnomer. But while the experts delve into the matter, we are at liberty to continue to use the term which is now so firmly established.

Little is known about the early ethnographic history of the Tarim basin. It is, however, certain that Iranians were neighbours of the Tocharians, and Tocharian contains words of Iranian provenance. It is assumed, as a working hypothesis, that the Tocharians represent the earlier Indo-European invasion. At an unknown date, but perhaps about the beginning of the second millennium, both Tocharian and Iranian gave way to Uigur, a member of the Turkic family, today the chief language of the Tarim basin.

THE STRUCTURE OF TOCHARIAN

Unless stated, the following material refers to Tocharian B (Kuchean, Western Tocharian) only.

Phonetics

The following conventions of the transcription may be noted:

ä is a vowel of undetermined (palatal?) quality; it may be pronounced as German ä.

ṅ is velar, *ñ* palatal.

ś is a sibilant of undetermined quality; it represents palatalisation of older *k* or *ts*.

ṣ is palatal *s*, *c* palatal *t*, *ly* palatal *l*.

ts is affricated *t*.

ṃ denotes nasalisation of preceding vowel.

Accidence

There are three genders, though only relics of the neuter survive. There are four numbers: in addition to singular and plural we find a (moribund) dual which denotes a fortuitously occurring duality and a paral which is used of natural pairs, e.g. *puwar* 'fire', du. *wi pwāri* 'two fires', pl. *pwāra*; *okso* 'ox', par. *oksaine* 'yoke of two oxen', pl. *oksain*.

The Tocharian declension of substantives is a kind of two-storeyed structure. The nominative, vocative, oblique (= accusative) and genitive are typical IE cases; a distinctive vocative is, however, restricted to a few words, while the nominative and oblique are often identical. But in addition to these primary cases, a number of others are formed by loosely affixing postpositions to the oblique case; such endings are thus the same for all genders and numbers, though phonetic adjustments may be involved in accordance with the phonology of Tocharian. Such a secondary case is the perlative *-sa*, which basically expresses the meaning 'across, over'.

Specimen declension; realisation of IE *ekwos* 'horse':

Sg.nom.	yakwe	Pl.	yakwi
obl.	yakwe		yakwem
gen.	yäkwentse		yäkwemts
per.	yakwesa		yakwentsa

Adjectives have comparable IE-type inflexions.

The Tocharian verb is predominantly synthetic and, in spite of far-reaching morphological innovations, remains in essentials true to the IE type. There are active and medio-passive voices, indicative and subjunctive. Tenses composed of a past participle and forms of the verb 'to be' (pres., imperf., pret.) have functions similar to our perfect and pluperfect. There are two numbers, with very rare traces of a lost dual. We illustrate the inflexions with the following indicative active tenses of the stem *klyaus-* 'hear':

Pres.sg.1	klyausau	Imperf.sg.1	klyauṣim	Pret.sg.1	klyauṣāwa
2	klyauṣto	2	klyauṣit	2	klyauṣasta
3	klyauṣäm	3	klyauṣi	3	klyauṣa
pl.1	klyausemo	pl.1	klyauṣiyem	pl.1	klyauṣāmo
2	klyauścer	2	klyauṣicer	2	klyauṣāso
3	klyausem	3	klyauṣiyem	3	klyauṣāre

Vocabulary

The greatest part of the Tocharian vocabulary is etymologically obscure, not surprising in the case of an isolated IE language attested at a relatively recent date, for phonetic changes alone have obliterated many ancient features which would have enabled philologists to detect equations no longer evident. Nevertheless, the etymological affinity of a very substantial number of Tocharian words is certain, and the examples below convey some idea of the basic lexical correspondences between Tocharian (A and B) and cognate languages:

A *kukäl*, B *kokale* 'wheel': Gk. *kúklos*, Skt. *cakrás*

B *mit* 'honey': Lith. *medùs*, Russ. *mëd*, also Skt. *mádhu* ('honey, mead'), denoting the drink only Eng. *mead*, Ir. *miodh*, Welsh *medd*, further Gk. *méthu* ('intoxicating drink')

A *pält*, B *pilta* 'leaf'. Ger. *Blatt*, with specialised sense Eng. *blade*

AB *tu* 'thou': Lat. *tū*, Lith. *tù*, Russ. *ty*, Alban. *ti*, Ir. *tú*, Welsh *ti*, further Gk. *sú*, Skt. *tvám*

A *rtär*, B *ratre* 'red' : Skt. *rudhirás*, Gk. *eruthrós*, Lat. *ruber* (*b* < **dh*) OCS *rŭdrŭ*, also *rŭdŭ*, Lith. *raûdas*, Eng. *red*, Ir. *rua*, Welsh *rhudd* A *kau-*, B *ko-* 'strike, kill' : Lith. *káuti* 'to strike', Russ. *kovát'* 'to forge, hammer', Eng. *hew*

Numbers (A and B): 1 *sas*, *ṣe*, 2 *wu*, *wi*, 3 *tre*, *trai*, 4 *śtwar*, *śtwer*, 5 *päñ*, *piś*, 6 *ṣäk*, *ṣkas*, 7 *ṣpät*, *ṣukt*, 8 *okät*, *okt*, 9 *ñu*, 10 *śäk*, *śak*, 100 *känt*, *kante*

Text

The following specimen is taken from the Tocharian (B) version of a lost Sanskrit work *Udānālaṁkāra* 'Ornament of Udānā' (E. Sieg and W. Siegling, *Die Udānālaṁkāra-Fragmente*, Göttingen, 1949, Fasc.1, p. 14, Fasc.2, pp. 9–10).

nanok pudñäkte   maskītra śrāvastī   spe
again Buddha-Lord was   Śrāvastī (a city) near

sāṅkampa.   kokaletstse īyoy   sū   prasenacī walo.
congregation-with charioteer   was-going this Prasenacī king

                                    ot   ṣem kautāte
(i.e. King P. was driving his chariot) then axle broke

koklentse waiptār pwenta kaskānte.   walo . . . ceu   preke
of-wheel apart   spokes were-scattered king . . . at-that time

śaultse   tāka sklokatstse.   jetavaṃne
life-with was anxious (i.e. feared for his life) Jetavaṃ-in (a grove)

pudñäkteś   masa. yarke   ynāñmñesa kokalentse
Buddha-Lord-to went reverence respect-with of-wheel

kautalñe preksa poyśiṃ   ot
breaking asked Omniscent then

walo:
king (i.e. with reverence and respect the king then asked the Omniscent about the breaking of the wheel)

mai ñi   tākam laitalñe wrocc-asānmeṃ laṃntuññe epe watno
if of-me be   falling great-seat-from kingly   or-also

śaulantse ñyātse ñi   ste nesalle?
of-life   danger of-me is   being
(i.e. if he were in danger of falling from his throne or losing his life)

wñāneś poyśi   karuntsa: mā tañ   ñyātstse śolantse, mā r-
spoke Omniscent pity-with not of-thee danger of-life   not either

asānmeṃ laitalñe. ceṃ sklok   ptārka palskomeṃ.
seat-from falling   this anxiety banish mind-from

14

ANATOLIAN

The discovery of Tocharian towards the end of the last century took the philological world by surprise. As we have seen, knowledge of Tocharian considerably widened the scope of Indo-European studies and led to a questioning of certain traditional views regarding the origin and dissemination of this linguistic family. But even more exciting events were in the offing. Within a few years of the discovery of Tocharian, the excavator's spade had brought to light in Asia Minor an entirely new group of IE languages which had been widely spoken there in the first and second millennia B.C. From its geographical location the new group received the name Anatolian. Research into these languages is proceding apace, and fresh knowledge is constantly being gained as their comparative philology is worked out. Furthermore, the raw material is being regularly increased by new findings in the field. Asia Minor is full of unexplored archaeological sites, so it may be confidently predicted that Anatolian studies will for a long time to come be a very lively part of IE linguistics.

The Anatolian story really begins in the winter of 1887–8 when near Tell el-Amarna, in Middle Egypt, the diplomatic correspondence of Pharaoh Amenophis III (1411–1375) and his son Amenophis IV/Akhenaton (1375–1358) was unearthed from the ruins of the latter's ephemeral capital Akhetaton. The correspondence has an international character. It is written mostly in Akkadian—the diplomatic language of the age—and refers among other things to dealings between Egypt and the kingdom of Heta. The existence of this kingdom was already known, for it is often mentioned in Assyrian and Babylonian documents under the name of Hatti. Naturally enough, these names had been connected with the Hittites of the Old Testament. It was clear that these were a powerful people in the second millennium, so powerful indeed that they had been able to threaten

Egypt. Their home lay somewhere north of Palestine, in Syria or Asia Minor.

It was now possible to consider the Hittite question in connection with other archaeological material. Since about the middle of the last century it had been known that scattered widely over Cappadocia, Cilicia and North Syria were a considerable number of archaic sculptures (fourteenth to fifth centuries B.C.) in a style very different from contemporary Egyptian or Assyrian-Babylonian. The sculptures often portray a distinctive anthropological type, the so-called Armenoid type, with prominent, curved nose and receding forehead. These monuments are not unfrequently accompanied by inscriptions in a peculiar hieroglyphic script. They could be ascribed with some confidence to the Hittites and just after 1870 Sayce introduced the term Hieroglyphic Hittite in reference to these inscriptions. But if this was the language of the mysterious Hittites, nothing could be said about its affinities, since the hieroglyphs remained undeciphered.

Among the Amarna correspondence were two items in cuneiform—the Arzawa letters as they came to be called—which were written in two languages. The introductory lines in both letters are in Akkadian, the rest in a language at that time unknown. The Akkadian lines disclosed that one of the letters had been sent to Egypt by the king of Mitanni and that the other was addressed by Pharaoh to the king of Arzawa. The characters in the unknown language could, of course, be read and attempts were made to establish the sense of various words. In 1902, Knudtzon published a study of the language of these letters. He considered the possibility that it might be Hittite, but he actually called it the "language of Arzawa". He identified, for instance, a nominative singular in -*s* and other IE-looking case endings, isolated the verbal endings -*mi* and -*ti*, and concluded that here was an IE language. But Knudtzon's views met with a bleak reception. His interpretations were disputed and, in the end, he withdrew his IE theory.

Finds at Boğazköy; Cuneiform Hittite

Learning that cuneiform tablets had been discovered on the surface at an archaeological site near the modern village of Boğazköy, 90 miles east of Ankara, Winckler began systematic excavations there in 1905. The site was soon revealed as Hattusa, the capital of a great Hittite Empire, the Heta of the Egyptians, the Hatti of the Assyrians and Babylonians. The city flourished from about 1700 until its destruction about 1200 B.C. The excavators had the good fortune to find almost at once the royal archives, a huge collection of over 10,000 baked clay tablets or fragments of tablets inscribed with cuneiform; the number has since grown to about 25,000. The tablets are written in various languages. Three of these were already understood: Sumerian (of unknown affinities), Assyrian and Babylonian (closely related East Semitic languages sometimes referred to jointly or indifferently as Akkadian), but by far the greater part of the tablets were inscribed in a fourth, unknown language. Decipherment, however, proceeded rapidly and the extensive material in the new language was seen to contain a varied literature which included versions of a legal code, royal decrees, treaties, annals, private and diplomatic correspondence, prayers, rituals, magic rites, legends, glossaries, and a manual on the training of chariot horses, All these texts were written during the two and a half centuries preceding 1200 B.C., although some are copies of works composed several centuries earlier. Perhaps the oldest of all is the account of the exploits of an early Hittite king, Anitta, datable to about the eighteenth century B.C. Here, at last, in cuneiform, was the long sought-after language of the Hittites, of which the two very imperfectly understood Amarna letters had been the only witnesses up to that time, apart from the supposed Hittite of the undeciphered hieroglyphs.

In 1915 Hrozný was able to issue a provisional report on the new language, which he described as IE. Two years later, on the basis of the material that had by then yielded to likely interpretation, he published the first Hittite grammar. But scholars were still generally unconvinced of the IE character of the language. As with the Amarna letters, the non-IE features seemed to outweigh by far the possible IE features. For a language so ancient—this would be by far the most ancient IE language recorded—one expected an involved synthetic structure, something like Vedic, but Hittite did not appear to be highly inflected. Moreover the vocabulary contained an overwhelming mass of very unIE-looking words. Yet, within three or four years, when more texts had become available, the basic IE character of Hittite could be established beyond doubt. It was then realised that the unIE features of Hittite were due to the profound influence exerted upon it by non-IE speech. When the Hittites entered Asia Minor, apparently from the north via the Caucasus, they encountered an earlier non-IE population. In the subsequent fusion of peoples, the IE language of the newcomers was drastically reshaped by the autochthonous population, whom we shall now identify.

Pre-Anatolian languages

By the early 1920s it had become evident that Hittite was not the only new language recorded on the Boğazköy tablets. It was noticed, for instance, that in ritual documents, the Hittite text sometimes states that the reciter will now speak *hattili* 'in the language of Hatti', whereupon sentences in this language follow. It is seen that these sentences are addressed to a Hattic deity. Then the wider context becomes clear. The Hittites are the overlords of the people of the land of Hatti and have added the gods of the subject people to their own pantheon, but continue to address them in the Hattic language. About the precise meaning of the sentences in Hattic nothing can be said, as they have so far defied full interpretation. But bilingual passages in Hittite and Hattic have also been found. From these, the sense of about 150 Hattic words has been worked out and some idea of the general structure of the language has been gained. In particular a system of verbal prefixes has been identified which has been said to bear some similarity to systems met with in the modern South Caucasian languages, so that it is not impossible that genetic affinity with these non-IE languages may one day be established. Perhaps the link with the Caucasus was provided by the Kaskian language. Between themselves and the Caucasus lay the territory often referred to by the Hittites as the 'Upper Country', a hostile, unconquered area, the home of the Kaskians. Their language is known only from names quoted in cuneiform sources, but these seem to contain prefixes and other characteristics of Hattic word formation, making it probable that Kaskian was a non-IE language akin to Hattic.

It was early observed that a number of Hattic words were in use in Hittite proper; clearly these are loan words. It is now evident that Hattic was the language of the indigenous population conquered by the IE invaders. Furthermore, the name Hattusa can now be better understood. It had been the name of the Hattic capital, which the IE Hittites had later made their own chief centre.

All this constituted an important advance in knowledge, but the discovery that the term *hattili* refers to the language of the autochthonous pre-IE inhabitants was disconcerting from the point of view of terminology, for it obviously means 'in Hittite'. Whatever the name Hittite may have denoted later in biblical times, it was certainly not the real name of the IE language found on the cuneiform tablets. But the term 'Hittite' was already too firmly established to be changed, and so Hittite and Hattic, though doublets of the same name, are used to denote quite different languages. The terminological problem was further complicated by the subsequent discovery of a native name for the IE language. The terms used are *nasili* (or *nisili*) and *nesumnili* meaning respectively 'in the language of Nesa' and 'in the language of those of Nesa', and Hittite has since occasionally been called Nesite. It is recognised that Nesa was one of the most ancient Hittite towns, though its location is still unknown. It is not unthinkable, however, that it is identical with the ancient town of Kanes, which lies due south of Hattusa across the Halys. The term *kanisumnili* 'in the language of those of Kanes' has been found in cuneiform, but the context is not entirely clear.

Just as we find inserted into the Hittite texts rituals recited *hattili* 'in Hattic', we also find rituals recited *hurlili* 'in Hurrian'. The Hurrians, whose wide territory—Mitanni—extended from Mesopotamia across to North Syria and Cappadocia, became subject to the Hittite kings, and the Hurrian deities went to join 'the thousand gods of Hattusa'. The Hurrians, an important people, are regarded as the ancestors of the Horites known from the Old Testament. Hurrian is a non-IE language which has affinities with Urartian, the language of the kingdom of Urartu ('Ararat'), centred on the area between the lakes Van, Urmia and Sevan; it flourished from the beginning of the first millennium to the sixth century B.C. The Urartians and the Hurrians appear to have fused with the immigrant IE Phrygians to form a new ethnic group, the Armenians.

Palaic and Luwian

Two further ancient languages were disclosed in the Boğazköy archives, both closely akin to Hittite. One could perhaps regard them as dialects of Hittite, but since they are referred to in the texts as separate languages, we shall do the same. They are Palaic (*palaumnili* 'in the language of those of Pala') and Luwian (*luwili* 'in the language of Luwia'). The earlier versions of the Hittite Code mention Pala and Luwia together with Hatti as the three provinces subject to Hattusa.

Palaic was spoken in an area to the north of Hattusa, say in the province later known as Paphlagonia. It occurs solely in interpolations in the Hittite text in connection with the cult of the god Ziparwa. Altogether about 190 complete words are known, of which some fifty have been adequately explained. The name Luwia disappears from the records by the thirteenth century, but the Luwian language is known to have continued in use in the provinces of Kizzuwatna and Arzawa. The former corresponds approximately to the present vilayet of Adana. The boundaries of the latter, in one text equated with Luwia, have not been clearly determined, but this province lay to the west of Kizzuwatna and included at least the southern half of the vilayet of Konya. To the north-east of Kizzuwatna, the Luwians were in contact with the Hurrians. Luwian, or more precisely Cuneiform Luwian, is known chiefly from interpolations in the Hittite texts, just like Palaic. But the records of Luwian are more plentiful than those of Palaic; they contain mythological and ritual matter for the most part, and several hundred words of Cuneiform Luwian are known. Both Palaic and Luwian have, like Hittite, been profoundly influenced by Hattic; in the case of Luwian, there is evidence of Hurrian influence too.

Hieroglyphs

Cuneiform writing originated among the Sumerians in Mesopotamia; it was later adapted for use in various languages and spread throughout the Near East. It was natural that the Hittites, too, should take over this mode of writing. But it was noticed that, in addition to cuneiform, a hieroglyphic script was also known to the Hittites and their kings used this kind of writing on their seals, some of which have been impresssed upon cuneiform tablets. The earliest examples have been dated to the sixteenth century B.C.

The hieroglyphs which came to light at Boğazköy were seen to be the same as the monumental script which had already received the name of Hieroglyphic Hittite. The discovery of Hieroglyphic Hittite among the tablets at Boğazköy seemed to confirm the supposition that Sayce's Hieroglyphic Hittite was indeed Hittite. On the other hand, the excavation of Hattusa posed new questions in connection with the Hittite monuments elsewhere. Hattusa fell about 1200 B.C., but the bulk of the other Hittite remains were later than this date. It looked as though the Hittites, or some of them, had survived the destruction of their old capital and had continued to live their national life in the southern part of the old empire, i.e. in Cappadocia, Cilicia and North Syria. Furthermore, the Hittites of the Bible cannot have been identical with the people of Hattusa; they must have been the later Hittites in the south. Subsequent excavations in Asia Minor and Syria have proved these suppositions to be correct.

Meanwhile work on the hieroglyphs was going forward. But the decipherment of this script, the signs of which contain both ideograms and phonetically spelt syllables, proved very difficult. By 1939, however, studies had so far progressed that it could be affirmed that Hieroglyphic Hittite was, after all, not Hittite, but had every appearance of being a form of Luwian. This view was strikingly confirmed by the discovery in 1946 of a long bilingual inscription of the eighth century in Phoenician (a known Semitic language) and Hieroglyphic Hittite. It now became certain that it would be more appropriate to speak of Hieroglyphic Luwian, and it could be concluded that the use of hieroglyphics at Hattusa was most likely a reflection of Luwian influence in the north. As far as can be ascertained, this unique hieroglyphic style was expressly developed as the national script of the Luwians.

Thus it became clear that the language of the later Hittite principalities, known to have flourished especially in North Syria, was in fact Luwian. But the people themselves were seemingly called Hittites, at any rate they are so named in the Old Testament. Presumably the appellation Hittite spread widely at the time of the Hittite Empire and so became attached to the Luwians as well.

New Anatolian languages

The Anatolian languages in cuneiform script may be termed Old Anatolian in contradistinction to New Anatolian which refers to languages recorded in Hellenistic or Roman times. Hieroglyphic Luwian bridges the gap between the two. We are, however, very inadequately informed about New Anatolian languages. The best known is Lycian, once spoken in the south-west corner of Asia Minor. It is found in some 150 inscriptions, mostly short, written in an alphabet derived from the Greek with the addition of several characters. The inscriptions all date from the fifth and fourth centuries B.C. Two somewhat differentiated dialects are found, usually called Lycian A and Lycian B. For no good reason, they are sometimes known as Termilian and Milyan respectively. In the fifth-century inscriptions the Lycians call themselves *Termmile* (Greek *Termílai*) and according to their own tradition they were settled in the country once known as *Milyas*. The total amount of linguistic material is not great, bilingual inscriptions are few, so that the texts are only imperfectly understood. All the same, enough of the inflexions and vocabulary is known to show that Lycian was an Anatolian language related to Luwian, as was established beyond doubt by Laroche in 1957.

We shall now mention two languages, of as yet unproved affinities, but sufficiently attested in inscriptions to allow us to hope for more. The first is the language of Lycia's neighbour to the north, Caria. The Carian language occurs in a few inscriptions in an alphabet derived from Greek. The value of certain letters has not yet been established and the interpretation of the scanty material is complicated by the fact that the inscriptions are written in continuous script, so that there is no way of telling where one word ends and the next begins. The second language, which is better understood, is Lydian, the speech of the once powerful and wealthy kingdom of Lydia which lay immediately to the north of Caria. The language survives in more than fifty inscriptions, mostly excavated at Sardes the Lydian capital between 1910 and 1913, all at least as old as the fourth century B.C. They are written in an alphabet based on an archaic Greek type. Such interpretation of the remains as has been possible is based mainly on a bilingual epitaph of 8 lines in Lydian and Aramaic (a well-known Semitic language). Certain endings are reminiscent of Hittite; accordingly, as a working hypothesis, many scholars regard Lydian as an Anatolian language.

In early times Asia Minor was a land of many tongues. Most of the terrain is difficult. The mountain tribes lived in considerable isolation and some of them succeeded in maintaining their independence in face of the encroachments of great powers. Such was the situation at the turn of the fifth century B.C. when the Greeks marched through the country, as is recounted in the famous *Anabasis*. Xenophon tells of mountain tribes who had never submitted to the Persian and more than once makes reference to the need for interpreters in negotiations with local tribes. Although the Greeks had by this time established colonies along the west and northern coasts of Asia Minor, one has the impression from Xenophon that Greek was not understood inland. Most likely Persian would be the most widely known foreign language in the interior of Asia Minor at this time. But in the following centuries, Greek influence was to become paramount in the area. It is assumed that, eventually, the indigenous languages were displaced by Greek before the coming of the Turks in the eleventh century.

The displacement of the indigenous languages by Greek was a gradual process and the Greeks themselves frequently refer to 'barbarian' languages in Asia Minor. In addition to Lycian, Carian and Lydian, already mentioned, we note the following languages of Asia Minor which finally gave way to Greek: Bithynian, Cappadocian, Cataonian, Cilician, Galatian, Isaurian, Lycaonian, Mariandynian, Mysian, Pamphylian, Paphlagonian, Pisidian, Phrygian, Pontic, Sidetic, Thracian. There are no literary records in any of these languages. In the case of Phrygian a few connected sentences are known, but the only linguistic material available in useful amounts for the study of most of these languages consists of personal and topographical names. By the nature of the case, these are difficult to interpret, but the acumen of philologists has nevertheless revealed a number of facts concerning the genetic relationship of several of them. It is certain that some of these languages were introduced into Asia Minor much later than Anatolian as a result of invasions from the north across the Dardanelles. These are Galatian, a Celtic language, and Phrygian and Thracian, which together with Armenian, form the Thraco-Phrygian family; Bithynian and Mysian may be described as Thracian dialects.

It is highly probable that several of the others are IE languages of the Anatolian type. In 1896, Kretschmer observed that in the indigenous languages of Asia Minor the personal names are formed with characteristic suffixes. The correctness of this observation has been confirmed by the large quantity of new epigraphical material which has come to light during the present century. Furthermore, some of these characteristic features have been traced back to the Old Anatolian languages. For example, the name *Armaziti*, found in Cuneiform Luwian, occurs in Cilician as *Armasētas*, the name *Panamu*, found in Hieroglyphic Luwian, appears in Pisidian as *Panamyas*— the ending in the Cilician and Pisidian forms is to be regarded as a hellenism. Doubtless there was a certain unity of culture in Anatolia which could lead to the diffusion of names originally confined to one people. On the other hand, it is evident that Luwian was once a widespread language, so that one is much tempted to consider the presence of Luwian names in Cilician and Pisidian as evidence that these languages were descendants of Luwian, or at any rate of allied stock, especially when one remembers that the provinces of Cilicia and Pisidia were situated on old Luwian territory.

Onomastic evidence suggests that the epichorial tongue of Lycaonia and neighbouring Isauria, provinces to the north of Pisidia, also had affinities with Luwian. It was in Lycaonia that the fickle crowd venerated Paul and Barnabas 'saying in the speech of Lycaonia, The gods are come down to us in the likeness of men' (Acts xiv.11)—this speech was, of course, incomprehensible to the Apostles. Finally, Luwian connections may be implied for Pamphylian, which was spoken on the coast due south of Pisidia. The Pamphylian port of Side is said by the Greek historian Arrian (second century A.D.) to have had a language of its own. Sidetic is present in short, not fully deciphered alphabetic inscriptions from the fifth and fourth centuries B.C.; one imagines it was a form of Pamphylian. Immediately to the west lay Lycia, where the language was certainly related to Luwian. It seems reasonable to suppose that languages descended from or closely akin to Luwian were widely spoken throughout the southern part of Anatolia in Hellenistic and Roman times. We recall that the area is particularly wild and inaccessible, being largely taken up by the formidable Taurus Mountains which isolate the coastal strip from the interior.

What of the other languages mentioned: Cappadocian, Cataonian, Mariandynian, Paphlagonian and Pontic? It has not been possible, so far, to say anything about the affinities of these languages. They, too, may be IE and as such be related to the languages identified above. But they could equally well be unrelated, non-IE languages. We have already seen that the invading IE Hittites found non-IE languages in use in Eastern and Central Anatolia: Hattic and the related Kaskian, and Hurrian. We know that Hattic and Hurrian yielded to IE languages (Hittite, Armenian), but we have no further information on the subsequent fate of Kaskian. How long would it survive? If we bear in mind that it was spoken in a remote area of the Pontic Mountains and that it was, to all appearances, in contact with Caucasian languages to the east, it would not be surprising if the language known to the Greeks as Pontic were a descendant of Kaskian.

Pre-IE peoples doubtless lived at one time in Western Anatolia, too, though none have been positively identified so far. In this connection, however, mention must be made of the Etruscan language, spoken in antiquity in what is now the Italian province of Etruria. According to a tradition first encountered in Herodotus, the Etruscans, whose language is considered to be non-IE (p. 21), immigrated to Italy from Lydia in the thirteenth century B.C. The Etruscans' own chronology put their arrival in Italy about three centuries later. Modern research can neither confirm nor disprove these traditions, so that we must at least reckon with the possibility that they may be evidence for non-IE speech in Western Anatolia towards the end of the second millennium B.C.

At what date all these various languages were supplanted by the Greek lingua franca cannot be stated exactly, but it is known that some of them continued in use well into the Christian era. We learn from patristic literature that Cappadocian, Galatian and Lycaonian were being spoken in the fourth century. Isaurian and Mysian are described as living languages in the sixth century. No doubt a period of bilingualism, actually attested in the case of Galatian, preceded the extinction of these minor languages.

THE STRUCTURE OF ANATOLIAN

At present we are only moderately well informed about one Anatolian language—Hittite. To be sure, there are still very many gaps in our knowledge, but it is evident that the material already to hand enables us to recognise the essential structure of the language. New discoveries will fill in details, but can hardly modify the general picture appreciably.

Phonetics

The study of Hittite sounds is made exceptionally difficult by the ambiguity of the cuneiform writing. One is entirely in the dark about accentuation. The script has no obvious means of indicating vowel length, so that although vowel quantity (long and short) is suspected, there is no indubitable evidence for it. Vowel quality, too, is imperfectly registered. Cuneiform does not distinguish at all between *o* and *u*; one uniformly transcribes 'u'. Nor can it always distinguish between *e* and *i*, and where it can, the Hittite scribes sometimes confused things. Even more confusing is the representation of the consonants. These are often written double, in some words certain consonants are always geminated, for reasons not yet ascertained. Chaos reigns in the writing of the occlusives: e.g., 'pa, ti, ku' may be used where 'ba, di, gu' are expected, and vice versa. On the other hand, in a limited number of cases, the script shows some consistency. For example, in some words (or forms of words) only 't' or only 'd' is used, but for reasons still not determined with certainty.

Cuneiform writing is syllabic, which means that it cannot write consonants except in connection with a vowel. Three patterns are possible: vowel + consonant ('ar'), consonant + vowel ('ka'), consonant + vowel + consonant ('kar'). With this system, consonant groups can only be represented approximately, e.g., *tri-* 'three' is written 'te-ri', *karpzi* '(he) lifts' is written 'kar-ap-zi'. Needless to say, the accurate reading of such syllables is impossible unless the word is identifiable by some other means. For instance, 'te-ri' can be interpreted as *tri-* only because its meaning has been established from the context and because the evidence of the other IE languages points unmistakably to initial *tr-*, not **ter-*.

But despite these orthographical uncertainties, one phonological feature of Hittite imposes itself on our attention at once. Hittite is seen to have 'h', standing for a laryngeal sound (or sounds), in inherited IE words where the related non-Anatolian languages show no sign of a laryngeal. For example, in initial position: Hitt. *hastai* 'bone', Skt. *ásthi*, Gk. *ostéon*, Lat. *os*; Hitt. *hant-* 'in front', Skt. *ánti*, Gk. *antí*, Eng. *and*; in medial position: Hitt. *eshar* 'blood', Skt. *ásṛk*, Gk. *éar*, Latvian *asins*; Hitt. *pahhur* 'fire', Gk. *pûr*, Eng. *fire*, Umbrian *pir*, Toch.A *por*. The commonest explanation is that here Hittite preserves a sound (or sounds) which other IE languages have lost, so that in this respect Hittite is more archaic than any other form of IE. This apparent archaism in Hittite then took on special significance when it was suggested that it might be possible to account for various irregularities in the phonology of other IE languages on the assumption that these irregularities were attributable to changes connected with a lost original laryngeal. This is the famous laryngeal theory. But the observed facts have not yet been reconciled to any consistent theory, so that the reason for the unexpected appearance of 'h' in a number of Hittite words is, in reality, still as mysterious as it ever was.

Accidence

Hittite distinguished two grammatical genders: common (a conflation of IE masculine and feminine) and neuter. The latter appears as a declining category, so that Hittite was on the way to becoming a genderless language. There are two numbers, singular and plural. Hittite preserves the inherited eight-case system of IE: nom. voc., acc., gen., dat., loc., abl., inst., the singular retaining the greater morphological diversity. However, even here the vocative is generally replaced by the nominative, and in later Hittite (after 1500), syncretism continues to reduce the number of distinct endings, e.g., dat. and loc. sg. fall together with the form of the dat. Hittite continues a number of IE declensional types. Sample paradigm (older language):

Sg.nom.	*antuhsas* 'man'	Pl.	*antuhses*
voc.	*antuhsa*		*antuhses*
acc.	*antuhsan*		*antuhsus*
gen.	*antuhsas*		*antuhsas*
dat.	*antuhsi*		*antuhsas*
loc.	*antuhsa*		*antuhsas*
abl.	*antuhsaz*		*antuhsaz*
inst.	*antuhsit*		*antuhsit*

Noteworthy in Hittite are the *r/n* stems. In other IE languages these constitute a small, decaying class, e.g., Lat. *femur* 'thigh', gen. *feminis*, but in Hittite they are numerous and productive. Examples: Hitt. *wātar* 'water', gen. *wetenas*, cf. Gk. *húdōr*, gen. *húdatos* ($a < n̥$). Germanic, too, inherited this class, but the recorded languages have in every case reshaped the declension, generalising either *r* or *n*: Eng. *water*, Icel. *vatn*.

Hitt. *pahhur* 'fire', gen. *pahhwenas*. Other IE languages have abandoned the *r/n* formation in this word, usually generalising *r*: Gk. *pūr*, Eng. *fire* etc., but *n* is found occasionally: Old Prussian *panno*, Goth. *fon*.

Hittite uses postpositions, not prepositions. They usually govern the dat.-loc., thus *suhha-* 'roof': *suhhi ser* 'on the roof', *suhhi sara* 'onto the roof'.

Adjectives have inflexions comparable to those of nouns.

There are two conjugations in Hittite, known from the endings of the first sg.pres.indic. as the *-mi* and *-hi* conjugations. The endings of both agree in most cases, and the later language tends to confuse the few differences found in the earlier period. There are two voices: active and medio-passive. The inherited IE system of moods and tenses has been drastically reduced. Of the former only the indicative and imperative are found, of the latter only the present and preterite. As in other IE languages, verbs fall into classes depending on the ending of the stem. Sample paradigms:

Active

Infin. *appanna* 'take, grasp'

	Pres.sg.1	*epmi*	Pret.	*eppun*
	2	*epsi*		**epta*
	3	*epzi*		*epta*
	pl.1	*eppweni*		*eppwen*
	2	*epteni*		*epten*
	3	*appanzi*		*eppir*

Imperf.sg. *ep*, pl. *epten*
Pres.part. *appant-*

Medio-Passive

Root *ar-* 'arrive', middle sense 'stand'

Pres.sg.	1	*arhahari*	Pret.	*arhahat*
	2	*artati*		*artat*
	3	*artari*		*artat*
pl.	1	*arwasta*		*arwastat*
	2	**arduma*		**ardumat*
	3	*arantari*		*arantat*

Imperf.sg. *arhut*, pl. *ardumat*

Numbers: Though of frequent occurrence, numbers are nearly always written with figures, so that the pronunciation of only the following is known: 2 *da-*, 3 *tri*, 4 *me(i)u-* (of mysterious origin, cf. Luwian *mawwa-*) 7 *sipta-*. (The Hittite form of certain other common words is similarly concealed behind ideograms, such as the terms for 'woman' and 'son')

Vocabulary

Other examples of the IE element include:

Hitt. *genu-* 'knee': Skt. *jắnū*, Gk. *gónu*, Lat. *genū*, Eng. *knee*, Armen. *cunr*

Hitt. *milit-* 'honey': Gk. *méli*, Lat. *mel*, Goth. *miliþ*, Alban. *mjaltë*, Ir. *mil*, Welsh *mêl*, Armen. *melr*

Hitt. *newas* 'new': Skt. *návas*, Gk. *néos*, Lat. *novus*, Russ. *nov*, Eng. *new*, Lith. *naũjas*, Ir. *nua*, Welsh *newydd*, Armen. *nor*

Hitt. *sup-* '(to) sleep': Skt. *svápiti*, Russ. *spit*, Icel. *sefur* (all meaning 'sleeps'), further the nouns Skt. *svápnas*, Gk. *húpnos*, Icel. *svefn*, Russ. *son*, Ir. *suan*, Welsh *hun* (all meaning 'sleep'), Lat. *somnus* 'dream'

A striking dialect isogloss: Hitt. *eku-* 'drink', Toch. *yok-*

Specimen text

In transcribing Hittite in Roman letters, the following conventions may be noted: $\underline{h} = h$, $\underline{i} = y$, *š* = *s*, $\underline{u} = w$, z = *ts*.

Cuneiform writing occasionally uses more than one sign for the same syllable. In such cases the most commonly occurring sign is not specially indicated in the transcription, but the less common signs are indicated by accents, e.g., an acute marks the second, a grave the third most commonly used sign.

In addition to phonetically written syllables, cuneiform script also employs ideograms and determinatives. Ideograms are non-phonetic signs standing for whole words. Certain words in the Hittite texts are always written with ideograms and consequently their phonetic form in Hittite cannot be recovered. It has become customary to spell out the ideograms according to their pronunciation in Sumerian, the oldest language written in cuneiform, and to print the transcription in capitals, e.g., IKU 'field'. Ideograms often take Sumerian endings, here shown by superior small capitals: IKU^{HI.A} 'fields'. Ideograms may also take native Hittite inflexions: ÍD-i 'to the river', where -i is the Hittite dative-locative ending. The Hittites themselves doubtless gave these ideograms their true Hittite values. Determinatives are classifying signs placed before certain groups of nouns. Thus, ^{LÚ} 'man' characterises all male persons: ^{LÚ}IŠ 'charioteer'. Being merely a graphic device, the determinative (printed in superior small capitals in the transcription) was not pronounced.

The Hittite texts regularly contain Akkadian words also. These are transcribed in italicised capitals: 3-*ŠU* '3 times'. It is not clear whether the Hittites regarded words like *ŠU* as loans words or whether they are a conventional way of representing native Hittite words.

As a now established convention of transcription, phonetically written syllables are, in Hittite words, separated by a hyphen, in Sumerian and Akkadian by a dot.

The following specimen text is a passage from the fourth tablet of the so-called *Hippologia hethitica*, a manual on the training of chariot horses dating from the fourteenth century B.C. It is described as having been composed by one Kikkuli, himself not a Hittite, but a Hurrian from the neighbouring state of Mitanni. Hurrian training methods must have been highly regarded in the Near East for in addition to the Hittite evidence fragments of a closely related text, this time in Assyrian, have recently come to light (first published 1951). It is therefore not surprising that the manual contains a number of technical terms borrowed from Hurrian. One of these occurs below: *auzumewa sīesa*. The first word means 'gallop(ing)', the second, though apparently corrupt, doubtless means something like 'double'. Our passage also contains the Hurrian word *uzuhri-* 'grass'. We have already noticed evidence for Aryan influence on Hurrian (p. 193) and a few technical terms from this source are found in the present treatise. We have below the example *nawartanni wasannasya* virtually identical with a Sanskrit **navartane* (haplology for **nava-vartane*) *vasanasya* 'for nine turns of the course'.

Syllabic transcription (Annelies Kammenhuber, *Hippologia Hethitica*, Wiesbaden, 1961, pp. 138–40); the numbers refer to lines:

(22) ma-aḫ-ḫa-an-ma-aš ar-ḫa la-a-an-zi na-aš a-a-an-te-it ú-e-te-ni-it
(23) ar-ra-an-zi nam-ma-aš ÍD-i kat-ta pí-e-ḫu-da-an-zi na-aš 3 *ŠU*
(24) kat-kat-ti-nu-an-zi nam-ma-aš tu-u-ri-ia-an-zi na-aš na-ua-ar-ta-an-ni (25) ua-ša-an-na-ša-ia 1 DANNA 80 IKU^HI.A-ia pár-ḫa-i
A.NA ua-ša-an-ni-ma (26) pár-ga-tar-še-it 6 IKU pal-ḫa-tar-še-it-ma
4 IKU^HI.A ua-ša-an-na-ma (27) 9 *ŠU* ua-aḫ-nu-zi ma-aḫ-ḫa-an-ma-aš
ar-ḫa la-a-an-zi na-aš aš-nu-an-zi (28) ša-ak-ru-ua-an-zi-ma-aš *Ú.UL*
nam-ma-aš *I.NA* É ^LÚIŠ an-da (29) pí-e-ḫu-da-an-zi nu-uš-ma-aš 1
UP.NA kán-za 1 *UP.NA* me-ma-al 1 *UP.NA* ŠE (30) 4 *UP.NA* ú-zu-uḫ-ri-in-na an-da im-mi-ia-an-da-an a-da-an-zi (31) nam-ma UD^KAM-an
ḫu-u-ma-an ú-zu-uḫ-ri-in ḪÁD.DU.A az-zi-ik-kán-zi (32) ne-ku-uz
me-ḫur-ma tu-u-ri-ia-an-zi na-aš ½ DANNA 20 IKU^HI.A-ia pí-en-nai
(33) na-aš a-ú-zu-mi-e-ua ši-i-e-ša *A.NA* 37 IKU^HI.A pár-ha-i (34)
EGIR-pa-ia URU-ri an-da pár-ḫa-an-du-uš ú-ua-an-zi nam-ma-aš
ar-ḫa la-a-an-zi (35) na-aš an-da ua-aš-ša-an-zi na-aš *I.NA* É ^LÚIŠ
an-da pí-e-ḫu-da-an-zi

Phonetic transcription (where possible) and literal
translation:

(22) mahhan-ma-s   arha lānzi   na-s
as-soon-as and them off   they-loose (i.e. unharness) now them

āntet   wetenit (23) arranzi   namma-s ÍD-i   *katta*
with-warm water   they-wash then-them to-the-river down

pehudanzi na-s   3 *ŠU*   (24) katkattinanzi namma-s
they-lead   now them 3 times   they-immerse then them

tūriyanzi   na-s   nawartanni   (25) wasannasya 1 DANNA
they-harness now them for-nine-rounds   of-the-course 1 'danna'

80 IKU^HI.A-ya parhai   *A.NA* wasannima (26) pargatar-set
80 fields   he-gallops for-the-course   length-its

6 IKU^HI.A palhatar-set-ma 4 IKU^HI.A wasannama (27) 9 *ŠU*
6 fields   breadth its and   4 fields   the-course   9 times

wahnuzi mahhan-ma-s   arha lānzi   na-s   asnuanzi
he-covers as-soon-as and them they-unharness now-them they-feed

(28) sakruwanzi-ma-s   *Ú.UL* namma-s *I.NA*
they-give-to-drink and them not   then them in

É   ^{LÚ}IŠ   anda (29) pehudanzi
the-house of-the-charioteer (i.e. stable) in   they-lead

nu-smas   1 *UP.NA*   kanza 1 *UP.NA*   memal 1 *UP.NA*   ŠE
now to-them 1 hand (of) wheat 1 hand (of) ?   1 hand (of) barley

(30) 4 *UP.NA*   uzuhrina anda immiyandan adanzi
     4 hand (of) grass   (in)   mixed   they-feed

(31) namma UD^{KAN}-an hūman uzuhrin HÁD.DU.A. azzikkanzi
     then   the-day   whole   grass   dried   they-eat

(32) nekuz   mehur-ma tūriyanzi   na-s   ½ DANNA
     of-evening time and   they-harness now them ½ 'danna'

20 IKU^{HI.A}-ya pennai (33) na-s   auzumewa sīesa   *A.NA*
20 fields   he-trots   now them gallop   double over

37 IKU^{HI.A} parhai   (34) EGIR-pa-ya URU-ri   anda parhandus
37 fields   he-gallops   back and   to-the-city in   galloping

uwanzi   namma-s arha lānzi   (35) na-s   anda wassanzi
they-come then them they-unharness   now them (in)   they-cover

na-s   *I.NA* É ^{LÚ}IŠ   anda pehudanzi
now them in   the-stable in   they-lead

('danna': about 7 leagues)

Note. Vowel length and consonant gemination are conjectures reached by means of comparative philology and/or a possible interpretation of the script, but they are not proved. Divisions of the type *ma-s* 'and them' are arbitrary, the separate words being *ma* and *as*, presumably contracting to *mas*.

INDEX OF LANGUAGES AND DIALECTS

Non-Indo-European languages and those of unknown or uncertain affinities are denoted by italics. Names of groups or families of languages are given in capitals.